D1610191

STUDIES IN WELSH HISTORY

Editors

RALPH A. GRIFFITHS, ERYN M. WHITE
CHRIS WILLIAMS

———————

26

DEVOLUTION IN WALES

CLAIMS AND RESPONSES, 1937–1979

DEVOLUTION IN WALES

CLAIMS AND RESPONSES, 1937–1979

by

JOHN GILBERT EVANS

Published on behalf of the
History and Law Committee
of the Board of Celtic Studies

CARDIFF
UNIVERSITY OF WALES PRESS
2006

© John Gilbert Evans, 2006

British Library Cataloguing-in-Publication Data
A catalogue record for this book is available from the British Library.

ISBN-10 0-7083-1990-4
ISBN-13 978-0-7083-1990-1

Printed in Great Britain by Antony Rowe Ltd, Wiltshire

EDITORS' FOREWORD

Since the foundation of the series in 1977, the study of Wales's history has attracted growing attention among historians internationally and continues to enjoy a vigorous popularity. Not only are approaches, both traditional and new, to the study of history in general being successfully applied in a Welsh context, but Wales's historical experience is increasingly appreciated by writers on British, European and world history. These advances have been especially marked in the university institutions in Wales itself.

In order to make more widely available the conclusions of original research, much of it of limited accessibility in post-graduate dissertations and theses, in 1977 the History and Law Committee of the Board of Celtic Studies inaugurated this series of monographs, *Studies in Welsh History*. It was anticipated that many of the volumes would originate in research conducted in the University of Wales or under the auspices of the Board of Celtic Studies, and so it has proved. But the series does not exclude significant contributions made by researchers in other universities and elsewhere. Its primary aim is to serve historical scholarship and to encourage the study of Welsh history.

To
MARIAN

CONTENTS

ACKNOWLEDGEMENTS

This study deals with a distinctive forty-two year period in the political history of Wales. It began in 1937 with a demand by MPs from all parties that a secretary of state be appointed and it ended in 1979 with a referendum on a Welsh assembly. The first major turning point was the setting up in 1949 of the Council for Wales and Monmouthshire, and then there quickly followed a minister for Welsh Affairs in 1951. The council recommended that a secretary of state be appointed and Labour acted on that proposal in 1964. Thereafter, the changing pattern of Labour thinking with regard to Wales and the nationalist challenges in the 1960s and 1970s are examined. The focus is on Wales, but in the 1970s the devolution issue became part of a wider debate within the United Kingdom and pertinent questions raised in that debate are also discussed. The referendum brought to an end a period in which both Labour and Conservative governments were forced to consider the Welsh question and made to think about the precise way in which Wales should be governed within the British state.

I am indebted to many people for the ready assistance which they gave me in preparing this book. I wish to express my gratitude to Professor Sir Glanmor Williams, University of Wales Swansea, who approved the study and thereby set me on my way, and to Peter Stead for his advice and guidance. I was very fortunate in that prominent individuals who had been actively involved during the period were prepared to discuss the subject with me, and the significance of their contributions cannot be overstated. I thank them most sincerely for their cooperation. My thanks are due also to those individuals, including the staffs of libraries and archives, public bodies, local authorities, government departments and political parties who acceded to my request for information. Their responses were particularly helpful. The Labour Party's role in all debates on devolution was crucial and I am most grateful for the assistance given by the then party officers: Hubert Morgan and J. Vaughan Jones in Cardiff, and Stephen Bird in London. R. K. Blundell and Les Rees also kindly allowed me to peruse materials in their possession. I must record my appreciation of the support given by Susan Charles, Dafydd Jones and Nicola Roper of the University of Wales Press and by the editors prior to publication. I thank Professor Ralph A. Griffiths and Professor Chris Williams for their invaluable contributions. They read each draft and offered many comments which greatly enhanced the work. The drafts were reproduced by Rhodri W. Evans and his effort too is greatly acknowledged. Some of the above mentioned are now deceased, but their contributions, nevertheless, should not be overlooked.

John Gilbert Evans
Penarth
August 2006

ABBREVIATIONS

AUEW	Amalgamated Union of Engineering Workers
CLP	Constituency Labour Party
EEC	European Economic Community
EETPU	Electrical, Electronic, Telecommunications and Plumbing Union
GMWU	General and Municipal Workers' Union
ILP	Independent Labour Party
NEC	National Executive Committee
NLW	National Library of Wales
NUM	National Union of Mineworkers
SNP	Scottish National Party
TNA	The National Archives
Wales TUC	Wales Trade Union Council

INTRODUCTION

From the 1930s onwards devolution was an increasingly important issue in Welsh politics, and Labour's ascendancy meant that the debate was, in Vernon Bogdanor's words, 'very largely the history of an internal Labour Party debate'.[1] Throughout the period under review Labour was associated with the national question. Indeed, it has been suggested that the debate was 'closer to Labour's heart in Wales than political allies or opponents were willing to concede'.[2]

In the 1930s, when the effects of the Depression were clearly visible, there were demands for the appointment of a secretary of state. MPs evidently thought that the government should transfer resources from the richer regions to the more deprived regions, and that being represented, as was Scotland, at the centre of government by a secretary of state would greatly assist in Wales's regeneration.[3] Therefore, the need to overcome Wales's economic and social problems was uppermost in MPs' minds, although cultural concerns were a consideration too.[4] In the early 1940s, when MPs and the South Wales Regional Council of Labour supported the appointment of a secretary of state, another and more general consideration was the need to give Wales as a nation recognition in government.

Following the election of a Labour government after the war, Wales's vulnerability as a region was again the basis for renewed demands for a secretary of state by the Welsh Parliamentary Party and by individual MPs, but the government adhered to the party's centralist philosophy: only if economic management were directed from the centre would the United Kingdom's outlying regions benefit and their standard of living be raised. The appointment of a secretary of state would not remedy Wales's economic problems –

[1] Vernon Bogdanor, *Devolution* (Oxford, 1979), 140.
[2] R. Merfyn Jones and Ioan Rhys Jones, 'Labour and the nation', in Duncan Tanner, Chris Williams and Deian Hopkin (eds), *The Labour Party in Wales, 1900–2000* (Cardiff, 2000), 241.
[3] Ibid., 246, 248.
[4] Ibid., 246.

problems that were no different from those experienced in other parts of the United Kingdom. This was certainly the view of some Labour MPs in industrial south Wales, who demanded that support from the centre be strengthened, rather than that changes in the machinery of government be made.[5] It could be argued that this socialist emphasis on centralization assisted the integration of Wales in the British state, thereby strengthening it.[6] Welsh Labour MPs, therefore, clearly held divergent views on how best to revitalize the Welsh economy. It was a disagreement about the effectiveness of government and its ability to solve the nation's economic and social ills.[7] Inevitably, perhaps, as the government succeeded in implementing its economic and social policies, the centralist view prevailed and the demand for a secretary of state temporarily receded.

From the 1950s onwards the Labour Party faced an ever-increasing dilemma of 'reconciling what was essentially a British party with Welsh aspirations'.[8] As a British party with a centralist philosophy, it had to respond to Welsh demands for recognition in the machinery of government, and was uncertain how to respond. Because of its ideology, it was not equipped to cope with nationalism when Plaid Cymru became a serious political threat in the 1960s:[9] when faced with Welsh demands Labour was always unsure of its ground, and it has been suggested that the party's 'struggles in this area replicate more clearly than those of any other party the ambiguous attitude held by the Welsh people towards devolution in the twentieth century'.[10] Labour's ambivalent attitude to devolution, however, resulted in policies that granted Wales greater recognition and a greater degree of autonomy.

After the Conservatives had appointed a minister for Welsh Affairs, attached to another government department, in the early 1950s Labour agreed to appoint a Cabinet minister, but without a department, to oversee Welsh affairs. Later, as the 1950s drew to a close, as a result of the influential report of the Council for Wales

---

[5]   Bogdanor, *Devolution*, 147.
[6]   John Davies, *A History of Wales* (London, 1993), 543.
[7]   Jones and Jones, 'Labour and the nation', 250.
[8]   Peter Stead, 'The Labour Party and the claims of Wales', in John Osmond (ed.), *The National Question Again: Welsh Political Identity in the 1980s* (Llandysul, 1985), 99.
[9]   Bogdanor, *Devolution*, 146.
[10]   Chris Williams, 'Introduction', in Tanner, Williams and Hopkin (eds), *Labour Party in Wales*, 16.

and Monmouthshire and pressure from its deputy leader, James Griffiths, Labour agreed, after much deliberation, to appoint a secretary of state and establish a Welsh Office. This policy was implemented in 1964. At that time there was a reassertion of Welsh identity – a phenomenon that is both 'subtle and elusive' – which had a dramatic influence on Welsh politics.[11]

After Plaid Cymru had won Carmarthen in July 1966, the party came very close to winning Rhondda West and Caerphilly in the south Wales mining valleys. It has been argued that the experiences and traumas of the 1930s had strengthened the attachment to locality, so that when the decline of the coal industry put these communities at risk, Plaid Cymru was able to appeal to this sentiment.[12] In these by-elections, Plaid Cymru emphasized the economic decline of the areas and took advantage of people's anxieties and insecurity in such conditions.[13] It 'combined protest with the restoration of hope and confidence'.[14] The voters in Rhondda West and Caerphilly, in voting for Plaid Cymru, were not voting for self-government, but protesting against the rundown of their communities and the social problems that resulted. The nationalists gained support because people felt that they had been let down by a Labour government and the newly created Welsh Office. When it was established in 1964, the Welsh Office was greeted with high expectations which, in the opinion of some, were not fulfilled.[15] Nevertheless, when the Welsh Office was created it did strengthen the idea of Wales as a territorial unit for administration.[16] As the centre of government administration in Wales, it became the subject of attack from nationalists and Labour supporters alike when it failed to prevent the rundown of the Welsh economy. In effect, it inflamed the discontent of nationalists in Wales.[17] The fact that economic matters lay outside its responsibilities made little difference. Plaid Cymru played up the economic decline of the Welsh valleys and drew comparisons between their plight and that

[11]   Bogdanor, *Devolution*, 144.
[12]   Kenneth O. Morgan, *Rebirth of a Nation: Wales, 1880–1980* (Oxford and Cardiff, 1981), 240.
[13]   Alan Butt Philip, *The Welsh Question: Nationalism in Welsh Politics, 1945–1970* (Cardiff, 1975), 181, 330.
[14]   Ibid., 205.
[15]   Morgan, *Rebirth of a Nation*, 388.
[16]   Davies, *History of Wales*, 666.
[17]   Morgan, *Rebirth of a Nation*, 389.

of the wealthier parts of England, and this gave the nationalists added support. It has been claimed that awareness that development was unequal was a key factor in the growth of nationalism.[18]

Plaid Cymru's by-election victory came at an opportune time for the party. Its victory coincided with an expansion of regional broadcasting services, particularly television, which helped to strengthen Welsh national consciousness and made all of Wales fully aware of Plaid Cymru's achievement in Carmarthen.[19] The repercussions were felt first in Rhondda West, and the result there in turn had its repercussions in Caerphilly. The growth in nationalism has been attributed to the increase in the power of the state and its control over people's lives, a control that was seen to be remote and bureaucratic.[20] However, this was not confined to Wales and Scotland. 'It was part of a wider uncertainty and disaffection with established forms of government and accepted values', prevalent throughout the United Kingdom.[21] Plaid Cymru and the Scottish National Party gave expression to grievances that also existed in other parts of the United Kingdom and brought the question of the need for a less centralized form of government to the British scene.[22]

Gwynfor Evans's success in Carmarthen in 1966 did not help those in the Labour Party who supported an elected Welsh council. It stiffened the resolve of those MPs who saw the creation of an all-Wales body (though operating only at local government level) as a concession to nationalism. After 1966 those Welsh Labour MPs did not wish to appear to be part of a nationalist agenda.[23] In the 1970s, following further nationalist successes, some Labour MPs were even prepared to join forces with the Conservatives to defeat their own government's devolution proposals. Plaid Cymru's successes in the 1960s and 1970s produced a backlash that 'led to a deep suspicion of any policies which sought to react constructively to them'.[24]

Those Labour MPs who opposed devolution were not, as a result, less Welsh than the pro-devolutionists in the party. Both groups wanted to see Wales thrive and prosper, but they had

[18]   Davies, *History of Wales*, 664.
[19]   Butt Philip, *Welsh Question*, 71, 109.
[20]   Bogdanor, *Devolution*, 4–5.
[21]   Morgan, *Rebirth of a Nation*, 407.
[22]   Bogdanor, *Devolution*, 4.
[23]   Butt Philip, *Welsh Question*, 292.
[24]   Davies, *History of Wales*, 670.

different perspectives on how this could be achieved.[25] The divide in the Labour Party in Wales occurred not because one group was more Welsh than the other; it was a divide 'between those Socialists whose national identity is as important as their socialist ideology and those other Socialists who are more influenced by the Marxist critique and the need to maintain the unity of the international working class movement'.[26] Whatever their viewpoint, Labour MPs genuinely believed that they were acting in the best interests of Wales and its people. After all, each of them represented a movement whose policies, when in office, had greatly benefited the nation.

Devolution was not one of Labour's fundamental beliefs, and so its policies on this issue (according to Alan Butt Philip) 'reflected the strength of Welsh demands for concessions to nationalism, of Labour's internal politics and of inter-party competitiveness'.[27] The debate within the Labour Party was an intense one, 'in which political priorities and programmes intersected with electoral calculation, cultural considerations and political analysis and commitment'.[28] It was indeed a divisive issue, and therefore the party sought to focus the debate on objectives that were pragmatic, rather than nationalistic.[29] In the 1950s, an emphasis on the need for more effective and efficient government eventually led to the appointment of a secretary of state in 1964. In no way was it an attempt to satisfy nationalist demands, although the need to grant Wales recognition in government was admitted. Devolution was proposed as a means of strengthening democracy at the expense of bureaucracy, rather than as a sop to nationalism.[30] In the 1970s the debate centred on the need to extend democracy: the creation of a Welsh assembly 'meant supporting public accountability and control and was a means of empowering and radicalising the people'.[31] The argument that devolution meant an extension of democracy was 'a far more acceptable ideological concept within

[25] Duncan Tanner, 'Facing the new challenge: Labour and politics, 1970–2000', in Tanner, Williams and Hopkin (eds), *Labour Party in Wales*, 281.
[26] J. Barry Jones and Michael Keating, 'The British Labour Party as a centralising force', *Studies in Public Policy*, 32 (1979), 23.
[27] Butt Philip, *Welsh Question*, 289.
[28] Jones and Jones, 'Labour and the nation', 242.
[29] Ibid., 260.
[30] Ibid., 251.
[31] Tanner, 'Facing the new challenge', 279.

the Labour Movement', but the diehard centralists remained scep-
tical.[32] In 1979 voters overwhelmingly rejected the Labour govern
ment's devolution proposals, for a variety of reasons, but it is evident
that in the circumstances current in the 1970s, political and
economic factors made the Welsh reluctant to support anything that
could be termed separatist: it was a mood that was as potent then as
in 1896, when the Cymru Fydd movement collapsed.[33]

Ideologically, the Labour Party was split on the need for a Welsh
assembly before and during the referendum campaign. Many of its
own supporters were either opposed to the policy or were lukewarm
in their support, and Labour consequently failed to campaign as a
united party to ensure a 'yes' vote in the referendum.[34] Not only was
this inability to maintain a united front a telling factor, but it was
also a very unusual occurrence in Wales, where the Labour vote was
always substantial and solid.[35] The result was interpreted as a
'defeat for Welshness', but that was as far-fetched as the claim 'that a
process of acculturation was in train'.[36] Many of those voters who
had rejected an assembly were just as committed to Wales as those
who had supported the proposal, but in their view that commitment
did not imply a commitment to devolution, as embodied in the
Wales Act 1978. Centralists and unionists claimed that the referendum marked the end of the devolution debate and, in Kenneth
O. Morgan's words, 'It was clearly destined to continue (if perhaps
less passionately) in years to come'.[37]

During the period under review in this book, governments at
different times faced demands from Wales for self-government, for
more parliamentary time for Welsh affairs and, above all, for more
administrative devolution and greater recognition in government.
These demands and the responses to them are discussed in the
following chapters. Self-government was never on the political

[32]   J. Barry Jones, 'The development of the devolution debate', in David Foulkes, J. Barry
Jones and R. A. Wilford (eds), *The Welsh Veto: The Wales Act 1978 and the Referendum*
(Cardiff, 1983), 24.
[33]   Morgan, *Rebirth of a Nation*, 405; Kenneth O. Morgan, 'Forward', in Foulkes, Jones
and Wilford (eds), *Welsh Veto*, ix.
[34]   J. Barry Jones and Michael Keating, 'The resolution of internal conflicts and external
pressures: the Labour Party's devolution policy', *Government and Opposition*, 17 (Summer
1982), 291.
[35]   Denis Balsom, 'Public opinion and Welsh devolution', in Foulkes, Jones and Wilford
(eds), *Welsh Veto*, 214.
[36]   Davies, *History of Wales*, 677.
[37]   Morgan, *Rebirth of a Nation*, 408.

agenda, but more parliamentary time was allocated to Welsh affairs, and, more significantly, there was a substantial increase in administrative devolution, though the development was uneven. At times, it seemed that the pace was slow, but at other times there was appreciable change, under both Labour and Conservative governments. During the period, the office of secretary of state was an important development. Initially, there were demands that such a post be created; thereafter there were demands that its functions be extended, and, finally, proposals were made to transfer many of its functions to an elected assembly. These developments give the period a definite unity.

In Wales, there was always dissension in the Labour Party whenever changes in the machinery of government were discussed, but up until the 1970s it managed to contain these differences of opinion. The party was able to reach a consensus, if at times an uneasy one. Labour's problems in this area are discussed at length hereafter, and discussion of the situation within the party in the 1970s includes the notable part played by a constituency party in south-east Wales in successfully mobilizing opposition to its own government's proposals for a Welsh assembly. Its action was totally unexpected and certainly unprecedented. Opposition from England, which was not anticipated, is another aspect of the discussion. MPs representing English constituencies joined economic planning councils and local authorities in opposing the assembly proposals, and their decisive role in the debate is critically examined.

This study is based on primary sources and on information made personally available to the author. Interviews were also conducted with prominent individuals who had been involved in the devolution debates, some over a considerable period, and their unique knowledge has helped to clarify and explain certain actions and decisions. These contributions were invaluable because documentary evidence does not always tell the whole story.

It is acknowledged that historians and others have written extensively on devolution in a Welsh context, not least in recent decades. This book provides a longer perspective on developments and places them in a wider context.

I

CLAIMS FOR RECOGNITION IN GOVERNMENT, 1937–1945

Towards the end of the nineteenth century, when Home Rule for Ireland was a major issue, there was an attempt to induce the Liberal Party, a centralist party, to pay more attention to Welsh problems. This resulted in the formation of Cymru Fydd (Wales to Be or 'Young Wales') in 1886. After merging with the North Wales Liberal Federation in 1895, it seemed that Cymru Fydd could become a nationalist movement embracing the whole of Welsh Liberalism. But that was not to be. In 1896, at a meeting in Newport, the South Wales Liberal Federation refused to become part of Cymru Fydd and the movement came to an end. Unlike in Ireland, in Wales most people saw themselves as both Welsh and British and had no inclination to break away from the British state. Rather, the objective was to ensure that Wales's distinctive needs were recognized within that state.[1] In Glanmor Williams's view, it is doubtful whether the Liberal leaders would have pressed 'the claims of Home Rule to the exclusion of all else'. To them 'Home Rule was a matter of tactics, useful for bringing pressure to bear on the Liberal Party, but which could be quickly dropped in face of a hostile Tory majority in the Commons'.[2]

By the 1930s, the Liberal Party had been displaced by the Labour Party as the major force in Welsh politics. The social and economic conditions prevailing in the 1920s had enabled the Labour Party to benefit in electoral terms, and it became associated with protests against these conditions. In 1900 Keir Hardie had been elected MP for Merthyr Tydfil Boroughs, and in just over twenty years the Labour Party had made a spectacular advance in Wales. The 1929 general election had seen Labour reach a new peak in Wales, with twenty-five MPs (the same number as it was to achieve in 1945), and nationally the party, led by J. Ramsay

---

[1]   David Williams, *A History of Modern Wales* (London, 1950), 280–1; K. O. Morgan, 'Welsh nationalism: the historical background', *Journal of Contemporary History*, 6 (1971), 165–6; Morgan, *Rebirth of a Nation*, 120.
[2]   Glanmor Williams, 'The idea of nationality in Wales', *Cambridge Journal*, December 1953, 157.

MacDonald, had been able to form a government. The election had also witnessed the arrival on the parliamentary scene of Aneurin Bevan (Labour, Ebbw Vale), Megan Lloyd George (Liberal, Anglesey) and Clement Davies (Liberal, Montgomeryshire). Following the 1931 general election, when Labour representation in Wales fell to sixteen (including an Independent Labour Party member), MacDonald formed a National government and remained prime minister until 1935. In the general election of that year the number of Labour MPs in Wales rose slightly to eighteen, and the party held every seat in industrial south Wales.[3] Nine of these Labour members were returned unopposed, together with a tenth, in Swansea East.[4] A National government again took office, under Stanley Baldwin, and Neville Chamberlain succeeded him as prime minister in 1937.[5] Before the outbreak of the Second World War, Welsh MPs were joined by James Griffiths (Labour, Llanelli) and Ness Edwards (Labour, Caerphilly), both of whom were elected in by-elections.[6] Griffiths, a Welsh speaker from industrial Carmarthenshire, was to be a key figure in the devolution debate within the Labour Party over the next thirty years or so. At the outbreak of the war nearly all the Labour MPs representing south Wales mining communities were miners' nominees. James Griffiths was a former president of the South Wales Miners' Federation, and S. O. Davies (Merthyr Tydfil) and Arthur Jenkins (Pontypool) were former vice-presidents. The other ex-miners were D. R. Grenfell (Gower), William Jenkins (Neath), E. J. Williams (Ogmore), George Hall (Aberdare), William John (Rhondda West), W. H. Mainwaring (Rhondda East), Ness Edwards, Charles Edwards (Bedwellty), George Daggar (Abertillery) and Aneurin Bevan, who was to achieve greater prominence than any one of the others.[7] Griffiths, Arthur Jenkins, Williams, Ness Edwards, Daggar and Bevan were former students of the Central Labour College, where Mainwaring had been a tutor and where the theoretical teaching in economics and historical science was based on Marxian theories.[8]

---

[3] David Butler and Anne Sloman, *British Political Facts, 1900–1975* (London and Basingstoke, 4th edn., 1975), 18, 20, 187–8.

[4] Beti Jones, *Parliamentary Elections in Wales, 1900–1975* (Talybont, 1977), 91–5.

[5] Butler and Sloman, *British Political Facts*, 22.

[6] Jones, *Parliamentary Elections*, 95–6.

[7] *Who Was Who*, vol. III (1929–40) (London, 1941); vol. IV (1941–50) (London, 1952), passim.

[8] W. W. Craik, *The Central Labour College, 1909–29* (London, 1964), 117, 147, 173–6, 184.

In the first quarter of the twentieth century, self-government had not been an issue in Welsh politics, but a Speaker's Conference had been held on the subject and E. T. John (Liberal, Denbigh East) in 1914 and R. J. Thomas (Liberal, Wrexham) in 1922 had introduced bills. Neither bill had proceeded beyond the first reading. In 1925, a year before the general strike, a Welsh Nationalist Party had been founded, demanding 'dominion status for Wales' and 'an almost complete severance from the political and economic fabric of England', but as a political force it was to make little impact until the 1960s.[9] In the 1930s, too, when the Depression was ravaging the Welsh nation, there was no clamour for a separate parliament, though a few MPs from all parties had come to favour the appointment of a secretary of state. On 29 October 1937 Clement Davies presented a bill 'to provide for and appoint a Secretary of State for Wales and Monmouthshire'. Ernest Evans (Liberal, University of Wales), Arthur Evans (Conservative, Cardiff South), William Jenkins, William John, Goronwy Owen (Liberal, Caernarvonshire), Reginald Clarry (Conservative, Newport), Henry Morris-Jones (Liberal National, Denbigh), Daniel Hopkin (Labour, Carmarthen), Gwilym Lloyd George (Liberal, Pembrokeshire) and Owen Temple Morris (National Conservative, Cardiff East) supported him.[10] Like so many private members' bills, it received only a first reading.[11] The Welsh Parliamentary Party, representing all the Welsh MPs, made the next attempt. A deputation from the party, led by the chairman, Morgan Jones (Labour, Caerphilly), met the prime minister, Neville Chamberlain, on 30 June 1938, to put the case for the appointment of a secretary of state and the creation of a Welsh Office. Chamberlain, in a reply sent on 27 July, maintained that the request could not be granted for several reasons. He explained that, where feasible, Welsh divisions had been established in government offices in London and that there were offices in Wales to deal with questions that could be handled locally. Therefore, there would be no advantage from the coordination of activities in one department that would, in any case, involve considerable expense, which was not justifiable at that time. Parity with Scotland was one of the arguments advanced by the deputation, but Chamberlain, like others after him, contended that the situations were not parallel,

[9]   Morgan, 'Welsh nationalism', 169.
[10] Secretary of State for Wales and Monmouthshire Bill (29 October 1937).
[11] Information from Public Information Office, House of Commons.

because Scotland had different legal and administrative systems from those of England. Even before the creation of the Scottish Office, the lord advocate was responsible for a separate Scottish department in London, and most of the administrative work relating to Scotland was performed in Scotland. Wales had always been closely united with England and there were therefore no distinct legal and administrative systems that required the attention of a separate department.[12] Thus, during a decade of depression there were no changes in the machinery of government in Wales.

During the war the proposal to appoint a secretary of state was supported by the South Wales Regional Council of Labour. This Council, consisting of Labour Party and trade union representatives, had been set up in 1937 to counter Communist influence in the region.[13] Its first secretary was George Morris. After a meeting with Harold Laski, a member of the Labour Party National Executive Committee, in October 1941, the Council appointed committees to investigate a number of subjects, including the machinery of government.[14] On 25 April 1942, a few weeks before the Council's annual conference, James Griffiths, who was becoming an increasingly important influence nationally in the Labour Party, declared in a speech at Caernarvon that the government should recognize Wales by appointing a secretary of state. He also discussed the possibility of a form of self-government emerging from the regional system established during the war, if that system were retained.[15] Such references by Labour politicians in Wales to self-government raised expectations, and were to cause embarrassment later when political opponents quoted them. Addressing the annual conference of the Regional Council on 16 May, Griffiths again stressed that there was in Wales 'a growing consciousness of nationhood' and that the Labour movement should recognize it. The conference followed his lead and carried unanimously a resolution submitted by Cardiff Borough Labour Party: 'That this conference is of the opinion that the time is now opportune to press for the appointment of a Secretary of State for Wales.'[16] At its next annual conference, on 15 May 1943, the year when Cliff Prothero,

---

[12] James Griffiths, *Pages from Memory* (London, 1969), 158–9.
[13] Cliff Prothero, *Recount* (Ormskirk and Northridge, 1982), 53.
[14] South Wales Regional Council of Labour, *Annual Meeting*, 16 May 1942, 4.
[15] *Y Cymro*, 25 April 1942.
[16] *Report of the Annual Conference of South Wales Regional Council of Labour*, 16 May 1942, 6, 15.

an ex-miner and former student of the Central Labour College, became its secretary, the Regional Council passed unanimously a resolution submitted by the executive committee reiterating its demand that the office of secretary of state should be created. That resolution went further than the one passed the previous year, in that it requested that the secretary of state's powers and responsibilities should be the same as those bestowed on the secretary of state for Scotland. It also urged the Labour Party to press for the creation of such an office in order to satisfy the claims of Wales for recognition.[17] Later in July, in an article in *Wales*, James Griffiths developed his ideas when he suggested that democratically elected regional authorities could administer a range of services, including water supplies, roads and bridges, electrical generation and distribution, and transport. There should also be decentralization from Whitehall, with the appointment of a secretary of state.[18] At the annual conference of the Labour Party in that year, a resolution supporting the demand for a secretary of state was not discussed and was referred to the National Executive Committee for consideration. On 29 September 1943 representatives of the National Executive Committee met the executive committee of the South Wales Regional Council of Labour to discuss the demand, but when they reported the National Executive Committee decided to defer a decision, pending the return of James Griffiths from abroad and consultations with Welsh Labour MPs. The executive committee of the Regional Council met Griffiths on his return and appealed to him to use his influence on the National Executive Committee in order to secure a favourable reply. No reply had been received from the NEC when the Regional Council held its annual conference on 6 May 1944.[19] At the conference another resolution, submitted by the Ogmore Constituency Labour Party and calling 'upon the Government to grant the unanimous demand of the Welsh people for a Secretary of State for Wales', was carried unanimously.[20] Iwan Morgan, who was to be the parliamentary candidate in Cardiganshire in 1945 and 1950, supported the motion.[21]

---

[17]   *Report of the Annual Conference of South Wales Regional Council of Labour,* 15 May 1943, 16; Craik, *The Central Labour College,* 180.

[18]   Jim Griffiths, 'Wales after the war', *Wales,* July 1943, 10.

[19]   South Wales Regional Council of Labour, *Annual Meeting,* 6 May 1944, 9.

[20]   *Report of the Annual Conference of South Wales Regional Council of Labour,* 6 May 1944, 16.

[21]   Jones, *Parliamentary Elections,* 101, 108.

In 1943, when the appointment of a secretary of state was supported by the South Wales Regional Council of Labour, Edgar L. Chappell, a prominent member of both Cardiff Rural District Council and Glamorgan County Council, published his own views on the reform of the machinery of government in *Wake Up, Wales!* and *The Government of Wales*. In the former he drew a distinction between delegation and devolution. He cited the Welsh Board of Health as an example of a body that had powers delegated to it, explaining that it would be devolution if such bodies were placed under a minister with sole responsibility for Wales. Such a minister would be able to advance Welsh claims, as in the case of Scotland. Chappell recognized that for such a demand to be successful it was necessary to convince the public of the need for reform. That was to be the role of the Welsh Parliamentary Party. Although a number of local authorities and a few political organizations had supported the appointment of a secretary of state, 'speaking generally', he said, 'the public are indifferent, while a substantial number of people are definitely opposed'.[22] That observation was probably just as true in 1964, when the office was eventually created. In *The Government of Wales*, Chappell argued that Wales, because of particular characteristics, had special problems and a different outlook in comparison with England. Consequently, more radical changes might be necessary, resulting in different arrangements. He also emphasized the need to consider Wales as a unit for government administration, and proposed that under the control of a secretary of state a Welsh planning authority should be established to direct economic activities. Chappell was more aware than most of his contemporaries of the weakness of local government, and his proposals for reform were probably more controversial at the time than the proposal that a secretary of state be appointed. In his view a national administrative council for Wales should be established as part of the reform of local government in Wales. Being a pragmatist, Chappell realized that there would be opposition to his plan and he was not afraid to say so:

> I do not expect my plan to be approved by the majority of local authority officials and members. The former – especially those holding part-time appointments – desire the continuance of the present system as they have a financial interest to protect. Many of the latter are more concerned with

---

[22]   Edgar L. Chappell, *Wake Up, Wales!* (London, 1943), 62.

their personal status and prestige than they are with efficient service. They love to be called Councillor, but too often they discharge the duties of the office in a very casual manner.

Although many of them bear the label Radical or Socialist, at heart they are diehard Conservatives, and will fight against any changes that are likely to affect the continuance of their public offices. Most of them are older in years than in civic knowledge and wisdom – the average age of the members of two public bodies on which I serve is above sixty years – their ideas are set, their vision is dimmed and their general attitude is one of resistance to change.[23]

Local government reform did not take place for another thirty years, and Chappell's observations were just as applicable later as they were in 1943. By 1943, Chappell, who had been an early member of the ILP in the Swansea Valley, had left the Labour Party, and the criticisms were obviously levelled at its local government leaders in south Wales.

In the 1940s the appointment of a secretary of state was being discussed by local authorities in Wales, and a conference convened by the Association of Welsh Local Authorities took place in Shrewsbury on 30 June 1943. This conference, attended by 233 representatives from 110 local authorities, unanimously passed the following resolution:

That this Conference is of opinion that proper administrative and legislative attention is not being given to affairs in Wales and Monmouthshire and that it is essential for the development and proper government of the people of Wales, that, as in the case of Scotland, opportunity is available for direct contact with the Government through the Cabinet, and that to this end and to ensure adequate and proper administrative and legislative attention being devoted to Welsh affairs, His Majesty's Government be urged to proceed immediately with the appointment of a Secretary of State for Wales and Monmouthshire.

It was agreed that the resolution should be sent to the prime minister, Winston Churchill, the deputy prime minister, Clement Attlee, the home secretary, Herbert Morrison, and every MP. In addition, each local authority was asked to communicate with the MP for its area requesting support for the proposal, and the Welsh Parliamentary Party was requested to seek a debate on the issue. The Welsh local authorities at their conference also appointed a

[23]   Idem, *The Government of Wales* (London, 1943), 68–9.

committee to discuss with the Welsh Parliamentary Party the prep-aration of evidence supporting the creation of the office of secretary of state. The local authorities felt that they should collaborate closely with the Welsh Parliamentary Party and that they should act jointly, because the creation of an office of secretary of state was an issue that vitally affected local government, and the local author-ities' practical experience would be invaluable. They considered that duties and powers in relation to education, health and housing, agriculture and forestry, the home department and planning should be vested in the secretary of state, and that he should be assisted by at least an under-secretary. A memorandum incorporating the fore-going proposals was submitted to the Welsh Parliamentary Party in March 1944.[24]

On 10 June 1943, just before the conference of Welsh local authorities, S. O. Davies raised the matter in the House of Commons. In reply, Attlee said that the prime minister would not introduce legislation for the appointment of a secretary of state for Wales. When D. R. Grenfell again raised the matter, on 6 July 1943, Churchill said that there was a tendency towards too many minis-ters so that careful consideration had to be given to new claims. Furthermore, in his view, to create an entirely new department was not a feasible proposition.[25] James Griffiths, secretary of the Welsh Parliamentary Party at that point, recalled later that there was unanimity on the demand for a secretary of state, but that there were many differences when the question of functions was discussed. The view that the demand should be restricted to the transfer of education and health, where there was some degree of devolution, prevailed. The replies given by Attlee and Churchill were discussed by the Welsh Parliamentary Party, and on 7 July a letter signed by the officers, including Aneurin Bevan, a vice-chairman, was sent to the prime minister. In the letter it was pointed out that the party had decided unanimously to examine the prob-lems of the machinery of government in Wales, and especially the creation of a Welsh Office with a secretary of state. A committee had been set up to formulate proposals to forward to the govern-ment and it was hoped that representatives of the Welsh Parliamentary Party would be received by the government to

[24]   UWS, S. O. Davies Papers, BI, Association of Welsh Local Authorities, memorandum to the Welsh Parliamentary Party, March 1944.
[25]   Parl. Deb., vol. 390, cols 845, 1928.

discuss them.[26] The committee appointed by the Welsh Parliamentary Party left the work of preparing a memorandum to Clement Davies and the former Liberal, R. Moelwyn Hughes (Labour, Carmarthen); the intention was that the memorandum should be sent to the prime minister, along with resolutions received from other bodies.[27] On 30 October the prime minister replied to Arthur Evans, chairman of the Welsh Parliamentary Party. He stated that the time was inopportune for making such a controversial appointment and therefore there was no advantage in receiving a deputation. On the other hand, he agreed that it was a matter that could be discussed when the war was over.[28]

When the Welsh Parliamentary Party was pressing the Coalition government for a secretary of state in 1944, Herbert Morrison proposed that a 'Welsh day' should be conceded to enable MPs to debate Welsh affairs. In a letter to the prime minister in February, he suggested that it would partly meet the demands of Welsh MPs, without conceding a secretary of state. He proposed that one or two ministers should speak for all ministers in the debate, but he did recognize that it might encourage Welsh members to seek further concessions.[29] The Cabinet approved the proposal, but Ernest Bevin, the minister of Labour and National Service, was adamant that if questions regarding employment in Wales were asked it should be stated clearly that there was one policy for the whole country.[30] On 17 October 1944, during what proved to be the first debate on Welsh affairs, members pressed the case for a secretary of state, on the basis that Wales was a nation and that the fact should be recognized. It was an argument that James Griffiths was to advance again and again in subsequent years. R. Moelwyn Hughes admitted that the claim was a nationalist one, but it was a nationalism that involved neither ostracism of, nor contempt for, others. Attention was drawn to the fact that Wales, unlike Scotland, did not have a minister whose responsibility it was to see that Welsh interests were not only safeguarded but also understood. Scotland with a secretary of state enjoyed definite advantages: financial assistance had been given by the government towards a hydroelectric scheme

[26]   Griffiths, *Pages from Memory,* 160.
[27]   NLW, J. Griffiths Papers, C2/3, A. Evans to J. Griffiths, 13 August 1943.
[28]   TNA, PREM. 4 36/9, Prime Minister to A. Evans, 30 October 1943.
[29]   Ibid., Home Secretary to the Prime Minister, 4 February 1944.
[30]   TNA, CAB. 65 41, WM (44) 27, 3 March 1944.

in order to develop the Highlands, and Scotland, unlike Wales, had a representative on the Forestry Commission. George Daggar thought that the demand for a secretary of state was a reasonable one, and he supported it. For his part, though, Aneurin Bevan condemned the whole idea of a Welsh affairs debate. In general, he did not think that it was needed, and the debate itself had proved the point. He conceded that Wales had 'a special place, a special individuality, a special culture and special claims', and he did not think that they could be properly discussed at Westminster. He thought that there was an argument for 'considerable devolution of government' and that Welsh problems should be discussed in Wales.[31] Unfortunately, he did not develop this point, and what Bevan actually meant remains a mystery. Writing in *Tribune* on 20 October, under the pen-name of 'Jack Wilkes', he criticized the proceedings, claiming that his fellow Welsh members had 'revelled in a debauch of oratory', and in a virtually empty chamber had spoken not so much to try to influence the government's policy, but in order to impress their constituents. As a result, 'almost every Welsh factory, dock, farm, road and school which claimed Government attention' had been mentioned. He believed that debates on the problems which afflicted the United Kingdom were likely to be more effective in securing social progress than those based on 'geographical areas'.[32] Subsequent debates were to confirm Bevan's judgement. The debate was given considerable press coverage in Wales, but it was not considered to be a debate of importance at Westminster. The party in opposition seemed to want the debate more than the party in government, and usually the sole participants were Welsh MPs and a few ministers. Bevan was surely right; it was and remained a futile exercise. R. Hopkin Morris (Liberal, Carmarthen) later shared Bevan's view about the standard of debate. In an article in the *Western Mail* on 27 November 1948, he wrote, 'An attendant with many years' experience of the House summed up the debate thus: "On the Scottish Day all parties unite to attack the Government; on the Welsh Day the Members attack one another." '[33]

On 10 November 1944 Megan Lloyd George, who had succeeded Arthur Evans as chairman of the Welsh Parliamentary

[31] Parl. Deb., vol. 403, cols 2315, 2251, 2243, 2240–1, 2256, 2298, 2311–14.
[32] 'Jack Wilkes', 'Lords and Commons', *Tribune*, 20 October 1944, 8.
[33] *Western Mail*, 27 November 1948.

Party, wrote to the prime minister to press for a decision regarding the appointment of a secretary of state. Attached to the draft reply submitted by one of his staff to the prime minister was this note: 'A non-committal and temporizing reply is submitted for your signature if approved.'[34] The draft reply stated: 'The difficulty is that a proposal of this nature has such far-reaching implications in the administrative sphere that detailed consideration has to be given to it by the many authorities concerned. These authorities are of course heavily burdened with war tasks.'[35] The prime minister saw no reason to change it, and the reply was sent on 2 January 1945.[36] The demand of the Welsh Parliamentary Party for a secretary of state was also turned down by the Coalition government's Machinery of Government Committee in February 1945, but the committee requested that a scheme be drawn up for an elected advisory council. A paper outlining two alternative schemes for a Welsh Council of State was prepared. The schemes were:

(a) A council drawn from local authorities and the University of Wales, with a number of members to be co-opted by the council itself.
(b) A council to be made up of representatives from all existing and future specialist advisory bodies.

The committee considered this paper in May 1945, but the general election prevented the committee from completing its deliberations.[37]

In the months prior to the general election in 1945, Labour candidates in north Wales supported the demand for a secretary of state. At a conference in February, it was decided that a resolution proposed by Huw Morris Jones (Merioneth), requesting the appointment of a secretary of state for Wales as a first step towards self-government, and proposing that Wales be treated as a unit during the post-war period of reconstruction, should be forwarded to the annual conference of the Labour Party, to be held in Blackpool. Eirene Jones (later White) (Flintshire) considered that the

[34]   TNA, PREM. 4 36/9, member of his staff to the Prime Minister.
[35]   Ibid., draft reply from the Prime Minister to Megan Lloyd George, 2 January 1945.
[36]   NLW, J. Griffiths Papers, C2/5, Prime Minister to Megan Lloyd George, 2 January 1945.
[37]   TNA, PREM. 8 1569 Part 2, MG (48) 5, 23 September 1948.

appointment of a secretary of state was the best practical proposal, but Goronwy Roberts (Caernarvonshire) was in favour of a stronger resolution.[38] D. Tecwyn Lloyd recalled later that at University College, Bangor, Roberts had been one of the founders of a movement known as Mudiad Gwerin (People's Movement), the aims of which had been to bring together nationalists and socialists in an attempt to secure self-government and a socialist economic order.[39] Roberts demanded a federal parliament and hoped that a national planning authority, on the lines of the Tennessee Valley Authority, would eventually lead to that.[40] Addressing the conference, James Griffiths agreed that Wales was a suitable unit for a scheme similar to the Tennessee Valley Authority.[41] In fact, the Welsh Nationalist Party had published in the early 1940s a pamphlet entitled *TVA for Wales*, in which it had advocated a Welsh economic authority. In support of its claims, it had quoted a US Congress committee:

> The Authority has recognised that planning can but suggest and that any development in the future, as it has been in the past, will be in the hands of local communities. The presence of this regional planning agency, decentralised from Washington, has stimulated the desire to solve the problems of the region.[42]

In July, the Caernarvonshire Constituency Labour Party, in its own election broadsheet *Llais Llafur*, supported the appointment of a secretary of state with responsibility for education and agriculture, and of a national planning authority on the lines of the Tennessee Valley Authority. It declared, too, that workers should not be transferred against their will and that a trunk road should be built linking north and south Wales. A broadcasting corporation for Wales should also be established. Later, in 1946, in the *New Statesman and Nation*, readers were to be reminded that the Labour government had turned down all five 'promises'. Actually, they were not Labour Party promises but the views of a constituency party. It was pointed out in the broadsheet that all candidates in north Wales were young

[38]   *Y Cymro*, 16 February 1945.
[39]   D. Tecwyn Lloyd, 'Cyfraniad y brifysgol i wleidyddiaeth', *Efrydiau Athronyddol*, 1974, 37.
[40]   The Tennessee Valley Authority is 'a public corporation established in 1930 to develop and control the natural resources of the Tennessee valley in the south-eastern United States', *Chambers's Encyclopaedia*, 13 (1973), 538.
[41]   *Y Cymro*, 16 February 1945.
[42]   Welsh Nationalist Party, *TVA for Wales* (Caernarfon, n.d.), 9.

and of exceptional ability, and very much part of the Welsh radical tradition. Electors were reminded of the Cymru Fydd movement and that these candidates had the same aspirations. It was recognized that socialism was an international movement, but the Welsh nation, like every other nation, should be given the right to govern itself in those matters that were particular to Wales as a nation. Welshness and socialism must be linked. In a personal message to the electors, Goronwy Roberts pledged that he would do his utmost to secure for Wales its rights as a nation. He supported the appointment of a secretary of state to give Wales parity with Scotland, but emphasized that securing a national planning authority similar to the Tennessee Valley Authority was more important, as this would give Wales a moderate degree of self-government.[43]

James Griffiths, however, speaking in Caernarvon in June, had stressed that the appointment of a secretary of state was the first priority, but that this should be followed by the reorganization of local government; from that combination he foresaw a new form of self-government emerging.[44] In 1943 Griffiths had supported a regional authority with a reduced number of local authorities beneath it, and in that same year he moved a National Executive Committee resolution on local government at the Labour Party conference.[45] The executive had proposed that 'New Local Government Regions should be created in which there would be (i) Regional Authorities and (ii) Secondary or Area Authorities', but although the resolution was carried it did not get the necessary two-thirds' majority, and so did not become official party policy.[46] At the very time when Griffiths was supporting the appointment of a secretary of state, the draft of a Labour Party leaflet entitled 'Labour and Wales', produced for the general election, included the ambiguous statement:

> To secure the freedom of Wales the irresponsible power of monopoly must be curtailed. In other words the true freedom of Wales depends not only on political control over her own life but economic control as well. True freedom for Wales would be the result and product of a Socialised Britain,

[43] *Llais Llafur*, 5 July 1945 (broadsheet supporting G. Roberts in the 1945 general election); *New Statesman and Nation*, 24 August 1946, 125.

[44] *Y Cymro*, 29 June 1945.

[45] Griffiths, 'Wales after the war', 10.

[46] *Report of the Annual Conference of the Labour Party*, 1943, 191; *Evidence of the Labour Party in Wales to the Commission on the Constitution*, 7 January 1970 (Cardiff, 1970), 19.

and under such conditions could self-government in Wales be an effective and secure guardian of the life of the nation.[47]

This statement and the statements of individual candidates meant that there was uncertainty at the time as to what was official party policy. A party worker from Bangor asked the general secretary of the Labour Party, Welsh-born Morgan Phillips, whether the party supported 'independence', 'self-government' or a 'secretary'.[48] In his reply, on 15 June, Phillips explained that while the South Wales Regional Council of Labour and the Welsh Parliamentary Party were in favour of a secretary of state, the Labour Party had not approved it centrally. He further explained that the reason for this was that during the war Labour ministers could see that the need to have separate legislation for Scotland had caused delay; in fact, there had also been delays with other matters because a number of ministries were concerned with the same problem. His own view was that it was 'impracticable political thinking' to believe that the appointment of a secretary of state would solve deep-seated problems, because Wales was affected by the same economic and social problems as those experienced by other parts of the country.[49] Phillips had been a student at the Central Labour College and his view was very much in line with that of other Labour leaders, such as Aneurin Bevan who, as Cledwyn Hughes (the Labour candidate for Anglesey at the time) later recalled, had dismissed as pure 'chauvinism' his suggestion that a specific Welsh policy should be included in the manifesto.[50] At the time of the general election in 1945, then, the party nationally had not come to any conclusion regarding the appointment of a secretary of state for Wales, but the party in Wales, together with the Welsh Parliamentary Party and the local authorities, considered that the post should be created.

Prior to the 1930s attempts had been made by MPs to secure a measure of self-government for Wales, but thereafter individual MPs and the Welsh Parliamentary Party, supported by the South Wales Regional Council of Labour and the local authorities, endeavoured to secure the appointment of a secretary of state. It

---

[47]   LPA, M. Phillips Papers, draft of a leaflet entitled 'Labour and Wales', June 1945.
[48]   Ibid., party worker in Bangor to M. Phillips, June 1945.
[49]   Ibid., M. Phillips to Labour Party worker in Bangor, 15 June 1945.
[50]   Craik, *Central Labour College*, 180; Lord Cledwyn, *The Referendum: The End of an Era* (Cardiff, 1981), 10.

was thought that Wales as a nation should be recognized in government administration, and also that such an appointment would help to protect and promote the country's interests. All these requests were turned down, but the Coalition government did make a minor concession – an annual debate on Welsh affairs. Following the end of the war renewed attempts were to be made to secure a secretary of state, and so began a thirty-five year period when there was to be increasing Welsh pressure both for greater recognition within the government and for a greater measure of devolution. Both the Labour Party – in essence a committed centralist party – and the firmly unionist Conservative Party were to make concessions when confronted with these demands.

II

LABOUR INTRANSIGENCE AND TORY CONCESSION, 1945–1951

'NO CASE FOR A SECRETARY OF STATE'

When the results of the general election were declared in July 1945, Labour had gained a landslide victory with 393 seats, and in Wales the party won twenty-five of the thirty-six seats.[1] Five MPs polled over 70 per cent of the total vote, seven, including George Hall, Ness Edwards, Aneurin Bevan, James Griffiths and S. O. Davies, polled over 80 per cent, and in Rhondda West, William John was returned unopposed.[2] For Labour Party workers the result was the realization of a lifetime's ambition.[3] Amongst the new Labour members were Goronwy Roberts (Caernarvonshire), Tudor Watkins (Brecon and Radnor), George Thomas (Cardiff Central), James Callaghan (Cardiff South), Hilary Marquand (Cardiff East), L. Ungoed-Thomas (Llandaff and Barry) and Peter Freeman (Newport), a former MP for Brecon and Radnor. Labour had consolidated its position in south Wales, and although R. Moelwyn Hughes had been defeated in Carmarthen, the party won one rural seat (Caernarvonshire) and came very close to winning Anglesey, Flintshire, Merioneth, Monmouth and Pembrokeshire.[4] Thus, Labour was a force in the rural areas as well as in the industrial areas and was on its way to becoming a truly national party. Welsh MPs figured prominently in the new government: Aneurin Bevan was appointed minister of Health, George Hall secretary of state for the Colonies, James Griffiths minister of National Insurance, Hilary Marquand secretary for Overseas Trade and Ness Edwards parliamentary secretary, Ministry of Labour and National Service.[5]

Following the general election, the question of a secretary of state was raised again in the House of Commons. In his maiden

---

[1] Butler and Sloman, *British Political Facts*, 184, 188.
[2] Jones, *Parliamentary Elections*, 99–104.
[3] Prothero, *Recount*, 58.
[4] Jones, *Parliamentary Elections*, 99–104.
[5] Butler and Sloman, *British Political Facts*, 32–6.

speech, on 17 August, George Thomas reminded the government that Welsh members were in agreement that the request should be considered, and on 21 August, Emrys Roberts (Liberal, Merioneth), in another maiden speech, called for the appointment of a secretary of state and the creation of a national development authority to develop the country's resources.[6] After the matter had been referred to the Machinery of Government Committee, on 16 October James Callaghan joined those who demanded that such an appointment should be considered.[7] At an earlier meeting of the committee, on 10 May, when the Coalition government was still in office, the home secretary had been asked to consider whether it could be arranged that he should be responsible for Welsh affairs. Following that decision, Chuter Ede, the new home secretary in the Labour administration, presented a memorandum to the Machinery of Government Committee on 1 October 1945. In his memorandum he indicated that he could not see how that proposal could be put into effect. Furthermore, if responsibility were assigned to the home secretary, he wondered whether his responsibility would be 'parallel with, or subordinate or superior, to the responsibility of the Minister concerned with the specific subject?' There was also the possibility that if MPs were dissatisfied with ministers' answers to parliamentary questions, they would redirect them to the home secretary. He concluded that a situation where one minister might become a court of appeal against the decision of another minister was unacceptable.[8]

Discussion of the administration of Wales and Monmouthshire was resumed at a meeting of the Machinery of Government Committee on 25 October, with George Hall and Aneurin Bevan present. Both Hall and Bevan were opposed to the appointment of a secretary of state; Bevan emphasized that the problems of Wales were those experienced in England and 'separation would be inimical to Welsh interests'. Furthermore, he suggested that the appointment would not be welcome in the densely populated and Anglicized parts of south Wales, namely Monmouthshire and Glamorgan. He also rejected the arguments for more administrative devolution unless local government could be reorganized on a

[6] Parl. Deb., vol. 413, cols 208, 510.
[7] Ibid., vol. 414, col. 918.
[8] TNA, PREM. 8 1569 Part 1, MG (45) 17, 1 October 1945.

regional basis. As minister of Health, he maintained that administrative devolution in the case of the Welsh Board of Health had not always resulted in administration that could be described as efficient.[9] The lord president, Herbert Morrison, as chairman, prepared the Machinery of Government Committee's report to the Cabinet. The committee recommended that the claim for a secretary of state should not be granted, for a number of reasons. It was thought that increasing the number of ministers would be undesirable, that the argument for a separate administration was not as strong as it was in Scotland, and that the appointment would not provide a remedy in the economic field, since the secretary of state for Scotland had no direct responsibility in economic affairs. Although it was admitted that there were historical, linguistic (in part) and cultural differences between Wales and England, if these were not supplemented by legal differences they did not in themselves provide a powerful case for the appointment of a minister. Neither could the committee recommend any alternatives, such as the appointment of a secretary of state without executive responsibilities or assigning to the home secretary responsibility for looking after Welsh affairs. The possibility of setting up an advisory council had also been considered, but the committee found that it was difficult 'to devise a plan by which such a Council would not become either a dead letter or a dilatory nuisance'. Such an unsatisfactory alternative to a secretary of state would only lead to demands for it to be made more effective. The committee recommended that the government should reject the claim for a secretary of state and that it should not propose an alternative, but that possible alternatives might have to be considered as a result of the reaction to the government's proposals.[10]

When the Cabinet discussed the matter on 28 January 1946, Aneurin Bevan referred to the fact that the demand had come partly from those who wished to see mid and north Wales 'achieve a separate identity' and partly from those who were concerned about the economic situation in south Wales. He thought that demand from the latter region would diminish as the government's economic policies succeeded. The prime minister, Clement Attlee, thought that the strongest demand had come from those concerned

[9]   Ibid., MG (45) 11, 25 October 1945.
[10] TNA, CAB. 129/6, CP (46) 21, 23 January 1946.

about the economic problems, and it was precisely in that sphere that the case for a secretary of state was weakest. The lord chancellor, Lord Jowitt, raised the question of meeting nationalist feeling and thought that the Welsh Reconstruction Advisory Council set up during the war could be retained for that purpose.[11] In fact, Percy Watkins, as chairman of the Wales Survey Board, had proposed in February 1943, in a memorandum to the Welsh Parliamentary Party, that the advisory council 'should be constituted a Permanent Welsh Advisory Council for all legislative purposes'.[12] Herbert Morrison thought that the advisory council was not doing useful work and he said he had thought of disbanding it, but he was prepared to retain it if 'its retention would be gratifying to Welsh national feeling'. Nothing was decided, and the Cabinet proceeded to reject the demand for a secretary of state.[13] It is evident that the main consideration was an economic one and not whether the Welsh nation should be given some form of recognition.

Although the Cabinet had reached its decision on 28 January 1946, that decision was not communicated to the Welsh Parliamentary Party. In a statement presented to the prime minister on 6 March, the Welsh Parliamentary Party was able to declare that no reply had been received and that there was no evidence that the matter had been considered. The Welsh Parliamentary Party again pressed the case for the appointment of a secretary of state, arguing that the House of Commons could not cope with the pressure of work and that there could not be effective coordination in London. The fact that Wales was an integral part of the economy of Britain was recognized, but Wales was also said to be a nation with its own language and culture, and a condition of the nation's continued existence was that its people could earn a living in their own country.[14] The minister, as envisaged in the memorandum, would coordinate government administration in Wales and undertake limited parliamentary duties. One of the other duties assigned to him would be that of submitting 'plans for development in every branch of industry and to keep an economic survey with a view to planning at

[11]   Ibid., 128/5, CM(46) 9, 28 January 1946.
[12]   Percy E. Watkins, *A Welshman Remembers* (Cardiff, 1944), 159; LPA, M. Phillips Papers, Percy E. Watkins, memorandum on the proposed appointment of a Secretary of State for Wales, February 1943.
[13]   TNA, CAB. 128/5, CM (46) 9, 28 January 1946.
[14]   LPA, M. Phillips Papers, Statement presented to the Prime Minister by the Welsh Parliamentary Party, 6 March 1946, 1, 9–10.

least five years ahead in all matters relating to the economic life of Wales'.[15] Shortly after a meeting in March between the prime minister and Welsh members on the question of a secretary of state, James Griffiths, who had attended the meeting, wrote to Attlee stating that he was convinced that some concessions should be granted, but he admitted that, in terms of the efficiency of the machinery of government, there was an 'overwhelming' case against a Welsh Office.[16] On 3 April Griffiths submitted a memorandum to the Machinery of Government Committee, in which he stated that it was essential that the claims of Wales to recognition within the government should be met, and he therefore thought that the matter should be reconsidered before a reply was sent to the representatives of the Welsh MPs. While appreciating the reasons why the claim for a secretary of state had been rejected he felt that some alternative means should be found to meet Welsh aspirations. He pointed out that both the South Wales Regional Council of Labour and the North Wales Federation of Labour Parties had called for the appointment of a secretary of state and for the direction of new industries to Wales, thus emphasizing that the appointment was requested for economic reasons. He was anxious that the reply should satisfy Labour people in Wales that the government was determined to solve their problems.[17] Griffiths, an astute politician, pointed out that Labour's opponents would exploit a negative response. As a prominent member of the government, Griffiths was facing a dilemma that was to remain with him for almost thirty years. As a socialist and trade unionist, he adhered to the centralist stance being taken by the government, but as a Welshman he desperately wanted to do something that would enhance Wales's identity as a nation. As J. Beverley Smith has pointed out, Griffiths had been greatly influenced by his early experiences as a member of the ILP. In 1911 he had been present at a meeting held in Carmarthen, and attended by representatives from north and south Wales, with the aim of creating 'within the ILP framework, a Welsh Labour Party committed to the task of co-ordinating the aspirations of Labour and of Welsh nationhood'.[18] In and out of office, Griffiths was to endeavour to reconcile his Welshness with his socialist beliefs.

[15]   Ibid., note presented to the Prime Minister by the Welsh Parliamentary Party, 6 March 1946.
[16]   TNA, PREM. 8 1569 Part 1, J. Griffiths to the Prime Minister, March 1946.
[17]   Ibid., MG (46) 4, 3 April 1946.
[18]   *James Griffiths and His Times* (Cardiff, n.d.), 70–1.

The question of how to achieve greater coordination between government departments in Wales was discussed at a meeting of the Machinery of Government Committee on 7 May 1946. It was said that if a coordinator at an official level were responsible to a non-departmental minister, the implication would be that such a minister had a responsibility for Wales. In effect, it would be 'introducing a Secretary of State for Wales in a disguised form'. The committee invited Ness Edwards to draft a paper outlining ways 'for securing closer co-ordination between Government Departments in Wales and Monmouthshire'.[19] Edwards prepared a memorandum later in May based on the understanding that the claim for a secretary of state had been rejected. He proposed that a non- departmental minister should be responsible for Welsh affairs, in order to secure greater coordination and to satisfy the people's demand for political recognition.[20] This second reason suggests that Edwards, an ardent opponent of political nationalism, supported the view that Wales was a nation and that some form of government machinery had to be devised to recognize that fact. At a meeting of the Machinery of Government Committee on 12 July 1946, Herbert Morrison circulated a Treasury memorandum on the proposals submitted by Ness Edwards, adding a rider that he and the chancellor of the Exchequer, Hugh Dalton, were in agreement with the Treasury view. The memorandum rejected Edwards's proposal for a non-departmental Cabinet minister and quoted the same objections that had led to the Cabinet's rejection of the appointment of a secretary of state. The government had not made up its mind at that stage regarding the quarterly conference of heads of government offices, the annual report and the one-day debate. The Treasury saw these as 'concessions' and emphasized that if they were to be granted the announcement should be accompanied by a 'clear pronouncement of the rejection of a Secretary of State for Wales'.[21] On 17 July the Machinery of Government Committee rejected Ness Edwards's proposal. George Hall, James Griffiths, Ness Edwards, Aneurin Bevan and Hilary Marquand were the Welsh members present at that meeting.[22]

[19] TNA, PREM. 8 1569 Part 1, MG (46) 1, 7 May 1946.
[20] Ibid., MG (46) 7, 17 May 1946.
[21] Ibid., MG (46) 10, 12 July 1946.
[22] Ibid., MG (46) 2, 17 July 1946.

On 31 July the prime minister, in a letter to its chairman, D. R. Grenfell, conveyed the government's conclusions to the Welsh Parliamentary Party. Attlee mentioned that a day for a general debate on Welsh affairs had been granted and that if it proved useful a similar debate could be held every year. Consideration was being given to the possibility of presenting an annual report prior to the debate, and ministers were to ensure that their offices in Wales were adequately staffed so that the application of government policy to specific Welsh conditions received due attention. Heads of government offices were to meet regularly, and departments had been instructed to ensure that there was maximum cooperation between the various offices. He emphasized that the government, which had so many ministers of Welsh descent, had a genuine desire to do what was best for Wales, and that the appointment of a special minister would lead only to extra work without any corresponding advantages. It was explained that Wales, unlike Scotland, did not have a system of law and administration that was different from that of England, and that Wales's economic difficulties would not be resolved since these matters would not form part of the responsibilities of the secretary of state. It was felt that United Kingdom departments should handle such matters, and so the government had come to the conclusion that the appointment of a secretary of state could not be justified.[23] The Welsh Parliamentary Party met in Cardiff on 14 August and D. R. Grenfell and W. H. Mainwaring, the secretary, sent a reply to the prime minister. The view was that Wales's claim to nationhood had been repudiated and that the prime minister's letter did not appear to understand the plea advanced on behalf of a people desiring to make a greater contribution to the government of Wales. The Welsh Parliamentary Party could not see that the machinery in existence, even with the proposed improvements, was adequate to achieve cooperation between the Welsh offices and to ensure that the application of government policy to conditions in Wales received due attention. These ends could be achieved, it was felt, only when there was suitable political machinery in existence, and therefore a ministerial appointment was essential.[24] In his reply to Grenfell, on 5 September, the prime minister stated that the Welsh Parliamentary Party's letter had not done justice to

---

[23]   LPA, M. Phillips Papers, C. R. Attlee to D. R. Grenfell, 31 July 1946.
[24]   Ibid., D. R. Grenfell and W. H. Mainwaring to C. R. Attlee, 14 August 1946.

the proposals and that the scheme should be given a fair trial.[25] In a further letter to the prime minister, on 2 October, Mainwaring reported that the Welsh Parliamentary Party had decided that the chairman and secretary should meet Attlee to explain the reasons for their claims and also to request a debate in the House of Commons.[26] Consequently, the prime minister and Herbert Morrison met Grenfell and Mainwaring, who made it clear that in the debate the Welsh Parliamentary Party wished to raise the question of a secretary of state for Wales. Morrison therefore suggested that the debate should not take place on the adjournment but, rather, on a government motion.[27] The Cabinet confirmed this decision on 17 October, after Morrison had said that a government motion would allow discussion of the proposal for a secretary of state.[28]

The debate followed on 28 October and was taken seriously by the government. A number of ministers were present for most of the time but, in contrast, only a small number of MPs from outside Wales attended. The debate was held on a Monday, and that did not help matters.[29] Speaking for the government in the debate, the president of the Board of Trade, Stafford Cripps, emphasized that the real problems of Wales were economic, and were no different from those of Durham and the north-east coast. Therefore, it was to Wales's benefit to be part of the strategy adopted for the country as a whole, rather than to be dealt with separately. Although in Scotland there was a secretary of state, economic matters remained a United Kingdom responsibility. He reiterated the points that had been made in earlier statements by the government, namely, that attention should be paid to Welsh matters by the relevant departments, that there should be liaison between the Welsh authorities and the departments, and that matters which were not part of wider administration should be decided in Wales. He asserted that there were no differences between England and Wales in the legal system, that a 'super' ministerial authority would lead to delay, since documents and decisions would have to pass through an additional channel, and that it would be impossible to maintain the high standard of administration that was possible when services were

25   Ibid., C. R. Attlee to D. R. Grenfell, 5 September 1946.
26   TNA, PREM. 8 1569 Part 1, W. H. Mainwaring to C. R. Attlee, 2 October 1946.
27   TNA, CAB. 129/13, CP (46) 378, 14 October 1946.
28   Ibid., 128/6 CM (46), 87, 17 October 1946.
29   *Western Mail*, 29 October 1946.

nationwide. His conclusion was that the idea of a secretary of state had to be abandoned. At the same time, he dismissed the idea of a minister with overall responsibility for Welsh affairs for, in his view, if other ministers had to consult him then administration would be slowed down, and if he was not consulted, then the appointment was pointless. The Welsh minister would be judging matters from a Welsh point of view and the departmental minister would be judging them from an United Kingdom point of view, and so many disputes would have to be decided in the Cabinet. For Cripps, such a minister 'would, in fact, at best be an empty symbol, or at worse a very great impediment to the efficient administration of Welsh and English affairs alike'. He emphasized that the government had considered the matter in conjunction with Welsh MPs who were members of the government, and was satisfied that the efforts of Welsh members would always ensure that Wales would get more than its rightful share of attention.[30]

In the debate that followed, D. J. Williams (Labour, Neath), another former student of the Central Labour College, said that the answer to Wales's problems lay not in the appointment of a secretary of state but in an 'economic planning authority'.[31] He was to declare two years later, in November 1948, that he had never advocated or associated himself with the request for a secretary of state.[32] James Callaghan, who had earlier requested that the appointment of a secretary of state should be considered, now declared that until a case had been prepared indicating the functions of a secretary of state or a minister for coordination he was not convinced that either would be able to do anything for Wales on the economic front. He argued that, with the advance of socialism, there was a case for greater devolution to ensure that the administration did not lose touch with the people, but that this would be the case not only in Wales but also in all parts of the country. He added, 'If the problem can be focused in Wales, if that comes as the first illustration of the need, then it is a thoroughly good thing'. When Aneurin Bevan, in attempting to justify the degree of executive devolution that had taken place since the government took office, referred to civil servants as 'executive agents of the Government', D. R. Grenfell interjected

[30] Parl. Deb., vol. 428, cols 312–17.
[31] Ibid., vol. 428, col. 367.
[32] Ibid., vol. 458, col. 1279.

the comment 'Irresponsible elements'. Bevan immediately admitted that as the government intervened more and more in economic matters it might have to examine the local government structure, as well as consider whether new constitutional machinery was necessary to enable elected representatives at the regional level to undertake a great deal of government administration. He thought that there was 'a lot to be said for that'. In his view, the effects on local government of the changes being implemented, as well as those proposed, would have to be considered. However, he was resolutely opposed to the appointment of a minister for Welsh Affairs, for if such a minister were to be appointed he would have to defend all aspects of administration in Wales. It would be impossible for one minister to do this: he would be consistently taking advice from his colleagues, so that he would be merely a 'Welsh messenger-boy'. He did not think that there was a place for a minister with overriding powers over other ministers in respect of the officers in their Cardiff offices: this would be 'a constitutional impossibility' which would 'not succeed in integrating Welsh administration', rather, it 'would succeed in disintegrating the Government'. He was convinced that constitutional changes would not solve acute economic problems. In the discussions within the government and between the government and the Welsh Parliamentary Party, the possibility that the secretary of state would have to be Welsh speaking was not mentioned, but Bevan, speaking for the Anglicized south-east of Wales, maintained that there was anxiety regarding the matter in some parts of the country. If the secretary of state and civil servants would have to be Welsh speaking, then the majority of Welsh people would not be able to participate in the government of their own country.[33] It may have been a genuine anxiety at the time, but we now know that if there were such fears they were in part ill-founded, because in 1968 George Thomas was to be appointed secretary of state, and he was not Welsh speaking.

W. H. Mainwaring, speaking in the debate for the Welsh Parliamentary Party, argued strongly that a minister was needed to deal effectively with Wales's economic and social problems, and to see that plans once devised were actually implemented. During the 1940s, it had been claimed repeatedly that Wales as a nation

---

[33]   Ibid., vol. 428, cols 347–8, 398–405.

deserved greater recognition, but Mainwaring, surprisingly, revealed a more overtly nationalist outlook when he stated:

> Wales will fight for what it considers to be justice for itself and no body of Englishmen, or of any other nation on earth, will prevent a Welshman with a sense of injustice from fighting as long as he can for that which he considers to be his just due.

Goronwy Roberts conceded that central economic planning was essential, but he added that Wales on the periphery was not 'receiving from the centre the central plan in quite its pristine force, urgency and relevance'. He thought that perhaps a minister without a department would be able to put the Welsh case to the Cabinet. Roberts, more so than any of the other participants in the debate, was interested in the wider issue of the machinery of government across the United Kingdom. He said, 'This House is overloaded, overworked and overtired. We give a cursory glance at most of the legislation and then fling it to the tender mercies of the bureaucracy.' In his view, the way ahead was not to delegate more and more work to bureaucrats, but to embark on democratic devolution. He urged that a Royal Commission be appointed to consider the feasibility of establishing a parliament to legislate broadly for the United Kingdom, and assemblies in Wales, Scotland and England to implement such policies at national level. Nigel Birch (Conservative, Flintshire) saw the claim for a secretary of state as a just one, since civil servants could not deal with political problems, and he agreed with those who felt that Wales would have done better in the past, would be doing better at the present time and would do better in the future with someone to press its case for it. There was no reason to believe that Wales would be isolated, any more than having a secretary of state isolated Scotland.[34] Apart from giving members an opportunity to express their views, the debate was rather pointless. The decision had been taken and the government had no intention of reconsidering the matter.

Following this debate, Wales's claims were discussed in *The Economist* on 2 November. Whilst that influential journal deplored the government's refusal to appoint a minister as chairman of the proposed quarterly conference of heads of government offices in Wales, it considered that a non-departmental Cabinet minister would be ineffective. It was of the view that the secretary of state for

[34]   Ibid., cols 393, 397, 380–1, 370–1.

Scotland was 'always in danger of becoming either a bottleneck or a dictator or both'. Since the demand for a secretary of state for Wales had been rejected, it considered that the reorganization of local government with one or more regional councils would be a partial solution.[35] On 29 October the *Western Mail* considered that some gains had been made which might lead to the appointment of a minister, and it suggested that it was now up to the Welsh people to show that they could be entrusted with the greater degree of autonomy which a future government would be forced eventually to concede.[36] In the post-war years, as Wales benefited from the government's social and economic policies, the demand for a secretary of state diminished somewhat, although a Secretary of State for Wales and Monmouthshire Bill was to be presented on 28 January 1949 by Henry Morris-Jones, supported by Clement Davies (now leader of the Liberal Party), D. R. Grenfell, D. A. Price White (Conservative, Caernarvon Boroughs), Megan Lloyd George, Tudor Watkins, R. Hopkin Morris and Robert Richards (Labour, Wrexham). It proceeded no further than its first reading.[37] The Labour government had resisted all demands for a secretary of state, but a decade or so later, when a different set of circumstances prevailed, the party was to endorse just such a proposal.

AN ADVISORY COUNCIL

In 1947 the Welsh Regional Council of Labour replaced the South Wales Regional Council of Labour and the North Wales Federation of Labour Parties; Huw T. Edwards, a north Wales official of the Transport and General Workers' Union, Huw Morris Jones and Goronwy Roberts were appointed to represent north Wales on its executive committee. At a meeting with ministers held in December 1947, representatives of the new Regional Council proposed 'a Council drawn from various bodies in Wales'. At that meeting the Council was asked to submit proposals.[38] By this time the Regional Council's executive committee had accepted 'that the proposal for a

[35]   'Welsh independence', *The Economist*, 2 November 1946, 699–700.
[36]   *Western Mail*, 29 October 1946.
[37]   Parl. Deb., vol. 460, col. 1245; information from Public Information Office, House of Commons.
[38]   TNA, PREM. 8 1569 Part 2, MG (48) 5, 23 September 1948.

Secretary of State for Wales was no longer practicable; and could not be fruitfully pursued', and so it proceeded to propose an alternative policy, in the hope that it would be acceptable to the government.[39] No doubt the executive was aware that a Scottish Economic Conference was under consideration by the government, and this may have influenced some members to support an advisory council for Wales. Huw T. Edwards, however, had shown interest in an advisory council ever since it was known that the request for a secretary of state had been turned down. In October 1946 he arranged for Morgan Phillips to receive a copy of Percy Watkins's memorandum to the Welsh Parliamentary Party, and Phillips had promptly sent it to Herbert Morrison.[40] At its meeting on 22 January 1948, the Cabinet recognized that the publication of a White Paper setting out proposals to meet Scottish demands for a greater degree of control over Scottish affairs could result in demands for greater devolution in Wales. It also accepted that there was strong support for the nationalists in the University of Wales and in colleges and schools, and that there was growing support in the industrial valleys. Therefore, whilst it was felt that concessions made to Scotland in the field of parliamentary business could not be granted to Wales, there was nonetheless a feeling that a body similar to the Scottish Economic Conference should be considered for Wales and that the initiative should be taken by the government. Accordingly, it was agreed that Herbert Morrison, Viscount Hall (now first lord of the Admiralty and formerly George Hall, MP for Aberdare), Aneurin Bevan and James Griffiths should consider what steps ought to be taken to meet Welsh demands for such a body.[41]

Goronwy Roberts was most active in pressing Welsh claims, and a few days after the Cabinet had reached its conclusion, a debate on 26 January on Welsh affairs gave him an opportunity to put forward his views. Government departments, he said, had 'decanted their powers . . . to appropriate Welsh offices', and although an attempt had been made to coordinate the work of those offices, there was no adequate supervision by elected representatives; an elected council should therefore be established to supervise government departments

---

[39]   Welsh Regional Council of Labour, *Annual Meeting*, 17 April 1948, 6.
[40]   LPA, M. Phillips Papers, E. Jones to M. Phillips, 8 October 1946; M. Phillips to H. Morrison, 9 October 1946; M. Phillips to E. Jones, 10 October 1946.
[41]   TNA, PREM. 8 1569 Part 2, CM (48) 6, 22 January 1948.

and to advise ministers. The government, however, was not likely to support a council with supervisory powers, since all responsibility for the supervision of their departments ultimately rested with ministers, and a directly elected advisory body would not be content just to advise, and so there would be conflict. Roberts also suggested that a Welsh development commission should be created under the supervision of a council of Wales with sufficient finance and powers to enable it to tackle the smaller areas of unemployment, for which there was 'no statutory instrument of resuscitation' at the time. The proposals, he thought, would give Wales the recognition as a nation to which it was entitled. When, on 2 February, the prime minister stated in a reply to Emrys Roberts that the government would be prepared to examine whether proposals in the Scottish White Paper could be applied to Wales, discussion of the matter was advanced.[42]

An advisory council for Wales was supported at the annual conference of the Welsh Regional Council of Labour in April 1948, and the executive committee and the Welsh Parliamentary Labour Party prepared separate proposals that were discussed at a conference in Cardiff on 19 June.[43] The MPs' proposals were far more comprehensive than those of the Regional Council; whereas the latter proposed an advisory council, the MPs advocated an advisory council with a minister as chairman who would act as a link between the council and the Cabinet.[44] In Scotland, it should be noted, the chairman of the Economic Conference was the secretary of state for Scotland.[45] The joint memorandum was submitted to the government in July 1948. Developments such as the Welsh affairs debate, the annual White Paper and the tendency to regard Wales as an administrative unit were welcomed, but it was pointed out that the quarterly conference of heads of government offices had its limitations. It had no liaison with the people or with the government; a civil servant chaired it, giving the impression that coordination of government activity was left to a bureaucracy; and it was 'in no sense a sounding board for Welsh opinion'. A council for Wales and Monmouthshire was proposed to act as a Welsh economic conference and as an advisory body to the government on social and cultural affairs. It was also intended that it should have

[42] Parl. Deb., vol. 446, cols 729–31, 1468–9.
[43] *Western Mail*, 21 June 1948.
[44] Ibid., 28 May 1948.
[45] Scottish Home Department, *Scottish Affairs*, 1948 (Cmd. 7308), 3.

oversight of the work of government offices in Wales, a function suggested by Goronwy Roberts during the Welsh affairs debate earlier in the year. It was further proposed that the chairman should be a cabinet minister, that he should be one of the ministers responsible for the Welsh affairs debate and that he should be responsible for the preparation and presentation of the White Paper. The Welsh affairs debate was considered to be 'too diffuse', and therefore two days in each session should be allocated to Welsh affairs. While no recommendation was made regarding the appointment of a minister for Welsh Affairs, it was maintained that this was the eventual aim.[46]

In a note to the prime minister on 19 August, Herbert Morrison said that he had consulted Aneurin Bevan, Viscount Hall and James Griffiths and had found that there was no agreement between them, so he feared that if he brought the memorandum of the Welsh Regional Council of Labour before them the resulting discussion would be inconclusive. The prime minister acceded to his request that he should be permitted to bring the memorandum before the Machinery of Government Committee, with which the three ministers could be associated. Morrison thought that this was the only way to formulate a definite view on the matter.[47] He then informed the Machinery of Government Committee of the prime minister's decision. He also made the point that ministers were not committed to the proposals submitted by the Regional Council and the Welsh Parliamentary Labour Party, and he expressed concern that in some respects the proposals were contrary to the guidance that had been given.[48] Quite obviously, they were not to his liking. Meanwhile, the machinery-of-government branch of the Treasury, in its own memorandum, said that if a council were set up it should function as the counterpart in Wales of the Scottish Economic Conference. The Treasury was opposed to the appointment of a minister for Welsh Affairs and expressed the view that the committee might 'think that to appoint a Minister as chairman would go too far in the direction of giving general Welsh responsibilities to a single Minister'. It felt that the grievance that there was no link between public opinion in Wales and the government could

---

[46]   LPA, M. Phillips Papers, Administrative Reforms: Wales and Monmouthshire, July 1948.
[47]   TNA, PREM. 8 1569 Part 2, H. Morrison to the Prime Minister, 19 August 1948.
[48]   Ibid., MG (48) 4, 26 August 1948.

be remedied by permitting the council to invite ministers to deliberate with it, about once a year.[49] When the Machinery of Government Committee met on 30 September 1948, Morrison's statement that it would not be advisable to condemn the proposal for a council out of hand might seem to confirm the view that the government was more sympathetic to Welsh demands partly because support for the nationalists was being taken more seriously. The committee accepted the Treasury view that a minister should not be the chairman, and it was agreed that the terms of reference should follow those of the Scottish Economic Conference. These would also include a reference to cultural affairs.[50]

In a letter of 9 October, Herbert Morrison told James Griffiths that in the memorandum to be submitted to the Cabinet the wording about the number of occasions on which a minister should attend council meetings had been left rather vague. He then added in his own hand: 'However, do not hesitate to put your view at the Cabinet if you wish', and this clearly suggests that Griffiths was not entirely happy with the arrangements.[51] In his reply of 11 October, Griffiths reminded Morrison that, in the Machinery of Government Committee, he had mentioned that a policy statement on Welsh affairs was due to be released at the Conservative conference. Griffiths felt that it was a factor that could not be ignored, and he thought that Welsh Labour MPs were certain to demand that a minister should be appointed chairman of the proposed council for Wales. He suggested that the Cabinet should not take a final decision until talks had been held with the Welsh Regional Council of Labour and Welsh Labour MPs. He was only too aware of the electoral implications and warned, 'I am anxious to avoid placing our own Members in what may become a politically impossible situation. 1950 will soon be upon us.'[52] He thought that a council with a minister as chairman was worthy of reconsideration because if it satisfied the demands of the Regional Council and Welsh Labour MPs, then the policy for the 1950 election would also be settled. If they considered that the proposals were unsatisfactory, then the matter would be raised again when the policy statement for the election was being drafted, and that was something he wanted to

[49]   Ibid., MG (48) 5, 23 September 1948.
[50]   Ibid., MG (48) 1, 30 September 1948.
[51]   NLW, J. Griffiths Papers, C2/7, H. Morrison to J. Griffiths, 9 October 1948.
[52]   Ibid., C2/8, J. Griffiths to H. Morrison, 11 October 1948.

avoid.[53] Replying on 13 October to Griffiths's plea that a decision should be delayed, Morrison said that, in his view, a decision on the constitution of the proposed council should be taken at the Cabinet meeting and that the matter should not be reconsidered in the light of the Conservatives' proposal to appoint a minister for Welsh Affairs. His actual words were: 'I don't think we should engage in an auction for Welsh votes by capping the Tories' impracticable proposal by an impracticable one of our own.'[54] Such statements as 'We consider that in all the circumstances it would be advisable to concede the request for a Council' and 'We . . . have reached the conclusion that the least objectionable arrangement would be for the Council to appoint a chairman from among its members', which appeared in Herbert Morrison's memorandum to the Cabinet of 11 October, indicate a lack of enthusiasm for such a council.[55] In a further note, dated 14 October, a member of the Cabinet office secretariat reminded the prime minister that any suggestion that ministers should attend all meetings should be resisted, because it would strengthen the demand for a separate minister.[56]

At the Cabinet on 15 October, Morrison stated that the committee was satisfied that the appointment of a minister as chairman would lead to greater demands for a secretary of state.[57] James Griffiths made the point that if Welsh MPs were to be convinced that contact with departmental ministers directly was preferable to contact via a minister as chairman, then the opportunities for such discussion should not be limited to just once a year.[58] The point seems to have been conceded, because the Cabinet agreed that Morrison, when discussing the proposals with the Welsh Regional Council of Labour, could promise that a Cabinet minister would attend each meeting. The Cabinet then approved the recommendation of the Machinery of Government Committee.[59] Accompanied by Hall, Bevan and Griffiths, Morrison met representatives of the Welsh Parliamentary Labour Party and the Welsh Regional Council of

[53]   Ibid., C2/28, notes by J. Griffiths for a speech on Welsh affairs.
[54]   Ibid., C2/9, H. Morrison to J. Griffiths, 13 October 1948.
[55]   TNA, CAB. 129/29, CP (48) 228, 11 October 1948.
[56]   TNA, PREM. 8 1569 Part 2, member of the Secretariat, Cabinet Office, to the Prime Minister, 14 October 1948.
[57]   TNA, CAB. 128/13, CM (48) 63, 15 October 1948.
[58]   NLW, J. Griffiths Papers, C2/28, Welsh Affairs, Cabinet, 15 October 1948.
[59]   TNA, CAB. 128/13, CM (48) 63, 15 October 1948.

Labour on 29 October 1948. The Welsh Regional Council of Labour's representatives included Huw T. Edwards, who, on Griffiths's recommendation, was to become the council's first chairman.[60] Goronwy Roberts, who was at the time the leading advocate of devolution within the Welsh Parliamentary Labour Party, was also a member of the deputation. Morrison reported that the government was opposed to the appointment of a secretary of state, to the appointment of a minister for Welsh Affairs, and to the appointment of a minister of Cabinet rank as chairman of the proposed council, as had been recommended in the joint memorandum from the Welsh Regional Council of Labour and the Welsh Parliamentary Labour Party. Although the scheme proposed by the lord president was accepted, the response of some MPs, as recorded in the minutes, is interesting:

> but some Members of Parliament expressed doubts and misgivings as to the possible attitude of their colleagues in the Group. It was stressed that this was a difficult matter on which to secure unanimity and, in fact the support of the Group for the scheme previously put up to the Government had not been unanimous but was that of a majority only. Some dissentient voices must be expected.

Herbert Morrison was urged to meet the group at a meeting attended by all members.[61] On subsequent occasions, when aspects of the machinery of government would be discussed, Welsh Labour MPs, like their predecessors in 1948, would be unable to come to unanimous decisions.

In the debate on Welsh affairs on 24 November 1948, Herbert Morrison defended the government's decision not to appoint a minister for Welsh Affairs. Such a minister, he argued, could have no executive power but would be used 'as a sort of ministerial court of appeal against the decision of the Departmental Minister', even though he would not be an expert on those matters that would be brought to his attention and in many cases the decisions already taken could not be reversed. Such a proposal, in his view, was 'really illusory window-dressing and political make-believe' and would not be feasible. Announcing the decision to set up an advisory council for Wales and Monmouthshire, Morrison quoted its terms of reference:

---

[60] *James Griffiths*, 42.
[61] NLW, J. Griffiths Papers, C2/15, Council for Wales and Monmouthshire, 1 November 1948.

(a) to meet from time to time, and at least quarterly, for the interchange of views and information on developments and trends in the economic and cultural fields in Wales and Monmouthshire; and

(b) to secure that the Government are adequately informed of the impact of Government activities on the general life of the people of Wales and Monmouthshire.

The Council to be appointed by the prime minister would consist of twenty-seven members: twelve members to be selected 'from a panel of persons nominated by Welsh local authorities'; eight members representing industry and agriculture (four representing the management and four representing the workforce); one member nominated by the University of Wales; one member nominated by the Welsh Joint Education Committee; one member nominated by the Welsh Tourist Board; one member nominated by the National Eisteddfod Council; and three members nominated by the prime minister. The chairman could not be a minister because he would be unable to associate himself with recommendations on matters falling outside his own department, but in order to provide an interchange of views ministers would be willing to attend meetings when the Council wanted to discuss subjects with them. Morrison stated that the Council would deliberate in private, since the government did not want it to be seen as a body competing with MPs. After stating that the proposals were a 'great advance', he said, 'We are unable as have been Governments before us, to think of anything better than this; we think this is good.'[62]

On the whole, Labour MPs who spoke in the debate supported the proposals. One who was relieved that they did not affect the powers, privileges and responsibilities of MPs was W. G. Cove (Labour, Aberavon) and he implored all concerned to 'rejoice and sing praises unto Herbert Morrison in a unanimous voice'. Both Robert Richards and L. Ungoed-Thomas agreed that the position of MPs, the elected representatives of the people, had to be protected. As a member of the government, James Griffiths defended the decision not to appoint a ministerial chairman, on the grounds that it was better for members of the Council to have meetings with the ministers responsible for the various subjects rather than have a ministerial chairman communicating their views to colleagues.[63] In J. Beverley Smith's words, he felt 'obliged to defend

[62]   Parl. Deb., vol. 458, cols 1262–77.
[63]   Ibid., cols 1289–90, 1348, 1353, 1370.

a position which was not of his choosing, but which, because of his natural fidelity, he felt bound to maintain'.[64] However, he emphasized that if, in the future, the devolution of government were considered it would mean reorganization at the centre and the reorganization of local government. Clearly, he had not abandoned his earlier stance in favour of a secretary of state accompanied by an elected council for Wales as the top tier of local government. George Thomas, like W. G. Cove, lavished exaggerated praise on Herbert Morrison. He congratulated him 'on being a well-intentioned Englishman' and 'on the understanding' he had 'revealed of the sentiments of the Welsh people, of their legitimate aspirations'. For Goronwy Roberts, the proposals had one merit at least, in that the government had recognized Wales as a nation. He admitted that, as a federalist, the proposals did not fulfil his desires, but in order to make any headway it was necessary to get the maximum agreement and that was one reason why the Council should be supported. In the past Welshmen had failed to agree on any definite proposal.[65] One can only concur with this judgement, for a lack of unanimity was consistently to slow down the devolutionists' cause throughout the period under review.

In this 1948 debate D. J. Williams argued, as he had done in the past, that the real problems of Wales were economic and social, and that those problems could not be 'overcome by some ingenious constitutional device, or by the setting up of some elaborate and complex piece of administrative machinery'. S. O. Davies, never one to conform easily, attacked the scheme in an uncompromising speech. In his view, it was 'emasculated, spineless', 'pointless and useless' and 'terribly offensive', and should be withdrawn. Clement Davies also made a bitter attack on the proposals. He commented: 'A whole mountain seems to have been shaken, and to have produced the smallest mouse ever presented as a substitute for a proper constitutional development.' He objected to it because, as a nominated body, it was an insult to the Welsh people's concept of democracy and it usurped the role of the Welsh Parliamentary Party, which had always put the Welsh case to the government.[66] The *Western Mail* even doubted whether the Welsh Parliamentary Party could survive.[67] It could be argued that the Welsh

[64]   *James Griffiths*, 58.
[65]   Parl. Deb., vol. 458, cols 1365, 1312, 1296.
[66]   Ibid., cols 1356, 1324–5, 1280–2.
[67]   *Western Mail*, 26 November 1948.

Parliamentary Labour Party had usurped the role of the Welsh Parliamentary Party, because Labour held two-thirds of the seats in Wales. According to Megan Lloyd George, Morrison had offered Wales a 'scraggy bone, without meat or marrow in it' and had 'offered it as a half-hearted concession – to Welsh public opinion'. That was undoubtedly an accurate assessment of the position. Her view was that if the Council were to be established Wales would have to consider whether the only answer was a greater degree of devolution than would be provided by a secretary of state and a Welsh Office. For her part, she thought that the solution was a parliament, on the lines of the one in Northern Ireland. This was quite a significant statement, and may well have been the first shot in what was later to become the Parliament for Wales Campaign. When this campaign was launched, its president was Megan Lloyd George. R. A. Butler reiterated the Conservatives' intention to appoint a non-executive Cabinet minister to represent Wales, co-ordinate the views of departments and chair meetings of civil servants. Nigel Birch did not think that a nominated council meeting in secret would lead to increased confidence about the way in which the country was governed.[68] The *South Wales Argus*, based in Newport, Monmouthshire, shared this view. It commented: 'Such a Council may inspire confidence if the public know what they are doing: it certainly will not if it is shrouded in secrecy.'[69] At the end of the debate, Morrison had every reason to be pleased with his achievement because the government had conceded nothing in terms of the devolution of government. There was every reason to believe that, like the proposals of other advisory bodies, the Council's proposals would more often than not be ignored.

In Wales, the *Western Mail* claimed that the Council was 'regarded even by most of the Welsh Socialists as useless and purposeless' and it thought that the only value the Council could have 'would be to provide overwhelming evidence of its inadequacy and thus prepare the way for a bolder measure'.[70] Meanwhile, in January 1949 the council of Undeb Cymru Fydd (New Wales Union), a voluntary non-political organization which had as one of its objectives 'the general surveillance of Welsh interests', sent the following resolution to the prime minister:

[68]   Parl. Deb., vol. 458, cols 1340–2, 1320, 1291–2.
[69]   *South Wales Argus*, 29 November 1948.
[70]   *Western Mail*, 26 November 1948; 25 November 1948.

> After earnest and careful consideration of the Government's plan to set up an Advisory Council for Wales, *Undeb Cymru Fydd* (the New Wales Union) expresses its grave disappointment that the Government has not so respected Welsh traditions as to grant Wales a greater measure of freedom to deal with her own national life. The Union trusts therefore that the Government will reconsider the whole matter.

Undeb Cymru Fydd could not support the Council because it ignored Welsh MPs and was undemocratic; its meetings would be in private, it had neither administrative nor executive power, and because of its constitution it was not in a position to deal with cultural matters.[71] Nevertheless, the proposals were acceptable to Welsh local authorities. By January 1949 seventy-nine authorities had expressed themselves in favour and sixty-four against, but on the basis of population there was a larger majority in favour.[72]

Herbert Morrison was so anxious to ensure that there were no misconceptions about the Council's role that he wrote to the prime minister seeking permission to address the first meeting of the Council on 20 May 1949.[73] The original draft of his speech, which he had submitted to James Griffiths for observations, included the following sentence: 'I am afraid that some folks have given way to the temptation to promise measures which must at first sight be attractive to every Welshman.'[74] In his response, Griffiths suggested that this should be deleted, explaining that practically every Welsh MP and the Regional Council had fallen for the temptation, and that Huw T. Edwards, the Council's chairman, had requested more than just a secretary of state.[75] Griffiths himself had fallen for the temptation, and he did not want opponents to make political capital out of it. In his opening address to the Council, Morrison stated that the government could have taken the easy option and yielded to the demands for a separate minister, but such an appointment would have led to confusion and delay. A council able to make direct contact with ministers was preferable to a 'buffer Minister' with responsibility for Wales. He thought that the Council should consider specific problems and the government would listen sympathetically

---

[71]   TNA, PREM. 8 1569 Part 2, T. I. Ellis, Secretary, Undeb Cymru Fydd, to the Prime Minister, 4 January 1949.

[72]   Parl. Deb., vol. 460, col. 20.

[73]   TNA, PREM. 8 1569 Part 2, H. Morrison to the Prime Minister, 18 October 1948.

[74]   NLW, J. Griffiths Papers, C2/31, draft speech by H. Morrison for the opening meeting of the Council for Wales and Monmouthshire.

[75]   Ibid., C2/32, notes by J. Griffiths on draft speech by H. Morrison.

to informed criticisms; ministers would turn to the Council for accurate information and for responsible, practical advice and guidance. He justified the fact that meetings were to be held in private on the grounds that it was an advisory body and it was essential that there should be open discussion between members and between the Council and the government. Morrison added that its success depended 'on the establishment of an intimate co-operation with the Government of the day which could only be frustrated by publicity for everything which is said in its discussions'.[76] The *Western Mail* was not impressed by the Council's membership and maintained that only 'outstanding personalities' could transform the Council into a 'living, forceful' body. However, after the Council's first meeting, the newspaper thought that it should be given a 'fair trial' and that 'it should be regarded as a new opportunity of proving . . . [Wales's] potentialities for self-government'.[77] The *South Wales Argus* welcomed the Council as a means of creating a more unified nation, but according to *The Times* 'nationalists' still argued that without a Cabinet minister with responsibility for the country, Wales would always be at a disadvantage.[78]

Hostility to the Council did not subside, and scathing comments were made about it in the Welsh affairs debate on 24 November 1949. D. A. Price White thought that 'It was hurriedly conceived, hastily born and is now suckling in secret while its foster mother, the Lord President of the Council, is busily making a play-pen in Battersea Park'. This was a reference to the Festival of Britain of 1951, for which Herbert Morrison had responsibility. In his attack on advisory councils, of which the Council for Wales and Monmouthshire was only one, W. J. Gruffydd (Liberal, University of Wales) pulled no punches. He declared that Wales 'has sickened under a thick pestilential rash of consultative councils; bodies which, for all practical purposes, are deaf and dumb and, for the most part, pathetically useless'.[79] James Griffiths was probably disappointed that his efforts to secure a secretary of state had failed, but his unfailing loyalty to the Labour movement impelled him to support the Council. In an article drafted for the *Western Mail* prior

---

[76]   Ibid., C2/31, draft speech by H. Morrison for the opening meeting of the Council for Wales and Monmouthshire.
[77]   *Western Mail*, 27 April 1949; 21 May 1949.
[78]   *South Wales Argus*, 20 May 1949; *The Times*, 21 May 1949.
[79]   Parl. Deb., vol. 470, cols 558, 553.

to the election in February 1950, he wrote, 'And I must not forget the much maligned Council for Wales; I am confident that the day will come when it will yet prove its value'.[80] It was certainly to prove its long-term value as far as Griffiths was concerned, because it was precisely this Council, conceded in 1948 in place of a secretary of state, which within a decade was to renew the demand for such an appointment.

In the 1950 election, the Labour government was returned with a much-reduced majority, though it did increase its Welsh representation. Nevertheless, Goronwy Roberts was deeply concerned about the political situation in Wales, and expressed his views and frustrations in a private letter to his friend Gwilym Williams, who was on Morgan Phillips's staff at Transport House. Roberts thought that there was an increasing awareness that the Labour movement was hostile to any form of devolution, and this was strengthened by the attitude of the Regional Council, and by the actions of government departments that had taken 20,000 acres (8,093 hectares) of land for afforestation in west Wales and 5,000 acres (2,023 hectares) in the Trawsfynydd area for military purposes. Roberts described the feeling in these communities: 'A dangerous feeling of helplessness in the face of arbitrary power exercised from outside is gripping our people. There is a feeling that Wales is being hacked about without regard to its national feeling entirely for the convenience of Whitehall.' In such a situation Labour Party workers were 'dispirited and frustrated'. It was difficult to counter the claims of the nationalists, and support for them was growing. Indeed, it was becoming difficult to find candidates of the right calibre for marginal seats, and Cledwyn Hughes had to be persuaded to stand again in Anglesey. Roberts added, 'Unless we change our attitude, we shall reap an inevitable whirlwind'. He was convinced that the demands for a degree of devolution would gain momentum and he asked, 'Is it that all sorts of concessions are to be given to Scotland, while Wales continues to be treated as a kind of box-room where the rubbish of the United Kingdom may be dumped?' He argued that Labour's Welsh policy should be redefined. Wales should be the unit for all government administration, the advisory Council for Wales and Monmouthshire should be a working party on specific

---

[80]   LPA, M. Phillips Papers, J. Griffiths's draft article for the *Western Mail*, 19 January 1950.

problems – which in effect it was – and the office of secretary of state or a national council should be created. Roberts was anxious that a policy for Wales should be in place for the next election which would probably come the following year. Despite his concerns, the number of Labour-held seats in the 1951 election remained unchanged: Plaid Cymru, which submitted candidates in a minority of seats, received 0.7 per cent of the votes cast.[81]

When Herbert Morrison left the office of lord president, responsibility for the Council for Wales and Monmouthshire passed to Ernest Bevin as lord privy seal. Huw T. Edwards met Bevin and convinced him that the claim for a body on the lines of the Catto Committee was a reasonable one, and Bevin suggested that names of possible members to serve on the committee should be submitted.[82] The Catto Committee was the Committee on Scottish Financial and Trade Statistics, appointed in July 1950 under the chairmanship of Lord Catto. Edwards's association with Bevin (a former general secretary of the Transport and General Workers' Union) could have been a major breakthrough for the Council but it never developed, because of Bevin's death; responsibility for the Council passed to Chuter Ede, who had not been sympathetic to any form of devolution.[83] The following February, in the Welsh affairs debate, Cledwyn Hughes, the new Labour member for Anglesey, repeated Edwards's request. He said, 'The information obtained from an investigation carried out by a fact finding committee of this kind is a vital prerequisite to any consideration of Welsh constitutional reform . . .'[84]

A 'WATCHDOG'

After the Labour government had rejected the proposal that a secretary of state be appointed, the Conservative Party was urged by its Welsh members to formulate a policy for Wales. The party conference of 1947 carried a motion to that effect.[85] By the

[81]   Ibid., G. Roberts to G. Williams, 8 August 1950; Beti Jones, *Etholiadau'r Ganrif: Welsh Elections, 1885–1997* (Talybont, 1999), 95.
[82]   TNA, PREM. 8 1569 Part 2, H. T. Edwards to C. R. Attlee, 5 May 1951.
[83]   Parl. Deb., vol. 491, col. 637.
[84]   Ibid., vol. 495, col. 743.
[85]   *Report of the Conservative Party Conference*, 1947, 106, 108.

following January it was quite apparent that the Conservatives were formulating a policy which was very much in line with a suggestion which the home secretary had been asked to consider by the Machinery of Government Committee, prior to the 1945 general election. In a debate on Welsh affairs on 26 January 1948, R. A. Butler stated that a Cabinet minister should be appointed to ensure that Wales was getting a fair deal. The minister, who would have the role of a 'watchdog', would also interest himself in the work of the quarterly conference of heads of government offices, meeting in Cardiff. Following the reference to a watchdog, S. O. Davies asked whether it would 'have anything other than a bark?' Butler's proposal was supported by D. A. Price White (who at the Conservative conference had moved the resolution calling for a Welsh policy), by Gwilym Lloyd George (who had been called in when the Coalition government's Machinery of Government Committee was discussing the request of the Welsh Parliamentary Party for a secretary of state) and, surprisingly, by Robert Richards, who considered that, compared with the government, Butler showed a deeper appreciation of what MPs had in mind.[86] During 1948, at a time when the Conservative Party was formulating its policy, J. Enoch Powell (joint head of the home affairs division in the research department) toured Wales.[87] Powell was a most appropriate choice because not only was he of Welsh extraction, but he was also Welsh speaking. The conference of that year, held appropriately at Llandudno, carried a resolution seeking assurances that the party, when next it achieved power, would appoint a minister for Welsh Affairs, and that when legislation was being framed Wales would be recognized as different from England.[88] R. A. Butler, speaking at Blaenau Ffestiniog during the conference week in October, said that the Conservative Party acknowledged that Wales and England were separate nations, but that both countries were intimately connected as an economic unit. The Conservative Party was therefore proposing that a Cabinet minister should be responsible for Wales: someone who would be in touch with Welsh needs and opinion and who would ensure that due account was taken of them by all government departments.[89] Winston Churchill confirmed this

---

[86] Parl. Deb., vol. 446, cols 693–5, 757, 736, 763.
[87] Information from Conservative Research Department; *Western Mail*, 7 May 1948.
[88] *Report of the Conservative Party Conference*, 1948, 71, 74.
[89] *The Times*, 8 October 1948; *Western Mail*, 8 October 1948.

when he addressed the conference as party leader. Aneurin Bevan's immediate reaction to the proposal was: 'It is not a watchdog. It is a carrot to deflect the attention of Wales from the real things.' In his view, the 'real things' were the country's social and economic problems and only ministers with executive power could resolve these.[90]

In February 1949, the Conservative Party published its policy document, *The Conservative Policy for Wales and Monmouthshire*, written by J. Enoch Powell, in which it set out its proposals.[91] The party considered that when government policy was being framed and executed there was a need to ensure that account was taken of Welsh conditions, where they were distinctive, and that Wales should be treated as a separate entity when the occasion demanded. The answer lay not in the appointment of a secretary of state, because some of the most important subjects would be outside his control, but, rather, in the appointment of a Cabinet minister to represent Wales when United Kingdom policy was being discussed. His responsibilities were clearly defined:

> He would be the Minister answerable in Parliament for the Government's policy as a whole in its effect upon Wales, presenting the Welsh reports, leading Welsh debates, presiding in Wales over the Welsh inter-departmental conferences, and helping to co-ordinate any plans for the whole or part of Wales which might involve two or more departments.

The statement that 'there would then be one person to whom Wales and Welsh interests could look' was significant, because it was inevitable that they would look to this person to put their case and defend their interests, and therefore the case for a secretary of state had been partly conceded. The Council for Wales and Monmouthshire would be retained, since it could perform a useful service as an adjunct to a minister with overall responsibility for Welsh affairs.[92] In the 1950 policy document *Labour is Building a New Wales*, Labour attacked the Conservative proposal as a 'piece of lip-service to Welsh sentiment'. The party added that the 'Minister suggested would be no more than a "sitter-in" at other Ministers' departments without separate responsibility, a position which no one of standing would accept'.[93]

[90]   *Western Mail*, 11 October 1948.
[91]   Information from Head of Information Section, Conservative Research Department, 4 December 1984.
[92]   Conservative Party, *The Conservative Policy for Wales and Monmouthshire* (London, 1949), 2–3.
[93]   Labour Party, *Labour is Building a New Wales* (Cardiff, 1950), 15–16.

The Labour government's attitude in the post-war years to the appointment of a secretary of state was no different from that of the wartime Coalition government. Ministers were adamant that problems could be resolved only when policies were directed from the centre, and as the government's economic and welfare programmes were implemented, the demand receded for a secretary of state. However, Wales received some recognition when the Welsh Regional Council of Labour and the Welsh Parliamentary Labour Party managed to gain a concession – the government rather reluctantly agreed to set up an advisory council – but, crucially, the request for a ministerial chairman was turned down. The 1940s ended not without irony, in that the Conservative Party, which had always been accused of being unsympathetic to Welsh aspirations, was now prepared, unlike Labour, to grant Wales a modest degree of recognition in government through the appointment of a minister for Welsh Affairs.

III

PAVING THE WAY FOR A SECRETARY OF STATE,
1951–1964

A MINISTER FOR WELSH AFFAIRS

In the 1950 general election, Labour increased its representation in Wales to twenty-seven members, whilst the Conservatives had three members and the Liberals five members. In 1951, when the Conservatives were returned to power, Labour still held twenty-seven seats and the Conservatives and Liberals held five and three seats respectively. The National Liberal and Conservative E. H. Garner Evans (Denbigh) held the remaining seat in 1950 and 1951. In both general elections members who were to figure prominently in the debates on devolution were elected. In 1950 David Llewellyn (Conservative, Cardiff North) and Eirene White (Labour, Flint East) entered the House of Commons, and in 1951 there followed Raymond Gower (Conservative, Barry), Peter Thomas (Conservative, Conway), T. W. Jones (Labour, Merioneth) and Cledwyn Hughes, who had defeated Megan Lloyd George in Anglesey.[1]

On taking office, the Conservatives kept their election promise and the home secretary, David Maxwell-Fyfe, was made responsible for Welsh affairs. The Labour government had turned down this arrangement after the general election of 1945. According to the prime minister, Winston Churchill, the choice had fallen on the Home Office, because it was the senior secretaryship of state.[2] The arrangement was criticized by members, who pointed out that it was perhaps the department that had the least impact on Wales. In fact, the prime minister was only following precedent because, as Frank Newsam was to explain later, the home secretary has since 1801 been 'responsible for all domestic affairs which are not the direct responsibility of some other Minister of the Crown'.[3] The Home Office has been described by Richard Clarke, permanent secretary, the ministries of Aviation and Technology from 1966 to 1970, as a

---

[1] Jones, *Parliamentary Elections*, 106–18.
[2] Parl. Deb., vol. 493, col. 75.
[3] Ibid., vol. 495, col. 736; Sir Frank Newsam, *The Home Office* (London, 1954), 25.

'conglomerate' because it is responsible for 'disparate subjects', none of which is sufficiently important to justify a minister's exclusive attention.[4] At the same time, the prime minister appointed an additional under-secretary of state at the Home Office, to assist the home secretary in his duties as the minister responsible for Welsh affairs.[5] The first holder of that office was David Llewellyn.[6] Thirty-five years later Llewellyn admitted that he had feared that the new arrangement would eventually lead to the appointment of a secretary of state and to a parliament for Wales. By that time, however, he accepted that successive secretaries of state had been 'effective champions of Wales', and was convinced that a parliament was no longer a serious proposition.[7] In an oral reply on 13 November 1951, the prime minister explained that the minister's functions would be 'to inform himself of the Welsh aspect of business by visiting the Principality and by discussion with representatives of Welsh life and to speak in Cabinet on behalf of the special interests and aspirations of Wales'. As minister for Welsh Affairs he would have no executive powers, and therefore the administration of services in Wales would still be the responsibility of United Kingdom ministers, but the prime minister added that he thought a better understanding of the Welsh viewpoint would result from the changes.[8] In December it was further explained that the under-secretary of state would be the chairman of the quarterly conference of heads of government offices in Wales, and that both ministers would have at their disposal all the government's senior officials with special knowledge of Wales.[9]

Attlee, speaking in the debate on the address as leader of the Opposition, described the items in the King's Speech relating to Scotland and Wales as 'somewhat window dressing'. He did not think that an additional under-secretary of state at the Home Office would exert more influence than an individual minister, such as James Griffiths. Of course we now know that, although Griffiths had tried desperately hard to influence government policy as it

[4]   Sir Richard Clarke, 'The number and size of government departments', *Political Quarterly*, 43, 2 (1972), 175–6.
[5]   TNA, CAB. 128/23, CC (51) 3, 2 November 1951.
[6]   Parl. Deb., vol. 493, xiv.
[7]   *Western Mail*, 13 January 1986.
[8]   Parl. Deb., vol. 493, cols 815–16.
[9]   Ibid., vol. 494, col. 2545.

affected Wales, he had not met with much success. In any case, Attlee's argument was weak because it was fortuitous that a Welshman happened to be a senior minister, and even so, he might be disinclined to put the Welsh viewpoint to his colleagues. In the debate, Welsh Labour MPs voiced their criticisms of the new arrangements. George Thomas suggested that the minister for Welsh Affairs would be a 'buffer' between members and ministers, and Cledwyn Hughes, in a maiden speech, alleged that David Maxwell-Fyfe's responsibilities as home secretary would prevent him from serving Wales adequately. In addition, Hughes did not think it helpful that the minister was not Welsh. He felt that the proposals fell short of the Welsh people's aspirations and were just 'crumbs from the rich man's table'. As a Welsh speaker he was concerned about the perilous state of the language, and he argued that it could be saved only if a measure of responsibility were placed in the hands of Welsh people in Wales.[10] Cledwyn Hughes's speech was his first parliamentary contribution to the debate on the machinery of government in Wales. Hughes, a solicitor and the son of a Presbyterian minister who had supported Megan Lloyd George, was steeped in the Welsh nonconformist radical tradition and, it would seem, a natural Liberal Party supporter. However, by the end of the war he realized that only the policies advocated by the Labour Party could remedy Anglesey's chronic social and economic ills. He had no difficulty in reconciling his Welshness with his socialism, which owed more to his nonconformist upbringing than to the teachings of Marx. Throughout his parliamentary career, Cledwyn Hughes would place Anglesey and Wales at the top of the political agenda, and he campaigned diligently and consistently for a greater measure of devolution, which would give Wales greater recognition as a nation.

In the Welsh affairs debate on 4 February 1952 David Maxwell-Fyfe gave an end-of-term report on his activities as minister for Welsh Affairs. Two government schemes, namely the siting by the War Office of a training ground in the Lleyn peninsula and the compulsory purchase of land by the Ministry of Agriculture in the Towy Valley for afforestation, had aroused strong opposition, which had been

---

[10]   Ibid., vol. 493, cols 62–3, 142, 422–3.

brought to the attention of ministers. Consequently, the War Office abandoned the Lleyn proposal for 1952, although it was to be reconsidered, giving due consideration to the views of the local community and agricultural requirements. It had also been decided that the compulsory purchase order for land in the Towy Valley should not be enforced.[11] As Maxwell-Fyfe recalled in 1964, in west Wales the building of modern works to produce steel and tin-plate had meant the closure of the old hand-mills. To prevent the decline of the area the Conservative government decided that new roads should be built to facilitate the introduction of industries allied to steel and tin-plate. In January 1953 David Maxwell-Fyfe put the matter before the House of Commons, and the government's action, including the decision to establish a committee under Lord Lloyd, the under-secretary, to consider proposals, was welcomed by MPs.[12]

The appointment of a minister for Welsh Affairs was an attempt by the Conservative government to meet the demand that Wales, as a distinct nation, should be given some form of recognition at ministerial level. It was a significant decision because it implied that special arrangements would be made for Wales, and also because it made further devolution more likely. As an arrangement, it paved the way for the appointment of a secretary of state, but at the time Labour refused to accept that the change was of any significance. During the Welsh affairs debate in February 1952, Ness Edwards reminded the House that, under the Labour government, the home secretary had been responsible for and had presided over meetings attended by all the Welshmen in the administration. J. Enoch Powell (now Conservative MP for Wolverhampton South West) quite rightly pointed out that the present situation was different, because although Welshmen had held responsibilities in past governments, those responsibilities had not related specifically to Wales. The Conservative innovation, said Powell, ensured for the first time that Welsh interests were not overlooked. It meant also that when the Welsh affairs debate was staged it was not necessary to appoint an ad hoc spokesman for that debate.[13] Aneurin Bevan still refused to accept that there was any merit in such an appointment. Speaking

[11]   Ibid., vol. 495, cols 654, 660.
[12]   Earl of Kilmuir, *Political Adventure* (London, 1964), 205.
[13]   Parl. Deb., vol. 495, cols 719, 726–7.

on 3 December 1953, he said: 'I have never been able to understand the animal at all. It was a constitutional device which sought
to create between the Government and the natural indignation of
the Welsh people a sort of constitutional shock-absorber.'[14] Despite
the lack of executive powers, the minister for Welsh Affairs did have
influence and the first holder of the office, David Maxwell-Fyfe, did
have some measure of success as an advocate for Wales. Of course,
the ever-present danger was that the holder of the office would, in
Vernon Bogdanor's words, 'come to be seen by his colleagues as a
nuisance' and his advice be 'regarded as interference' to be 'politely
ignored'.[15]

A Cabinet reshuffle in October 1954 saw the appointment of
Gwilym Lloyd George as home secretary and minister for Welsh
Affairs. Having been defeated in Pembrokeshire in 1950, he had
been re-elected in 1951 as the Conservative member for Newcastle
upon Tyne North. As a Welsh speaker and as a member of the most
distinguished political family in Wales, Gwilym Lloyd George
seemed a most appropriate choice, but Huw T. Edwards later
doubted whether it had been an advantage to have a Welsh speaker
in such a position. He felt that a Welsh speaker was always afraid
that he would be accused of favouritism, and therefore was reluctant to take any decisions likely to be controversial.[16] A new
under-secretary of state, Lord Mancroft, was appointed, but in
November the minister was pressed by E. H. Garner Evans to
request the appointment of a minister of state for Welsh Affairs.[17]
Not surprisingly, Labour had not seen fit to select a spokesman to
shadow the minister for Welsh Affairs when the office was created in
1951. In February 1956, S. O. Davies rather belatedly drew attention
to this, in a forthright letter to the secretary of the Parliamentary
Labour Party, stating that it was a matter that had 'either been overlooked, or possibly, as usual, contemptuously ignored'. He said that
this was an insult to the Welsh people, gave ammunition to other
parties and added to the problems of those MPs endeavouring to
retain their seats.[18]

[14]   Ibid., vol. 521, col. 194.
[15]   Bogdanor, *Devolution*, 134.
[16]   Huw T. Edwards, *Troi'r Drol* (Dinbych, 1963), 13.
[17]   Parl. Deb., vol. 532, col. 1009; vol. 533, col. 1345.
[18]   UWS, S. O. Davies Papers, A2, S. O. Davies to C. Johnson, Secretary, Parliamentary
Labour Party, 16 February 1956.

When he became prime minister in 1957, Harold Macmillan decided to give responsibility for Welsh affairs to the minister of Housing and Local Government. He decided to do so because that ministry was closely involved with Welsh needs, was affected by both social and economic developments in Wales, and had a strong Welsh office. In addition, the minister for Welsh Affairs would be able, through his executive power as minister of Housing and Local Government, to take initiatives of his own in order to meet Welsh needs.[19] The new arrangement was considered an advance on the previous one, but there was the contrary view that the home secretary, because he was in a more detached position, was better placed to take an overview, and of course he was a more senior member of the government. When the change was announced, no provision was made for an under-secretary to be appointed. When Conservative members David Llewellyn and David Gibson Watt (Hereford) raised the matter on 11 February, Henry Brooke, the minister of Housing and Local Government, replied that if there were to be an under-secretary he was not prepared to hand over his responsibility to him and be a 'Minister by proxy'.[20] Eventually, in response to the report in the *Third Memorandum* of the Council for Wales and Monmouthshire, Lord Brecon was appointed a minister of state, in December 1957.[21] In his capacity as minister for Welsh Affairs, David Maxwell-Fyfe had been sensitive to the intense opposition to the training ground in the Lleyn peninsula and the afforestation scheme in the Towy Valley, and he had used his influence to safeguard the interests of the communities affected. By contrast, Henry Brooke, as minister for Welsh Affairs, refused to respond when many people of different political persuasions in Wales expressed opposition to the construction of the Tryweryn reservoir. Instead, he used his executive authority as minister of Housing and Local Government to tip (in the words of Megan Lloyd George) 'the scales in favour of the Liverpool Corporation against the united wishes of the peoples of Wales'. Brooke defended his action on the grounds that the water was of no commercial value to Wales, and he chose to ignore protests on behalf of the

---

[19]   *Government Administration in Wales. Text of a letter addressed by the Prime Minister to the Chairman of the Council for Wales and Monmouthshire*, 11 December 1957 (Cmnd. 334), 4.
[20]   Parl. Deb., vol. 564, cols 943, 995, 1025.
[21]   *Government Administration in Wales*, 5.

Welsh-speaking community in Merioneth.[22] The Tryweryn episode and resignations from the Council for Wales and Monmouthshire in 1958 were to mar permanently Brooke's period as minister for Welsh Affairs, but the encouragement given to the Central Electricity Generating Board to site a nuclear power station in north Wales, which provided employment, is seldom recalled.

In April 1963 the government announced that a new office, to be known as the office of the minister for Welsh Affairs, was to be created, and that housing and local government would be part of it. The links that the Housing and Local Government and Welsh Affairs staffs had with all aspects of Welsh life and with the local authorities were to be retained, and the new office was to keep the minister informed of the implications for Wales of government policies. If, as was claimed, the minister for Welsh Affairs had always been kept informed, the change would not have been a significant one, except that, according to the minister, Keith Joseph, the Welsh office would now be better equipped to advise the minister.[23] On 11 April Harold Macmillan explained that the office would be responsible 'for carrying out a long-term survey of the prospects for Wales, and for producing plans for the economic and social development of the Principality'.[24] Joseph stated in July that it would be assisted in this work by an economic intelligence unit.[25] By July of the following year this office employed thirty-seven professional staff and could call on the services of the staff of the Ministry of Housing and Local Government in London and Wales.[26] Joseph, like his predecessors, maintained that as minister for Welsh Affairs he had influence, and he assured MPs that he was consulted before any decisions were taken regarding possible railway closures in Wales.[27] At the end of the thirteen-year period of Conservative government, then, Wales had not only a minister for Welsh Affairs but also a minister of state and the beginnings of a Welsh Office in Cardiff. It had transpired that the decision taken by the Conservative Party in 1948 had been of far greater significance than had been appreciated at the time.

[22] Parl. Deb., vol. 580, cols 127, 146, 148.
[23] *Western Mail*, 11 April 1963.
[24] Parl. Deb., vol. 675, col. 1477.
[25] Ibid., vol. 682, cols 53–4.
[26] Ibid., vol. 699, cols 55–6.
[27] Ibid., vol. 697, col. 754.

HOME RULE

On 1 July 1950 Undeb Cymru Fydd, which had found the proposal to set up a Council for Wales and Monmouthshire unacceptable, called a national conference at Llandrindod Wells to reconsider the question of home rule for Wales.[28] On the very same day, a Labour Party rally was held in Newtown. Already, the executive committee of the Welsh Regional Council of Labour had adopted an uncompromising stance, and at its meeting on 27 March it passed the following resolution, opposing the conference: 'That this Regional Council disassociates itself with this Convention and therefore calls upon the whole of the Labour Movement in Wales not to send any representatives to the Convention and further, that any question of devolution for Wales can be discussed inside our Movement.'[29] Cliff Prothero, speaking for the executive committee, said that it was a 'frivolous' demand by a minority who were not representative of Welsh opinion; as it turned out, that was a fairly accurate assessment of the situation.[30] At the conference at Llandrindod Wells, delegates passed unanimously a resolution supporting home rule for Wales. S. O. Davies had taken a prominent part in proceedings, and Gwilym Williams drew Morgan Phillips's attention to that fact.[31] Following the conference an article in *The Economist* on 8 July interpreted the demand for self-government as 'a protest against the power of any government in a planned economy', but pointed out that the attitude of Whitehall was just as 'exasperating and callous' towards the regions of England as it was towards Scotland or Wales. The writer thought that since the influence of the individual was being diminished, any move to reverse the trend should be supported, and if Scotland and Wales gained self-government then perhaps it might encourage someone 'to demand a little freedom for the patient English'.[32] Meanwhile, the national conference called by Undeb Cymru Fydd had elected a committee and, after preliminary work, the Parliament for Wales Campaign was launched at the Llanrwst National Eisteddfod in 1951. The aim was to secure a parliament, on the Northern Ireland model, with legislative

[28]   Parliament for Wales Campaign, *Parliament for Wales* (Aberystwyth, 1953), 3.
[29]   Welsh Regional Council of Labour, *Annual Meeting*, 13 May 1950, 11.
[30]   *Western Mail*, 29 March 1950.
[31]   LPA, M. Phillips Papers, G. Williams to M. Phillips, 4 July 1950.
[32]   'Home rule', *The Economist*, 8 July 1950, 60.

and administrative powers. The Welsh parliament would be responsible for matters closely affecting Wales, while the Westminster
parliament would retain control of matters of 'wider concern', and
so there would be no need for a reduction in the number of MPs
representing Welsh constituencies. A petition, to be presented to
parliament, was to be organized by the campaign committee.[33]

The five Labour MPs who associated themselves actively with the
campaign were S. O. Davies, Cledwyn Hughes, T. W. Jones,
Goronwy Roberts and Tudor Watkins.[34] Peter Freeman also
supported the principle and in November, soon after the campaign
was launched, he requested the home secretary to introduce legislation granting self-government to Wales.[35] Hughes and Roberts had
inherited the ideals of the Cymru Fydd movement; the involvement
of Davies, Watkins, Jones and, particularly, Freeman is more difficult to explain.[36] When the campaign got under way, the five rebel
MPs found themselves in a difficult situation within the Labour
movement. In October 1953 Cliff Prothero, in a letter to Morgan
Phillips, named the MPs as well as Huw T. Edwards (vice-president
of the Parliament for Wales Campaign), but S. O. Davies was
singled out because he had appeared on a Plaid Cymru platform
in support of a parliament for Wales. The executive committee of
the Welsh Regional Council of Labour was not only against a
parliament, but was also against its members sharing a platform
with the nationalists.[37] In November 1953 the Labour Party's assistant
national agent, Sara E. Barker, wrote to Tudor Watkins and T. W.
Jones, on behalf of Morgan Phillips, informing them that the Welsh
Regional Council of Labour had considered correspondence from
the Rhondda Borough Labour Party and the Rhondda East
Constituency Labour Party which protested against the participa-
tion of both MPs in a meeting to be held in the Rhondda on 27
November 1953 under the auspices of the Parliament for Wales
Campaign. Both MPs were advised of these objections and told
that the Welsh Council of Labour disapproved of their action. In
his reply to Barker, on 25 November, Watkins stated that the local
member had been informed and had no objections. Watkins added

---

[33]   *Parliament for Wales*, 3, 7–8.
[34]   LPA, M. Phillips Papers, C. Prothero to M. Phillips, 6 October 1953.
[35]   Parl. Deb., vol. 494, col. 57.
[36]   Lord Cledwyn, *Referendum*, 8.
[37]   LPA, M. Phillips Papers, C. Prothero to M. Phillips, 6 October 1953.

that the meeting was not being arranged by a political organization, and that since he was in favour of the petition he would be criticized if he failed to attend. The position would have been different if the Labour Party had announced that it was opposed to a parliament for Wales; if that had been the case, he would have sought advice and abided by it. In his reply, on the same day, Jones said that he had promised to attend a non-party meeting after ascertaining that the local member had no objection. He was anxious not to harm the party in any constituency, but he was wholly convinced that the best course in the interest of all concerned was for him to honour his commitment and attend.[38] When the five MPs issued a press statement in January 1956 inviting all Labour Party members to sign the petition for a parliament, the executive committee of the Welsh Regional Council of Labour unanimously decided to report them to the National Executive Committee 'with a view to appropriate action being taken'.[39] Steps were evidently being contemplated against the MPs, and Cledwyn Hughes later confirmed that Cliff Prothero sought to bring the 'force of the Labour Party machine against those advocating devolution'.[40] He also recalled that the MPs' activities caused considerable ill feeling in the Welsh Parliamentary Labour Party, and that there was talk of expelling them; but Aneurin Bevan, who had opposed the party line on other issues, defended their right to hold their views.[41] It is interesting to note that S. O. Davies, Cledwyn Hughes, Goronwy Roberts and Tudor Watkins had, in fact, supported Bevan in the past, for instance, when he defied the party line in voting against the Statement on Defence in 1952.[42] Although he did not share the MPs' viewpoint, Bevan did not make any move against them. Perhaps this was surprising because, as Tudor Watkins later recalled, the campaign faced 'opposition in the mining valleys'.[43]

The Parliament for Wales Campaign put pressure on the Welsh Regional Council of Labour to reconsider its policy. A motion at the annual conference in 1952 calling for a policy for Wales was referred to the executive committee, which in turn set up a

[38]   Ibid., S. E. Barker to M. Phillips, 24 November 1953; T. E. Watkins to S. E. Barker, 25 November 1953; T. W. Jones to S. E. Barker, 25 November 1953.
[39]   Welsh Regional Council of Labour, *Annual Meeting*, 26 May 1956, 13.
[40]   Interview, Cledwyn Hughes, 29 March 1983.
[41]   Lord Cledwyn, *Referendum*, 10.
[42]   Parl. Deb., vol. 497, cols 559–60.
[43]   Interview, Tudor Watkins, 5 March 1983.

subcommittee on Welsh affairs, on which the Welsh Parliamentary Labour Party was represented.[44] At its first meeting in September 1952 the subcommittee agreed that Wales had special problems, and that it was the committee's right to prepare a memorandum outlining ways of resolving them.[45] These were very important decisions, because one of the main arguments against any form of devolution was the argument that Welsh problems were no different from those of the regions of England. Once the point had been conceded officially that Welsh problems were indeed different, Labour had to offer a solution unique to Wales. The absence of a Labour Party policy statement on its attitude towards a parliament for Wales was causing problems for the Welsh Regional Council of Labour, and on 6 October 1953 Cliff Prothero wrote to Morgan Phillips requesting the National Executive Committee to consider the matter and make known its views. The executive in Wales demanded action and declared that 'the Labour Party is having the ground taken from underneath its feet because we do not make a declaration one way or the other'.[46] Nevertheless, no statement was forthcoming from the National Executive Committee, and on 27 October Prothero wrote a further letter to Phillips, informing him that the Regional Council had decided, in answer to the National Union of Mine-workers' request for a policy statement, to make a declaration against a parliament for Wales.[47] Still there was no response from the NEC, but the Regional Council persisted in its demand for action, and at a meeting of the Welsh Parliamentary Labour Party attended by representatives of the Council and the NEC, the following resolution was passed:

> That this Joint Committee recommend the National Executive to affirm that a Welsh Parliament would be detrimental to the best interests of Wales. Further, an explanatory statement should be issued together with an indication of the measures a Labour Government would initiate to meet the social and economic problems of Wales.

In November, immediately following this, the Welsh Regional Council's Welsh affairs subcommittee decided to begin discussions with the Welsh Parliamentary Labour Party and the National

[44] Welsh Regional Council of Labour, *Annual Meeting*, 29 May 1954, 10.
[45] Idem, *Annual Meeting*, 2 May 1953, 8.
[46] LPA, M. Phillips Papers, C. Prothero to M. Phillips, 6 October 1953.
[47] Ibid., C. Prothero to M. Phillips, 27 October 1953.

Executive Committee on a proposal to establish a Welsh Grand Committee, and to ascertain whether a Cabinet minister with responsibility for Welsh affairs (but without a department) was feasible.[48] In the policy statement *Labour's Policy for Wales*, which appeared in March 1954, there was a firm commitment to appoint a minister for Welsh Affairs with a seat in the Cabinet and a promise to review the arrangements for the scrutiny of Welsh affairs by Welsh MPs. In addition, an attempt would be made to allocate more parliamentary time to Welsh affairs, and the constitution of the Council for Wales and Monmouthshire would be revised to make it a more effective and representative body.[49] In other words, major changes in the machinery of government were not contemplated. The decision to appoint a Cabinet minister with sole responsibility for Welsh affairs was only a slight advance on the position under the Conservatives, who had appointed the home secretary as minister for Welsh Affairs, but the party was moving – if slowly – in the direction that the devolutionists wanted. The policy document was subsequently overwhelmingly endorsed by the regional conference on 29 May 1954, and a much-relieved Cliff Prothero was able to include the following statement in a report on the conference: 'It now goes on record that the Welsh Labour Movement is against a Parliament for Wales, because it considers it would not be in the interests of the people of Wales.'[50]

S. O. DAVIES'S BILL

Stephen Owen Davies was not typical of those south Wales Labour MPs sponsored by the miners, in that he always displayed a marked degree of independence and adopted a specifically nationalist position in relation to the government of Wales. He could, in Gwyn A. Williams's words, 'embrace a species of Welsh nationalism and a species of communism in a Welsh socialism which had him repeatedly excluded from the Labour Party'.[51] On 15 December 1954 he

[48]   Ibid., minutes of the Welsh Regional Council of Labour's Welsh Affairs Committee, 16 November 1953.
[49]   Labour Party, *Labour's Policy for Wales* (Cardiff, 1954), 11–12.
[50]   *Report of the Annual Conference of the Welsh Regional Council of Labour*, 29 May 1954, 5.
[51]   Gwyn A. Williams, *When was Wales?* (London, 1985), 266.

presented a private member's bill 'to provide for the better government of Wales', and it received a second reading on 4 March 1955. Goronwy Roberts, Cledwyn Hughes, T. W. Jones, Tudor Watkins and Peter Freeman supported Davies.[52] Davies sought help to frame the measure, and Eryl Hall Williams, a lecturer in law at the London School of Economics, and D. Watkin Powell, a barrister and a member of Plaid Cymru's executive committee, were named as legal advisers. They met as a group about once a week in the House of Commons. Freeman did not attend one meeting, while Watkins, though supporting the principle, was not too interested in questions of constitutional law, and Jones followed from a distance. Thus, those most closely involved were Davies, Hughes, Roberts and the legal advisers.[53] Apart from the fact that he was a Welsh speaker and came from a Nonconformist background, Davies had little in common with the two north Wales MPs who were his principal supporters.

As D. Watkin Powell later recalled, the fact that it was a private member's bill meant that there were certain financial constraints, and after a lengthy discussion it was agreed to adopt a simple scheme, on the lines of the Government of Ireland Act 1914.[54] Hughes and Roberts tried to persuade Davies to frame a less ambitious measure. They proposed a scheme limited to the appointment of a secretary of state and the creation of an elected national assembly that within three years would be consulted by the secretary of state, regarding proposals for the future devolution of powers to it. In the meantime, the assembly would have deliberative, initiative and executive functions. Hughes thought that, since it was a private member's bill, a more modest scheme was more appropriate, would win support in Wales and in parliament, and could be defended because of its simplicity. He said that 'a fight on a narrow and defensible salient will be more valuable and profitable than a battle over a wide and scattered front'. He claimed that the secretary of the Parliament for Wales Campaign was finding it difficult to secure canvassers, and that a major setback in parliament would only dampen the enthusiasm of the campaign's supporters. In his view, it was premature to seek a parliament before securing a secretary of

[52] Parl. Deb., vol. 535, col. 1772.
[53] Information from D. Watkin Powell, 10 January 1985.
[54] Ibid.

state and a Welsh Office. The proposal for an elected assembly was a vital element in the scheme, because once that was established everything would be possible.[55] Roberts was fully prepared to support the measure, but felt that the position of colleagues in an election year should be taken into account. He thought that the scheme could be defended because it was Labour Party policy to appoint a minister for Welsh Affairs and make the Council for Wales and Monmouthshire more representative. It was his view that if the minister for Welsh Affairs were to be different from the Conservative minister for Welsh Affairs he would have to be allocated executive functions, and that the Council for Wales and Monmouthshire could be made more representative only by being transformed into an elected body. The aspect that was not Labour Party policy was the request that the secretary of state consult the assembly before the end of a three-year period. Roberts considered that the scheme had 'substance, logic and a high promise for future development'.[56] Hughes and Roberts obviously thought that the bill, in Peter Stead's words, 'went much too far and was disastrously the wrong bill at the wrong time'.[57] They fully appreciated the intense opposition to self-government within the Labour Party and realized that it could be achieved only in the longer term; so great was the hostility within the Labour Party that it was a question of one step at a time. Davies, however, was adamant that the measure as proposed should not be modified. An alternative scheme would not be acceptable to the Parliament for Wales Campaign's supporters and would be ridiculed by opponents of self-government; three years would be too long a time to wait, and a secretary of state would, he felt, be simply the 'creature of the British Government'. He saw himself as having no alternative but to introduce such a measure by means of a private member's bill, since both major parties were hostile to the idea. The debate would inform public opinion that the House of Commons was overburdened with work, and it would underline to the people of Wales their right to govern themselves.[58]

[55]   UWS, S. O. Davies Papers, B3, C. Hughes to S. O. Davies, 14 January 1955.
[56]   Ibid., G. Roberts to S. O. Davies, 9 January 1955.
[57]   Stead, 'Labour Party and the claims of Wales', 104.
[58]   UWS, S. O. Davies Papers, B3, S. O. Davies to C. Hughes and G. Roberts, 19 January 1955.

Davies would not accept Hughes and Roberts's view that his bill was too ambitious. Opening the debate on 4 March 1955 he referred to it as 'a modest Bill . . . on which a considerable measure of self-government could be built in the future'. He could foresee a similar demand coming from Scotland and probably from some parts of England. A real anxiety was the fact that so much legislation was delegated, which meant (in Davies's words) 'that the rights and privileges of elected Members of Parliament are taken away from them and handed over to an impersonal, unelected and unrepresentative service'. The diminishing role of MPs was of major concern to him.[59] In the Welsh affairs debate in January 1948 he had complained about the arbitrary acquisition of land by the War Office, a sensitive issue which had aroused the anger of the Welsh people. Before that action was taken there had been no consultation with MPs.[60] Although unhappy with the bill, Hughes and Roberts gave the measure maximum support. Hughes maintained that there were Welsh problems, that they were inadequately dealt with because of the congestion of business in the House of Commons, that such government action was taken with the majority of the electorate in mind, and that that majority resided in England. The establishment of the Council for Wales and Monmouthshire and the appointment of a minister for Welsh Affairs recognized that Wales had its own special problems, and if it had control over its affairs such problems might arise less frequently and with less intensity. He viewed with apprehension the increase in administrative devolution over the years, because it had meant an increase in bureaucracy without a corresponding increase in democracy. The sovereignty of the United Kingdom parliament was not at risk, and it would retain responsibility for foreign policy, defence, trade and taxation. Therefore, Wales would continue to send a full complement of MPs to Westminster. The bill, said Hughes, would give Wales a status befitting a nation and a greater voice in the affairs of the United Kingdom. It would ensure a more effective solution to Wales's problems and that the establishment of a new organization was undertaken smoothly. The senate or parliament would not be an 'emasculated, powerless body' since it would have control over the executive in most aspects of government, and there was an

[59] Parl. Deb., vol. 537, cols 2442–3.
[60] Ibid., vol. 446, col. 774.

allowance 'for a margin of economic initiative'. Its powers would be both legislative and deliberative, and it would also have limited taxation powers. The functions to be transferred would be those of the Welsh Board of Health, the Welsh Department of Education, the Welsh Department of Agriculture and the Welsh office of the Ministry of Housing and Local Government, and the senate would receive the Welsh residuary share of reserved taxes and taxes paid directly to the Exchequer of Wales. Hughes argued that the bill, which was based on the Northern Ireland model, would strengthen democracy, result in more efficient administration and ensure that the Welsh nation was protected against economic and political storms in the future.[61] This last assertion was the most difficult to defend because the economy of Wales is inextricably linked with that of England. Roberts did not see the United Kingdom as a unitary state but as a federation, and so he considered the bill as the first step in the development of a federal state. He reproached colleagues who had wasted time arguing against republicanism and dominion status when the real issue was federalism. The passing of the bill would not mean economic separation, and he made the point, anticipating opposition from south Wales Labour MPs like Ness Edwards, that a unified coal board for the United Kingdom would remain and that, as in Northern Ireland, a unified British trade union movement would operate in Wales. Roberts refused to accept that the standards of social and welfare services were lower in Northern Ireland. Nevertheless, James Callaghan claimed that he was putting forward an argument that was purely theoretical.[62]

Meanwhile, the Welsh Regional Council of Labour had rejected the entire concept of a parliament for Wales. At its conference, James Griffiths had spoken for the movement and he now led his party's general opposition to the bill. He argued that if a parliament were established it would lead to the break-up of the economic unity of the United Kingdom and of social services, and it would take Welsh MPs out of the mainstream of British politics. He was only too aware of the historic failure of the Cymru Fydd move-ment, and he reminded the House that the views of the populous counties of south Wales – Carmarthenshire, Glamorgan and Monmouthshire – had to be taken fully into account. Griffiths had

---

[61]   Ibid., vol. 537, cols 2447–55.
[62]   Ibid., vol. 537, cols 2519, 2521–4.

always abided by the party's decisions with regard to Wales, even when he disagreed with them, but on the home rule issue his views were very much in line with those of his party. He believed that the answer was the diversification of the structure of the economy and the rehabilitation of rural areas; local government needed to be strengthened and the Council for Wales and Monmouthshire given added powers and made more representative of local government, but he did not think that the Council should be directly elected. He advocated more administrative devolution and welcomed the decision to appoint a minister for Welsh Affairs with a seat in the Cabinet.[63] Not only was Griffiths opposed to a parliament, but he also avoided having the slightest contact with the campaign. It seems that supporters of the Parliament for Wales Campaign sought an interview with him after the bill was presented, in order to discuss the point that there was no trade restriction between Ulster and the United Kingdom, but he refused to meet them, and his reasons for doing so do not appear to have been particularly convincing ones.[64] Speaking in this same debate, Ness Edwards refused to accept that a 'nationalist policy' was required to solve Wales's economic problems. These problems, he felt, would be solved – along with similar problems in the rest of the United Kingdom – only by adopting a particular social policy.[65] D. J. Williams, in a prepared speech, argued that the people of Wales were indifferent to constitutional changes, that the bill was too lengthy and too complex for a private member's bill, and that there had never been a demand for separation from the United Kingdom. Interestingly enough, before the bill was presented Cledwyn Hughes and Goronwy Roberts had made the point to S. O. Davies that it was too complex. Williams, like other Labour MPs, thought that the economic argument against any form of separatism was overwhelming, and that although Davies meant well he was inviting 'the people of Wales to take the road to economic ruin'.[66]

For the government, Gwilym Lloyd George assured MPs that in respect of administrative devolution the end of the road had not been reached, but the question that now had to be answered was

[63]   Ibid., vol. 537, cols 2514–17.
[64]   UWS, S. O. Davies Papers, B3, Cyril O. Jones to S. O. Davies, 4 January 1955.
[65]   Parl. Deb., vol. 537, col. 2480.
[66]   UWS, D. J. Williams Papers, C7/8, typescript with manuscript draft of a speech by D. J. Williams attacking S. O. Davies's bill for a Welsh Parliament, 1954.

whether the 'Welsh nation should become the Welsh State'. The Northern Ireland precedent was not a valid one for other parts of the United Kingdom, and a parliament unable to tackle economic problems would not serve Welsh interests. Furthermore, if Wales determined its own domestic policy, there was no case for sending thirty-six MPs to Westminster. Conservative backbenchers also voiced their opposition to the bill. David Llewellyn thought that Wales's problems could be solved only by a combination of private enterprise, diversification of industry and, somewhat unexpectedly, state planning. He supported demands for a Welsh Grand Committee, but feared that Glamorgan and Monmouthshire would dominate a parliament. Peter Thomas pointed out that that would mean not only the domination of the rest of the country by urban south Wales, but also the domination of Welsh-speaking rural areas by a predominantly Anglicized region. Labour was the dominant party in the urban areas and would inevitably control a Welsh parliament, but of course, as Raymond Gower noted, a reduction in the number of Welsh MPs would give the Conservative Party a distinct advantage at Westminster. Gower thought that the bill's promoters were too far ahead of public opinion. He demanded the appointment of a secretary of state, and was the only one among those opposed to the bill to make an alternative proposal of any substance.[67] The following day the *Western Mail* supported this demand for the appointment of a secretary of state to give Wales equal standing with Scotland.[68]

When the House divided, the bill was defeated. In the division only fourteen members voted for it, while forty-eight voted against: neither Aneurin Bevan nor Peter Freeman, one of the bill's sponsors, participated in the vote. Herbert Morrison attended and voted against the bill.[69] That he bothered to do so may seem surprising, but he was the deputy leader of the Labour Party and his opposition was a clear indication of where the party stood on this issue. The combined vote of Labour and Conservative members (George Thomas and David Llewellyn acting as tellers) ensured a heavy defeat, but the bill had at least drawn attention to the machinery of government in Wales and in that respect had served a useful

---

[67]   Parl. Deb., vol. 537, cols 2469, 2472–3, 2461, 2458.
[68]   *Western Mail*, 5 March 1955.
[69]   Parl. Deb., vol. 537, cols 2526–8.

purpose. More than anything, the debate had demonstrated once again that the Labour Party was just as sharply divided on the 'Welsh question' as the Liberal Party had been sixty years earlier. On 24 April 1956, Goronwy Roberts presented a petition to the House of Commons on behalf of the Parliament for Wales Campaign. The petition, signed by 240,652 Welsh people, concluded: 'We pray your honourable House to promote an Act of Parliament to secure for Wales a Parliament with adequate legislative authority in Welsh affairs.'[70] The number of signatures was a disappointment to its promoters. By that time the campaign had effectively come to an end, and presenting the petition was merely a symbolic act, of little real consequence.

It would seem that among Labour MPs, those supporting devolution were the only ones thinking about ways of improving the machinery of government. In the main this was true, but the contribution made by Ness Edwards, to whom nationalism was anathema, should not be overlooked. In the same year that S. O. Davies's Government of Wales Bill was debated, Edwards published *Is This the Road?*, a pamphlet in which he outlined what he considered to be a policy for 'radical thinkers', which would give a 'greater purpose' to people's lives. Although he rejected what he considered to be 'narrow nationalism', he was equally opposed to the centralization of power because, in his words, when 'power is centralised local democracy becomes atrophied and the citizen becomes a cypher'. He suggested a number of ways whereby power could be returned to the people in their own localities. The Council for Wales and Monmouthshire should become, he proposed, an indirectly elected body with responsibility for the work of advisory bodies which 'offend the democratic principle'. This type of development should also take place in Scotland and the regions of England, but there was 'no reason why Wales should not blaze the trail'. He also thought that the whole question of the accountability of the boards of nationalized industries ought to be re-examined, because 'Public ownership under bureaucratic control can be as monstrous as unchecked private ownership'. From the inception of the National Health Service, Edwards had drawn attention to the violation of the democratic principle. He saw no reason why responsibilities below regional level could not be shouldered by local

[70]   Ibid., vol. 551, col. 1589.

authorities and joint local authority boards. By then Aneurin Bevan had published *In Place of Fear* and had recognized that nomination to the various health service boards was a defect, and that election was 'a better principle than selection'. Bevan thought that if local government were reorganized, the revised units could be responsible for the administration of hospitals, but he emphasized that he was not thinking of regional authorities because they 'would not be local government units in any proper sense of the term'.[71] Ness Edwards also thought that joint local authority boards might be allocated responsibilities for gas and electricity. Then, as now, the majority of MPs were mainly concerned with policies and their effect on people's lives, but Edwards warned that 'we should all be doing much more thinking and agitating about the form, structure and nature of Government in a society where the State must inevitably play an increasing role in the life of the community'.[72] Ness Edwards, like those MPs advocating devolution, recognized that the machinery of government could have an effect on the quality of life of their constituents.

THE COUNCIL FOR WALES AND MONMOUTHSHIRE

The Council for Wales and Monmouthshire, Labour's substitute for a secretary of state, had not been appointed to advise the government on any specific matter, and the chairman later admitted, in an article in *Wales*, in November 1958, that no one had been able to say what its role was or how it was to be executed.[73] The Council proceeded on the basis that it would not discuss matters of purely local interest unless they affected matters of national interest covered by its terms of reference.[74] At the outset, members agreed that, whatever the task, it should not be approached on party lines, and that principle was strictly adhered to while Huw T. Edwards was chairman.[75]

---

[71]   Aneurin Bevan, *In Place of Fear* (London, 1952), 91, 188.

[72]   Ness Edwards, *Is This the Road?* (Cardiff and Wrexham, n.d.), 5, 13.

[73]   Huw T. Edwards, 'Why I resigned', *Wales*, November 1958, 4.

[74]   The Council for Wales and Monmouthshire, *A Memorandum by the Council on its Activities*, October 1950 (Cmd. 8060), 4.

[75]   Edwards, 'Why I resigned', 4.

Included in the Council's first memorandum, published in October 1950, was the report of a panel on the depopulation of rural areas. This panel drew the attention of the Council to the need for a more authoritative inquiry into 'all aspects of Welsh administration, including the general position of local government in Wales and the relationships between Government Offices in Wales and the central Departments'. This, the panel said, should be undertaken with the government's full authority and with the help of an independent secretariat. The Council endorsed the panel's request.[76] In these early years the Council spent a good deal of time examining the possibility of securing extended functions for government departments in Wales. As a result of a meeting between the Council and government officials a new office of the Ministry of Local Government and Planning was established, in the charge of an under-secretary. This office was responsible for all those functions relating to town and country planning in Wales which had formerly been located in London, and for the Welsh Board of Health's functions relating to housing and local government. After discussions with officials of the Ministry of Agriculture, Fisheries and Food, it was agreed that the status of the secretary, Welsh Department of Agriculture, should be raised to that of under-secretary, and that he should be consulted on all matters of Welsh interest or when it was essential that the Welsh viewpoint should be considered. Following a meeting between representatives of the Council and the minister of Education, the government decided to establish a new unit of the Welsh Department of Education to handle day-to-day matters relating to primary and secondary schools. The Council was disappointed that the government had not implemented proposals that the work in Wales of the Agricultural Land Service and the National Agricultural Advisory Service should be the responsibility of the Welsh Department of Agriculture, and that the permanent secretary of the Welsh Department of Education should be located in Wales. Its representatives submitted the Council's proposals for administrative devolution when they met ministers in June 1951. They made it quite clear that their long-term objective was 'parity with Scotland': that meant a secretary of state with responsibility at least for agriculture, education, health, and housing and local government.[77]

[76]   The Council for Wales and Monmouthshire, *A Memorandum*, 48, 65.
[77]   Idem, *Second Memorandum by the Council on its Activities*, July 1953 (Cmd. 8844), 8–9.

After it had been requested by the government to suggest ways in which the rural areas could be rehabilitated, the Council, in its *Second Memorandum*, published in July 1953, advocated a Welsh rural development corporation. After nine months' delay the government not only refused to implement the proposal, but also failed to discuss its own proposals with the Council.[78] In the debate on rural Wales in December 1953 the minister for Welsh Affairs, David Maxwell-Fyfe, defended the government's inaction. He stated that the government's own proposals were published in the form of a White Paper, and that to have discussed them with the Council in advance of publication would have been improper since the government's responsibility was to the House of Commons. The Council, meanwhile, had refused to accept that its role was purely advisory, and had issued a statement after the publication of the White Paper on rural Wales declaring that the government had not given its views due consideration.[79] Naturally, relations between the Council and the government were strained, and it was only after representatives of the Council met David Maxwell-Fyfe (who had been praised in the *Second Memorandum* for the manner in which he discharged his duties) that relations improved.[80] They deteriorated again in the following year, when the Council submitted its report on the difficulties facing the Welsh ports. Again, the Council was not consulted by the government and was not informed of progress made in order to solve the problem.[81]

In 1954, the Council decided, in accordance with its decision in 1950, that it would investigate the administrative arrangements for the exercise of central government functions in Wales. A panel was appointed, with William Jones, a former clerk of the peace for Denbighshire, as chairman; its terms of reference were: 'To examine the machinery of Government administration in Wales, and report.' The earlier investigation by the Council had been confined to those departments that were envisaged as the responsibility of a secretary of state, but the new panel would be able to assess the position in all departments in Wales. It set itself three tasks, namely, to discover whether as much appropriate business as possible was being settled in Wales; whether the heads of Welsh

[78]   Edwards, 'Why I resigned', 4–6.
[79]   Parl. Deb., vol. 521, col. 1823.
[80]   The Council for Wales and Monmouthshire, *Second Memorandum*, 8.
[81]   Edwards, 'Why I resigned', 6–7.

offices carried enough weight at their headquarters' offices in London; and whether sufficient account was being taken of Welsh aspects when wider policy matters were under consideration. The panel's report was included in the Council's *Third Memorandum*, published in January 1957. It concluded that there was room for improvement in the way in which government functions were administered, and that more recognition should be given to 'distinctive Welsh conditions and to the many differences between Wales and the remainder of Great Britain'. The main weakness identified was the insufficient coordination of the work of the departments' Welsh offices. The quarterly conference of heads of government offices in Wales, established in 1946 to secure a degree of liaison, was unable to take decisive action, because each head of department did not have the authority to make the final decision regarding his department's business. The appointment of a minister for Welsh Affairs in 1951 was an attempt to increase coordination, but, lacking executive authority, it was unlikely to be able to exert much influence. The panel was also of the view that heads of Welsh offices did not have sufficient influence on policy decisions taken in London, and that too much Welsh business was administered there. Although a separate nation, Wales was not treated differently from the regions of England, except that the word 'regional' was not part of the title of heads of government offices in Wales.

The panel examined the arrangements within government departments and made a number of recommendations. The secretary, Welsh Department of Agriculture, did not have responsibility for important functions that were the responsibility of his counterpart in Scotland, and he had no control over technical officers, although in other departments they came under the office located in Wales. The panel noted that the Arton Wilson Committee, set up to examine the provincial and local organization of the Ministry of Agriculture, Fisheries and Food, agreed that Wales was a nation and that the secretary in Wales did not have the autonomy that other heads of government offices possessed. The committee and the panel accordingly recommended that the secretary in Wales should have greater authority than the English regional controllers. The panel was frank enough to declare that it had been afforded the opportunity of submitting oral and written evidence to the Arton Wilson Committee and that therefore that committee's findings had been influenced by the panel, which in turn utilized them in support of its own viewpoint. The Welsh Department of Education was headed by a permanent secretary who was able to influence policy decisions, but it was not equipped, like the Welsh Board of Health, to carry out extensive day-to-day work in Wales, and therefore the permanent secretary was unable to control such work completely. The panel thought that it would be more beneficial for the permanent secretary and his staff to be located in Wales, where they would be in close contact with the country's special educational problems. The Welsh Department should also be strengthened to enable it to deal with all aspects of the Ministry's work in Wales. In fact, the Welsh Board of Health was the only office in Wales with statutory backing, and it was responsible for all the duties that in England were the responsibility of the Ministry. The panel was impressed by the willingness of the Ministry of Health to delegate responsibility, and considered that the Welsh Board of Health was a model that should be examined by other government departments to see whether they could adopt a similar pattern.

However, the panel thought that a more fundamental change was needed than was covered by these recommendations. It proposed that a secretary of state with a seat in the Cabinet should be appointed, and a Welsh Office established to handle those problems that were different from those prevailing in other parts of the United Kingdom. Such a minister would be responsible for agriculture, education, health, housing and local government, the work of the Central Office of Information, and some Transport, Board of Trade and Home Office functions. The heads of Welsh offices not under the control of the secretary of state should be of a higher status than their counterparts in the English regions, to enable them to exert greater influence when their departments in London considered Welsh matters. The departments mentioned were the Board of Trade, the Ministry of Labour and National Service, the Ministry of Works, and the Ministry of Fuel and Power. It was also necessary for the Ministry of Transport and Civil Aviation to have a Welsh office, under the control of an under-secretary, to coordinate its activities in Wales. The new Welsh Office should be located in Cardiff, but there should also be a liaison office in London to enable the secretary of state to maintain close contact with other government ministries. The panel envisaged two major functions for the secretary of state: he would exercise full control over the functions vested in him, and he would also be Wales's voice in the Cabinet and be able to safeguard Welsh interests in matters beyond his statutory responsibilities. The panel emphasized that when legislation was being prepared for England and Wales in areas subject to the control of the secretary of state, the Welsh Office and the government department sponsoring the legislation should work closely together, in order to ensure that due attention was given to the special needs of Wales.[82]

After the Council for Wales and Monmouthshire had published its *Third Memorandum*, the question of whether or not a secretary of state should be appointed became a major issue in Welsh politics. In the debate on Welsh affairs on 11 February 1957, James Griffiths welcomed the panel's proposals and made the point that the proposed secretary of state's functions were so limited that the economic unity of the United Kingdom would not be impaired. Other Labour MPs expressed their doubts. Walter Padley (Labour, Ogmore) was not sure whether it was the right course to take; even if it was, he was not sure that it should be on the scale proposed. He thought that administration could suffer, and that the argument that a secretary of state had been beneficial to Scotland was questionable, because Scottish housing was the worst in the United Kingdom. Padley feared that Wales would have less impact on United Kingdom policies, and he reminded the House that during the post-war years Wales's impact on the country's policies, and on social policy in particular, had been greater than Scotland's. After stating that he considered the real issues to be housing, education and fear of unemployment, Harold Finch (Labour, Bedwellty) made the inexplicable remark that he had decided to 'leave abstract arguments about a Parliament for Wales to other hon. Members' when the debate centred on the appointment of a secretary of state.[83]

On the Conservative side, Raymond Gower and E. H. Garner Evans, who from the early 1950s had supported the appointment of a secretary of state, welcomed the memorandum.[84] Peter Thomas's view was that it was a first-class report and that the conclusions reached by the Council for Wales and Monmouthshire were inescapable. Successive governments had long recognized Wales's

[82]   The Council for Wales and Monmouthshire, *Third Memorandum by the Council on its Activities*, January 1957 (Cmnd. 53), 9, 12, 14, 49–53, 55–9, 80, 84–5.
[83]   Parl. Deb., vol. 564, cols 981–2, 1023–4, 953.
[84]   Ibid., vol. 564, cols 971, 1002; vol. 523, col. 239; vol. 521, cols 1905–6.

status as a nation, and a policy of administrative devolution had been implemented which could only lead, eventually, to the appointment of a minister with executive powers. Commending the Council's proposals, Thomas emphasized the fact that they were not the proposals of those who supported separatism. The fiercest critic among Conservative members was David Llewellyn, who thought that the Council had outlived its usefulness; he considered the report to be its 'death sting' because there was little else for it to investigate. In fact, it was to be the implementation of the major recommendation in the report that would hasten the Council's demise. Llewellyn also made the point that since the Council's inception there had been little consultation between the Welsh Parliamentary Party and the government, and that that had been anticipated when the Council was established. David Gibson Watt argued that there was no reason why heads of government offices in Wales should be given powers over and above those of their counterparts in the English regions. In his view an organization that was unwieldy might be a hindrance to efficient administration.[85]

The government's reply to the Council's *Third Memorandum* was eagerly awaited. During the year, the local authorities' subcommittee of the Welsh Joint Education Committee objected to the Council's recommendations regarding the Welsh Department of Education, and in June the minister, Lord Hailsham, supported the authorities. Addressing the subcommittee, he said, 'I am entitled to accept your opinions as the authentic judgment of the people of Wales on the relationship between the Ministry and education, in preference to those of some other bodies not, on this topic, either as knowledgeable or as representative.'[86] One member of the government had therefore made public his opposition, while the prime minister, Harold Macmillan, was still considering the proposals. The minister for Welsh Affairs, Henry Brooke, gave assurances that Hailsham would withdraw his remarks, but in fact he did not do so. The government took over a year to reply, and during that time the Council was not consulted once. The chairman, Huw T. Edwards, conceded that if the government chose to distance itself from the Council, very little could be done about it.[87] Eventually the reply came, in the form of a letter sent on 11 December by the prime

85   Ibid., vol. 564, cols 961, 963–4, 943–4, 994–5.
86   *Western Mail*, 15 June 1957.
87   Edwards, 'Why I resigned', 9.

minister to the chairman of the Council. The government rejected
the recommendation that a secretary of state should be appointed,
and the reference in the letter to disadvantages being more
apparent to those with 'close experience of the machinery of
Government administration from within' was insensitive, to say the
least. In rejecting the proposal, the prime minister said that Wales
had only half the population of Scotland and was also different
from Scotland, and therefore it would be surprising if a half-scale
model of the Scottish system were to meet the nation's distinctive
needs. Wales also had the same legal system as England, and the
economic ties with England were very strong. The Welsh offices to
be transferred to a secretary of state would be isolated from the
large United Kingdom ministries, and it did not seem that such
drastic changes were needed in those fields. The prime minister
took the opportunity to say that he had considered and rejected
what was actually Labour Party policy at the time, namely a
Cabinet minister without a department, because experience proved
that a minister could be effective only if he had the power to act.[88]
The Economist, later in the month, agreed that a minister without a
department 'whose sole purpose was to sound the voice of Wales on
every issue would soon come to be regarded by his colleagues as a
confounded and squashable nuisance'.[89] The prime minister
proposed, rather, to appoint a minister of state who would spend
most of his time in Wales and who would, in the absence of the
minister for Welsh Affairs, take the chair at the quarterly conference
of heads of government offices.[90] Passing judgement on that decision, *The Economist* declared that although it did no harm, it did
make the Conservatives look rather silly.[91] A committee of the quarterly conference was to be established, on which all Welsh
departments concerned with economic growth would be represented. The committee's task was 'to ensure co-ordination of the
study of economic developments, needs and prospects in all parts of
Wales, and to initiate fresh lines of study as they are required'. A
minor change was that the under-secretary responsible for the
Welsh office of the minister for Welsh Affairs and the minister of
Housing and Local Government was to be known as the Welsh
secretary. Other changes announced were that the minister of

[88] *Government Administration in Wales*, 4–5.
[89] *The Economist*, 21 December 1957, 1033.
[90] *Government Administration in Wales*, 5–6.
[91] *The Economist*, 21 December 1957, 1033.

Education proposed to strengthen the office in Cardiff, the secretary, Welsh Department of Agriculture would be responsible for a staff of 900 out of a total staff of 1,400 (though the technical staff would still be outside his authority), and that the minister of Transport and Civil Aviation would place a senior general administrative officer in Wales.[92]

In the Welsh affairs debate on 16 December 1957, the home secretary, R. A. Butler, announced that the government had been 'fortunate in securing for the post of Minister of State the services of a Welshman with wide experience of public life, business knowledge, and an intense interest in Welsh problems and aspirations'.[93] The new minister of state was D. V. P. Lewis, chairman of the Conservative Party in Wales and Monmouthshire; he became a life peer, with the title of Lord Brecon. The peculiar way in which this appointment had been made led *The Economist* to comment on 21 December:

> How an obscure Brecon county councillor, visiting London (in his tweed suit) for the University Rugger match, was called to Downing Street to be made a baron and a Minister of State, represents one of the most curious political appointments since Caligula made his horse a consul.[94]

Labour spokesmen derided the choice of an 'unoffending, unobtrusive county councillor', in George Thomas's words, but the important factor was the calibre of the person appointed and not his position. Labour members criticized the appointment of a peer, on the grounds that he could not participate in their debates, but the government justified the choice by saying that he would have more time to spend in Wales.[95] There had been similar murmurings in November 1952, when Lord Lloyd had been appointed as a joint under-secretary of state.[96] Now Goronwy Roberts declared that the appointment of Lord Brecon was a 'sham', while in Clement Davies's opinion the minister of state's role would be that of a 'lapdog', fetching and carrying for the minister. Since the government had stated categorically that it would not implement the Council for Wales and Monmouthshire's recommendations, Goronwy Roberts urged that a select committee of the House of Commons should

[92]   *Government Administration in Wales*, 6.
[93]   Parl. Deb., vol. 580, col. 35.
[94]   *The Economist*, 21 December 1957, 1034.
[95]   Parl. Deb., vol. 580, cols 45, 120, 151.
[96]   Ibid., vol. 508, col. 618.

examine the whole issue of devolution in Wales and also the arrangements for the discussion of Welsh affairs at Westminster. He had, over a period of several years, advocated a Grand Committee to debate Welsh issues, with the appropriate ministers present.

James Griffiths continued to believe that a secretary of state should be appointed, but he had modified his earlier views. He had come to the conclusion that too many functions would be trans-ferred, and that if some of the proposals were implemented Wales would be taken 'out of the mainstream of the economic and social development of the United Kingdom'. He accordingly proposed that only the responsibilities of the departments dealing with educa-tion, local government and agriculture should be transferred. This may have been a tactical move on his part, arguing for more limited functions in order to win the support of those in his own party who were not entirely convinced that any functions should be transferred to a secretary of state. Raymond Gower and E. H. Garner Evans continued to support the appointment of a secretary of state, and the latter dismissed the government's response in these words: 'We are now fobbed off with a Minister of State whose powers are as nebulous as one can make them.' Henry Brooke defended the government's decision to maintain the existing arrangement, on the grounds that to be the head of a large department as minister for Welsh Affairs made him an effective force. David Llewellyn pointed out that as a result of the new arrangements there were significant changes. Previously, the three under-secretaries at the Home Office had had to share their time between Wales and other work, none of the civil servants had day-to-day contact with Wales and, as far as he was aware, not one of them was Welsh speaking. The minister for Welsh Affairs, on the other hand, had a department in Wales. Surprisingly Peter Thomas, who in the February debate had welcomed the report, also supported the government. Thomas now justified the government's action, on the grounds that the proposals sought 'drastic constitutional changes' and change could only be brought about gradually, but he thought that ultimately a minister with executive authority would be appointed. In fact, in 1970 he would be the first Conservative secretary of state.[97]

The Council discussed the prime minister's letter on 20 December and it was decided that a panel under William Jones's

[97]   Ibid., vol. 580, cols 123–4, 63, 95–6, 73, 102, 152, 52–3, 86, 88.

chairmanship should formulate a reply. The Council unanimously approved the reply on 25 April 1958. In it, the Council maintained that the prime minister had responded to the detailed memorandum in 'vague and general terms' and that was to be regretted. The Council considered that it was 'an integral part of the machinery of Government' and therefore 'the Government should have sufficient confidence in the Council . . . to permit a free and full exchange of views'. The Council pointed out that the minister for Welsh Affairs had executive responsibility in Wales only as minister of Housing and Local Government, and the civil servants ultimately responsible to him exercised responsibility in England and Wales. The argument that the population of Wales was half that of Scotland was not a plausible one, since Northern Ireland, with half the population of Wales, enjoyed legislative devolution and the departments, if linked, would not be as small as was suggested by the prime minister. In addition, as there would be an interchange of staff between the Welsh Office and other ministries there was no danger of isolation. The Council was not pleased with the appointment of a minister of state for Welsh Affairs because he had no executive responsibilities, and it seemed that the Welsh workload of the minister of Housing and Local Government was also outside his responsibility. One of the weaknesses of the quarterly conference of heads of government offices was that its members had no authority to take final decisions, and in that respect the economic committee would be no different, while the duties and the powers of the under-secretary – to be known as the Welsh secretary – remained unchanged. The Council had come to the conclusion that the arrangements in the Welsh Department of Education were different from those of other government departments simply because the Ministry of Education had such a small office in Cardiff. In conclusion, the Council maintained that its own proposals were 'in line with Welsh views and aspirations'. However, whatever merits lay in the Council's proposals, it could not claim that there was a popular demand for them. Harold Macmillan remained unconvinced and informed the chairman of the Council accordingly in July 1958.[98] Huw T. Edwards recalled how he had discussed the matter privately with Macmillan, who talked endlessly

[98] The Council for Wales and Monmouthshire, *Fourth Memorandum (Government Administration in Wales) and the Reply of the Prime Minister*, January 1959 (Cmnd. 631), 6, 11–14, 22, 24, 27, 29–30, 34–5.

without making any reference to the actual content of the memorandum. Furthermore, Macmillan was unable to give him any satisfactory explanation as to why the findings in the memorandum had been rejected.[99]

After the government finally rejected the Council's demand for a secretary of state, Huw T. Edwards commented in September that the proposal had not been abandoned and that there was no likelihood of resignations.[100] Yet in October he resigned from the Council. He explained that he had taken this action in order to focus attention on the fact that Wales was not receiving 'a fair and square deal'. Other factors also influenced his decision. The Council's relationship with the government had deteriorated over the past three years, and the transfer of responsibility for Welsh affairs to the Ministry of Housing and Local Government had not been a success. He also thought that the 'grip of "Whitehallism" had become tighter' and that ministers were 'weak-kneed in the presence of the gods and goddesses of the Civil Service'. Immediately following his resignation, he declared that the appointment of a secretary of state would be only a first step, since his ultimate aim was legislative devolution, and that meant a parliament.[101] Huw T. Edwards had been a leading member of the Labour Party in Wales since the early 1940s, and, unlike some prominent local government and trade union leaders, had always been interested in the machinery of government. Writing in *Wales* in 1944, he described how in those early years he had supported self-government for Wales, and had attended an annual conference of the Labour Party at which there was insufficient time allocated to discuss resolutions seeking the appointment of a secretary of state for Wales. He had come away feeling very disillusioned and expressed his disgust: 'The impression I got was that the platform had not the slightest sympathy with either resolution.' He therefore proposed the formation of a Welsh Socialist Party to formulate policies affecting Wales, affiliated to the party in England and to the International Socialist movement.[102] By the early 1950s, as he explained in *They went to Llandrindod*, because the Labour government's policy of diversification of industry had given the Welsh people a standard of living comparable to that in England, he had thrown 'completely

99   Edwards, *Troi'r Drol*, 34–6, 128, 14, 26, 28.
100   *Western Mail*, 26 September 1958.
101   Ibid., 25 October 1958.
102   Huw T. Edwards, 'What I want for Wales', *Wales*, January 1944, 13.

overboard the idea of a parliament for Wales as something impossible of accomplishment'. However, he suggested that Welsh parliamentary secretaries should be appointed to the Ministries of Health and Agriculture and to the Board of Trade, that the Council for Wales and Monmouthshire be changed to an elected body with delegated functions and that a Welsh economic council be appointed.[103] Within a few years he had changed his views again and was a leading member of the Parliament for Wales Campaign, alongside Megan Lloyd George, S. O. Davies, Cledwyn Hughes, T. W. Jones, Goronwy Roberts and Tudor Watkins. At that time too, he recalled in *Troi'r Drol*, he was becoming disillusioned with the Labour Party, and in his speeches he attacked the party for its failure to make a declaration on the nation's claims. Cliff Prothero was sufficiently concerned to seek confirmation that he had actually said what had been reported in the press.[104] After his resignation as chairman of the Council for Wales and Monmouthshire, he left the Labour Party to join Plaid Cymru at the Caernarvon National Eisteddfod in 1959, convinced that it was the only party that gave expression to the nation's claims. Edwards had given notable service to Wales, but unfortunately his attitude towards devolution and the form it should take lacked consistency, and that perhaps undermined his credibility. On 7 August the *Western Mail* judged him 'an impractical idealist whose political vacillation has in recent years cast doubt on his judgement, undermined his influence, and thus done a disservice to those Welsh purposes his natural abilities once so greatly assisted'.[105]

Edwards's decision to resign at the close of the Council's October meeting took members completely by surprise, and one member summed up the general attitude: 'I think Alderman Edwards should have remained until the position had been cleared up. We are left in a vacuum.'[106] Trevor Vaughan, chairman of Newport Education Committee and a fellow member, who was himself to resign later, had noticed a lack of enthusiasm for the Council on Edwards's part prior to his resignation.[107] Since the resignation came at the end of the meeting and no advance notice had been given, the Council was left without a chairman, and it did not have a vice-chairman

[103] Idem, *They went to Llandrindod* (Wrexham, Cardiff and Oswestry, n.d.), 8–9, 15, 40–2.
[104] Idem, *Troi'r Drol*, 36.
[105] *Western Mail*, 7 August 1959.
[106] Ibid., 25 October 1958.
[107] Telephone interview, Trevor Vaughan, 2 October 1984.

who could take over pro tem. Consequently, its first task at the next meeting would have been to appoint a chairman, but Harold Macmillan intervened and on 14 November 1958 appointed Henry Brooke, the minister for Welsh Affairs, as the Council's chairman. Labour spokesmen gave the appointment a mixed reception. George Thomas was critical of it, but Ness Edwards, who was opposed to the creation of the Council in the first place, was not too concerned. William Jones declared that members of the Council would not have a chairman imposed on them by the government. He added that they had arranged a meeting to appoint a chairman but that the prime minister had forestalled them; it was the Council's prerogative to appoint its own chairman after the prime minister had made the initial appointment in 1949.[108] From the beginning, William Jones had presided over the Council in the absence of Huw T. Edwards, and his fellow members probably would have appointed him as chairman.[109] On 18 November the executive committee of the Welsh Regional Council of Labour decided to protest to the prime minister because it maintained that he had acted in an unconstitutional manner.[110] On 20 November the prime minister defended his action in the House of Commons, on the grounds that the relationship between the Council and the government should be closer and the arrangement would provide an opportunity to consider how this could be achieved. The minister for Welsh Affairs, as chairman, would be able to assist in the task of creating a better structure. The Council was an independent body appointed to advise the government, but, as Cledwyn Hughes reminded the prime minister, with a ministerial chairman that would no longer be the case.[111]

When Henry Brooke presided at his first meeting, on 28 November, William Jones, Richard Davies, a councillor from Ebbw Vale, and Dafydd Williams, a former mayor of Caernarvon, resigned in protest. William Jones maintained that the appointment of the minister as chairman was intended 'to silence the Council' and 'to ensure a pretence of consultation in a hole-and-corner manner'.[112] William Jones's resignation was a major loss to the

[108] *Western Mail*, 15 November 1958.
[109] Ibid., 24 June 1959.
[110] Ibid., 18 November 1958.
[111] Parl. Deb., vol. 595, cols 1323–4.
[112] *Western Mail*, 29 November 1958.

Council because he was probably its driving force before Edwards's departure, and was, in the words of Trevor Vaughan, the 'brain behind the report' which had a far-reaching effect on Welsh politics.[113] At the close of the meeting, Trevor Vaughan informed the minister of his intention to resign because of the prime minister's decision to appoint a ministerial chairman to review the Council's role.[114] In his letter to the prime minister, Vaughan wrote that the Council's membership was fairly representative of Welsh interests and its terms of reference were sufficiently broad. He could not accept the prime minister's 'diagnosis of the ills of the Council' and was convinced that members' feelings of frustration were caused by the excessive time taken to reply to the Council's recommendations and the fact that they were dismissed in a brief statement. The relationship between the government and the Council had also deteriorated and there had been no contact with Lord Brecon, even though he had been in office for nearly a year. He also emphasized the fact that a Cabinet minister would advocate government policy, while the Council expected its chairman to plead for changes in government policy.[115] He had no doubt that it would be the voice of the Council that would be 'muffled'. However, Ifan ab Owen Edwards, founder and president of Urdd Gobaith Cymru (Welsh League of Youth), who had rejoined the Council in November, justified the appointment of a ministerial chairman on the grounds that the Council had an opportunity to meet the minister regularly every two months. In his view it was a 'wonderful opportunity' to put their case to the minister.[116] Brian C. Smith, writing in 1969, was to make the point that advisory bodies may be set up, not because advice on a particular subject is required, but to satisfy regional or ethnic demands. However, if insufficient notice is taken of the advice proffered or if it is ignored, frustration follows. The Council's advice had been ignored and its prerogative to appoint its own chairman had been withdrawn, and so it was 'an example of a disgruntled advisory body'.[117] Henry Brooke remained chairman until 30 September 1959. It seems that during his chairmanship the

---

[113] Interview, Trevor Vaughan, 8 October 1984.

[114] *Western Mail*, 1 December 1958.

[115] Trevor Vaughan to the Prime Minister, 29 November 1958 (Trevor Vaughan, personal archive).

[116] *Western Mail*, 1 December 1958.

[117] Brian C. Smith, *Advising Ministers (A Case Study of the South West Economic Planning Council)* (London, 1969), 12.

Council reviewed its role and informed the prime minister accordingly. The prime minister then announced in November that if he were returned to power he would reconstitute the Council, so that it would be an independent body broadly representative of Welsh life, with the power to elect its own chairman and to co-opt other people to its panels or committees. In order to maintain close contact with the government, the minister for Welsh Affairs or the minister of state would chair meetings over and above the ordinary meetings, and the Council could therefore discuss matters with them. The minister would also chair a meeting that he would be empowered to call at any time in order to discuss with the Council matters of urgency.[118] While the Council would be given some independence, the government would still have an involvement in its activities.

In 1960 R. I. Aaron, Professor of Philosophy at the University College of Wales, Aberystwyth, who had been a member of the Council since 1956, was appointed as its chairman. Aaron emphasized in 1962 that a close relationship had developed between the Council and the government, due in the main to the efforts of Henry Brooke and Lord Brecon, and the following year he felt it necessary to refer to this again.[119] In a foreword to the *Report on the Welsh Language Today*, he thought it appropriate to state what he considered to be the Council's role. The aim was to offer advice 'in a spirit of friendly persuasion', and although it was not assumed that the advice would be automatically accepted, it was expected that there would be a better understanding of Welsh needs. The Council thought that that had proved to be the case.[120] Under Aaron's chairmanship, it seems as if the Council was particularly anxious to focus attention on the improved relationship with the government. This may have been due partly to the efforts of ministers, but more particularly to the Council's willingness to accept that its role was purely advisory.

When the Council was reconstituted in 1963, one of its long-standing members, G. R. Beeston, a former chairman of Bedwas and Machen UDC, was appointed chairman, and at the first meeting the minister for Welsh Affairs suggested that a study of the

---

[118]   Parl. Deb., vol. 613, cols 196–7.

[119]   The Council for Wales and Monmouthshire, *Report on the Rural Transport Problem in Wales*, September 1962 (Cmnd. 1821), 2; idem, *Report on the Welsh Holiday Industry*, March 1963 (Cmnd. 1950), 2.

[120]   Idem, *Report on the Welsh Language Today*, November 1963 (Cmnd. 2198), 2.

provision made for the arts in Wales would be useful. It seems that the previous Council had recommended such a study. The choice of subject for investigation was entirely a matter for the Council itself, but its relationship with the government may have become too close, and consequently the minister for Welsh Affairs was able to exercise considerable influence. On the other hand, by selecting subjects for examination without reference to the government, the Council ran the risk of having its advice rejected because it was not requested. If a subject was suggested by a minister, government action would at least be more likely. In a foreword to the last report, entitled *Report on the Arts in Wales* and published in May 1966, G. R. Beeston attempted to evaluate what had been the Council's achievements. He emphasized that the Council's role was purely advisory and that it could function only as long as the government required it. He went on to declare that if advice was 'sound and acceptable' it was acted upon and that the advice tendered by the Council had 'suffered no better and no worse fate'. He considered one of the lasting benefits of the Council's investigations to be the wealth of information that it had made available to enable a proper study to be made of problems. By putting forward its solution to such problems the Council had stimulated extensive discussion, both in Wales and at Westminster. In this way the Council had 'contributed to the moulding of public opinion and public policy', and if it had 'succeeded in turning the spotlight of public attention on important Welsh problems', it had justified its existence.[121] The Council had certainly justified its existence when Huw T. Edwards, the tough trade union negotiator, was its chairman, but during that period it had refused to accept that its role was merely advisory. The Council's end came in 1966 because the changes in the machinery of government since 1949 had diminished the need for such a council. It had advocated some of the changes itself, and therefore was partly responsible for its own demise.

LABOUR ENDORSES A SECRETARY OF STATE AND A WELSH OFFICE

After the Council for Wales and Monmouthshire proposed that a secretary of state should be appointed, the Labour Party was imme-

---

[121]   Idem, *Report on the Arts in Wales*, May 1966 (Cmnd. 2983), 6, 3.

diately put under pressure to reconsider its policy towards Wales. On 11 February 1957, the very day when MPs debated the Council's proposals, the Welsh Parliamentary Labour Party met to discuss the report and 'Members generally accepted the principle of a Secretary of State for Wales, with Cabinet status and rank, and the creation of a Welsh Office'.[122] A reference to the Welsh Parliamentary Labour Party's decision was included in the Labour Party's annual report, published in September; immediately, Cliff Prothero wrote to Morgan Phillips stating that the Welsh Regional Council of Labour's executive committee was concerned about its implications and that it was not in favour of the appointment of a secretary of state, as recommended by the Council for Wales and Monmouthshire.[123] At the annual conference of the Regional Council in May, a motion requesting the conference to endorse the recommendation of the Council for Wales and Monmouthshire that a secretary of state be appointed had been remitted to the executive committee.[124] The following May, in its report to the conference, the executive committee stated that the policy agreed in 1954 had been confirmed and that it would continue to press for the appointment of a Cabinet minister with responsibility for Welsh affairs.[125] Thus, the Welsh Regional Council of Labour, unlike the Welsh Parliamentary Labour Party, took a conservative approach to the reform of the machinery of government. As it happened, the possibility of further devolution was also being discussed by the Labour Party in Scotland. Since Scotland had its own secretary of state, the deliberations centred on the proposal to establish a Scottish parliament. The executive committee of the Scottish Regional Council, which was instructed by its annual conference 'to examine all the economic and constitutional issues involved in the proposal to establish a separate Scottish Parliament', favoured greater administrative devolution.[126]

In 1959, the Labour Party's National Executive Committee formed a committee, known as the tripartite committee, to consider its policy for Wales. The committee consisted of representatives of the NEC, the Welsh Regional Council of Labour and the Welsh

[122] *Labour Party Annual Report*, 1957, 67.
[123] LPA, M. Phillips Papers, C. Prothero to M. Phillips, 17 September 1957.
[124] *Report of the Annual Conference of the Welsh Regional Council of Labour*, 18 May 1957, 16.
[125] Welsh Regional Council of Labour, *Annual Meeting*, 17 May 1958, 10.
[126] *Labour Party Scottish Regional Council Annual Report*, 1957, 19.

Parliamentary Labour Party. Aneurin Bevan was a member but he did not attend the first meeting, on 16 April. At that meeting James Griffiths, the chairman of the committee, supported the creation of a Cabinet minister with responsibility for those functions exercised in Wales by the ministers of Health, Education, and Housing and Local Government. Ness Edwards disagreed with this view and asked what would be the attitude of other ministers to the loss of their responsibilities. He thought that once a Welsh Office was established the outcome would be to concede a Welsh parliament. In his opinion, the minister would have too much responsibility, and so inevitably power would be in the hands of civil servants. He maintained that the Welsh Board of Health was inefficient and had been found to be an obstruction by Aneurin Bevan when he was minister of Health. Furthermore, when the Labour government had considered the question of a secretary of state, all the Welshmen in the government, except James Griffiths, had opposed it.[127] The tripartite committee's recommendation in June to the home policy committee, a subcommittee of the NEC, was that there should be a Cabinet minister without a department.[128] James Griffiths had evidently failed to sway the committee, and there was no change in Labour's policy. When the home policy subcommittee, under Griffiths's chairmanship, considered the tripartite committee's policy statement on 6 July it was agreed that, except for the section dealing with constitutional matters, it should be submitted to the National Executive Committee. The resolution to delay a decision on the constitutional question was taken after the leader of the party, Hugh Gaitskell, had expressed a desire that he and Griffiths should discuss it further with the Welsh Parliamentary Labour Party. Depending on the outcome of that meeting, the section of the policy statement dealing with constitutional matters should be submitted to the NEC, or a further meeting of the tripartite committee should be convened before the meeting of the NEC.[129] It was Gaitskell's initiative – undoubtedly as a result of Griffiths's influence as deputy leader – that prevented the original decision of the tripartite committee being endorsed by the home

[127] LPA, Tripartite Committee on Welsh Policy Statement, report of first meeting, 16 April 1959, 1–6.
[128] Ibid., Tripartite Committee, draft for consideration by Home Policy Subcommittee, Re. 576/June 1959, 20.
[129] Ibid., Home Policy Subcommittee, minutes, 6 July 1959, 2.

policy subcommittee. This is confirmed by Griffiths himself, who recalled how he had been 'agreeably surprised' when Gaitskell supported his point of view.[130]

At the reconvened meeting of the tripartite committee chaired by Griffiths on 21 July, with Aneurin Bevan and Ness Edwards present, Gaitskell said that as a result of his discussion with the Welsh Parliamentary Labour Party he could not agree with the proposal for a minister without departmental responsibilities. In his view the secretary of state should be responsible for education, health, and housing and local government. The representatives of the Welsh Regional Council of Labour made it quite clear that the Council was unanimous in its opposition to Gaitskell's proposal, but the leader's view prevailed.[131] When, the following day, Griffiths presented a verbal report of the meeting to the NEC, he stated that the tripartite committee's recommendation was that a secretary of state with departmental responsibilities should be appointed. The NEC approved the recommendation. Those present at this meeting included Aneurin Bevan, James Callaghan, Richard Crossman, Hugh Gaitskell, Eirene White and Harold Wilson.[132] What is interesting is that Bevan was present at the NEC meeting and also attended the final meeting of the tripartite committee, when the decision to support the appointment of a secretary of state and a Welsh Office was taken, and yet there is no record that he opposed the proposal, even though it is well known that the idea did not appeal to him. By then he was on better terms with Gaitskell, who had appointed him shadow foreign secretary in 1956, and Cledwyn Hughes's view was that once Gaitskell had approved the proposal, Bevan just accepted it.[133] On the other hand, Ron Evans, his agent in Ebbw Vale, thought that his close friend Archie Lush, who was sympathetic to devolution, might have influenced him.[134]

James Griffiths justified the decision to support the appointment of a secretary of state on the grounds that there was a demand for administrative devolution; equally important, he considered that such an appointment was necessary in order to give greater recognition to the Welsh nation.[135] In its policy document *Forward with*

[130] *James Griffiths*, 43.
[131] LPA, Tripartite Committee, minutes of Fifth Meeting, 21 July 1959.
[132] Ibid., NEC minutes, 22 July 1959.
[133] Lord Cledwyn, *Referendum*, 11.
[134] Interview, Ron Evans, 11 December 1984.
[135] Griffiths, *Pages from Memory*, 164.

Labour (Labour's Plan for Wales), the party, too, maintained that there was a demand for such recognition.[136] However, it is doubtful that the electors were interested either in different systems of government or in gaining a greater recognition for the Welsh nation. The Labour Party changed its policy towards Wales after the departure of the old guard of Attlee and Morrison, who had resisted demands for a secretary of state, both as members of the wartime Coalition government and as prime minister and lord president in the postwar administration. By 1959 Griffiths, a former chairman who had served on the NEC since 1939, had become a very prominent figure in the Labour Party, and he was extremely loyal to Gaitskell, who had a high regard for him. Philip M. Williams quotes Gaitskell as saying later, 'I really do consider myself extraordinarily lucky in having such a wonderfully loyal and thoroughly decent person as the Deputy Leader'.[137] That close relationship between Gaitskell and Griffiths was a major factor in committing the Labour Party to the appointment of a secretary of state, and the creation of the office in 1964 by the Labour government was the most significant development in the machinery of government as it affected Wales prior to 1999, when a Welsh assembly was created after the people had voted for it in a referendum.

Prior to the 1959 election, the Conservatives made no attempt to match Labour's proposal for a secretary of state, and in its editorial on 16 September 1959 the *South Wales Echo* suggested that this was because they did not think that it was a vote-winner. The paper added, 'if there were a few more marginal seats in Wales, and a few less where the Labour vote engulfs the opposition, the Conservatives might have felt it necessary to offer at least as much as the Socialists'.[138] The Conservatives may have been right, because constitutional reform is seldom a vote-winner.

A WELSH GRAND COMMITTEE

Ness Edwards, who was opposed to the appointment of a secretary of state with departmental responsibilities, was one of a very small

[136]   Labour Party, *Forward with Labour (Labour's Plan for Wales)* (Cardiff, 1959), 19.
[137]   Philip M. Williams, *Hugh Gaitskell* (London, 1979), 425.
[138]   *South Wales Echo*, 16 September 1959.

group of Welsh MPs to have shown a particular interest in the machinery of government. Another was Goronwy Roberts. Roberts was only too aware of the deficiencies of the Welsh affairs debate, and had suggested in that debate in 1953 and again in 1956 that a Welsh Grand Committee should be established.[139] In July 1958 Ness Edwards took the first formal steps to secure such a committee when he submitted a memorandum to the Select Committee on Procedure. In his memorandum, Edwards reiterated Goronwy Roberts's earlier argument that debates on Welsh affairs were 'uncommitted in theme and inevitably diffuse', and he argued that debates on the floor of the House should be on matters of importance to the United Kingdom. Constituency and regional matters were important, but they should be discussed in committee and not in a chamber deserted by all except Welsh MPs. The Grand Committee's role would be to discuss and scrutinize the activities of government departments in Wales. The date of the Welsh affairs debate was a matter for the government, and often it was held several months after the publication of the report on government action in Wales and the digest of Welsh statistics; that in itself was unsatisfactory. Edwards suggested that the principal topics discussed in the documents should each be debated in turn in committee on six mornings in every session. Giving evidence before the Select Committee on Procedure, Edwards, who was chairman of the Machinery of Government Committee of the Welsh Parliamentary Labour Party, stated that while he was putting forward his own proposal, his party was aware of it and he felt that he was speaking for most of his colleagues. After restating the case, he said that he was prepared to forego the time allocated for the discussion of Welsh affairs on the floor of the House. His main concern was that MPs should have a greater opportunity to discuss regional matters and that there should be adequate supervision of administration. Edwards explained that there were valid reasons why Wales should be treated differently from the regions of England: 'There is a long historical tradition, and there are still some elements of Welsh nationalism there; I think we must recognise that, and we must see to it that the thing is dealt with not arrogantly, but is dealt with sympathetically.' He informed the committee that he had been in a minority of one in opposing the creation of the nominated Council

---

[139]   Parl. Deb., vol. 510, cols 485–6; vol. 548, cols 680–2.

for Wales and Monmouthshire, and he felt strongly that ministers should not consult advisory bodies, rather than the people's elected representatives, in a committee such as the one he proposed.[140] When it reported, the Select Committee on Procedure raised no objection, and stated that if more time were needed for the discussion of Welsh matters in addition to the debate on the floor of the House, the method could be tried so as to avoid further encroachments on the time available in the House itself.[141] The committee then supported the proposal, in the interests not so much of Wales, but of the House of Commons.

When the report was debated in the Commons in July 1959, R. A. Butler, for the government, maintained that a case had not been made for a Welsh Grand Committee, but the government was prepared to listen to members' views. Welsh members, said Cledwyn Hughes, were at a disadvantage compared with Scottish members, and so the Welsh Parliamentary Party considered that the committee's recommendation would go some way towards providing sufficient time for the discussion of Welsh affairs, though the party did not wish a Welsh Grand Committee to replace debate on the floor of the House.[142] Following discussions between Butler and Henry Brooke, the minister for Welsh Affairs, who thought that it was a sound proposal, the government agreed that a Welsh Grand Committee should be constituted, though Butler reserved the government's position in relation to the actual details. Ness Edwards immediately warned that existing time on the floor of the House would not be conceded unless there was considerable compensation.[143] The committee was established in 1960 and the Standing Order read that:

> There shall be a standing committee to be called the Welsh Grand Committee, which shall consider –
>
> a) bills referred to it; and
> b) such specified matters relating exclusively to Wales as may be referred to it and shall consist of all Members sitting for constituencies in Wales, together with not more than five other Members to be nominated by the Committee of Selection, which shall have power from time to time to

---

[140] Minutes of evidence taken before the Select Committee on Procedure, 15 July 1958, 131–6.
[141] *Select Committee on Procedure, 1958–59, Report, vol. 1*, Paper 92, par. 48.
[142] Parl. Deb., vol. 609, cols 44, 121.
[143] Ibid., vol. 617, cols 145–6.

discharge the Members so nominated by it and to appoint others in substitution for those discharged.[144]

The 1950s – that often-maligned decade – had been a vital period in the development of the machinery of government in Wales. A minister for Welsh Affairs had been appointed and a Welsh Grand Committee established, and there had been changes in the way in which government was administered. Throughout the period after 1951, the Conservatives had been in power at Westminster, but in Wales itself they had failed to make any headway against Labour. The nationalists had secured their best result in Merioneth in 1959, when their candidate, Gwynfor Evans, polled 22.9 per cent of the votes cast, but as in previous decades they had not been a threat to any of the major parties.[145] Compared with the pre-war years, it was a period of greater prosperity, and that had made it somewhat easier to initiate and sustain a debate on the machinery of government. This debate lasted virtually the entire decade. Before the 1955 election, the Parliament for Wales Campaign forced the Labour Party to address the 'Welsh question', whilst after the election the Council for Wales and Monmouthshire, under Huw T. Edwards's leadership, provided Labour with a proposition which it could accept, albeit only after James Griffiths had exerted considerable influence. During these eventful years, not only had important changes been made to the machinery of government, but a vital decision had been taken, which would lead in time to an even more momentous change.

IV

A SECRETARY OF STATE AND THE NATIONALIST
CHALLENGE, 1964–1974

A PLEDGE REDEEMED

The general election of October 1964 was a crucial one for a
Labour Party that had lost the previous three encounters. Under
the leadership of Harold Wilson, the party's hopes were high, but
though in the end Labour managed to win, it was with only a small
majority. In Wales, Labour continued to dominate the political
scene and regained Swansea West, where Alan Williams was
elected. The Welsh Parliamentary Labour Party, now led by the
septuagenarian James Griffiths, included Leo Abse (Pontypool),
John Morris (Aberavon), Ifor Davies (Gower) and Aneurin Bevan's
successor in Ebbw Vale, Michael Foot.[1] Labour had promised to
appoint a secretary of state, and so the return of a Labour government was felt to be of particular significance for Wales. When
Harold Wilson formed his government the manifesto commitment
was honoured, and on 18 October 1964 James Griffiths was
appointed, in the prime minister's words, the 'Charter Secretary of
State for Wales'. Apparently there were other contenders (Ness
Edwards was mentioned), but Griffiths, with his enthusiasm for the
office and his experience of government as a former minister of
National Insurance and secretary of state for the Colonies, was the
obvious choice to establish the new department.[2] As minister of
National Insurance from 1945 to 1950, Griffiths 'had effected a
quiet revolution' in the lives of the poor, and his first task had been
to create a new department to implement the insurance scheme
that was a vital part of the Labour government's welfare
programme; that task is often overlooked when Griffiths's considerable contribution to the achievements of the Attlee government is
assessed.[3] This experience was to prove invaluable nearly twenty

---

[1]   Jones, *Parliamentary Elections*, 133–8.
[2]   *James Griffiths*, 44.
[3]   Francis Beckett, *Clem Attlee* (London, 1997), 244.

years later when he again entered the Cabinet to launch another new department, of which he had always been a firm advocate. Incidentally, only Griffiths and the prime minister had previous Cabinet experience. Griffiths's appointment was a crucial one, because so much depended on the holder of the office and on developments in the first year or so, as Griffiths himself was only too aware. On 20 November the *Western Mail* thought likewise: 'The future pattern of and changes in the Welsh Office will be dictated in no small measure by the office holder, especially in the early months. The man will make the office.'[4] As in 1945, Welsh MPs were given prominent posts in the government. James Callaghan was appointed chancellor of the Exchequer, Walter Padley, Cledwyn Hughes and Goronwy Roberts became ministers of state and George Thomas, Eirene White and Harold Finch under-secretaries.[5]

After Griffiths's appointment, Richard Crossman, the minister of Housing and Local Government, noted that it was 'an idiotic creation . . . a completely artificial new office . . . all the result of a silly election pledge'.[6] Significantly, Crossman did not mention that he had been present in 1959 when the National Executive Committee of the Labour Party agreed that the office should be created. In a later comment, Richard Clarke argued that the appointment could indeed be justified. He explained that:

> the political advantage for the cohesion of the whole community which results from the specific representation of this particular section of the community may be regarded as outweighing the economic loss to the whole community from the failure to get the economies of scale in the administration of the various services and from whatever misdirection of resources may occur.[7]

Soon after his appointment, Griffiths explained that the office was established partly for administrative reasons, but also to give greater recognition to the Welsh nation.[8] Politicians tend to claim that the majority of the electorate supports their viewpoint, and in that respect Griffiths was no exception. Whether the desire for a secretary of

[4] *Western Mail*, 20 November 1964.
[5] Butler and Sloman, *British Political Facts*, 45–50.
[6] Richard Crossman, *The Diaries of a Cabinet Minister*, vol. I (London, 1975), 117.
[7] Clarke, 'Number and size of government departments', 178.
[8] Coleg Harlech, J. Griffiths Papers, J. Griffiths, 'Launching a new ministry: the Welsh Office', 1.

state was as extensive as he claimed is doubtful, if later evidence is any guide. In an attitude survey conducted in 1970 for the Royal Commission on the Constitution, 1969–73, only 56 per cent knew the office existed, 30 per cent did not think that it existed and 14 per cent had no viewpoint – while very few had any idea as to its responsibilities.[9] It was pointed out in the *Spectator* on 30 October that if the experience of Scotland was relevant, Wales would not benefit and, of course, the secretary of state for Scotland had both statutory power and the support of a large department, without which the secretary of state for Wales was going to be 'a lone voice'.[10] The secretary of state himself thought differently. The 1964 Labour manifesto for Wales, *Signposts to the New Wales*, had stipulated that the secretary of state would have 'executive responsibility over a wide field, including education, health, housing and local government, and agriculture', but some Welsh Labour MPs still adhered to the view that the secretary of state should be merely a watchdog keeping an eye on the work of other departments.[11] James Griffiths's view was that if he were merely a watchdog there would be conflict between him and other ministers; this was also the view of Thomas W. Phillips, who had served under him as permanent secretary when he was minister of National Insurance. Phillips's advice to Griffiths was:

> You must be of course, a watchdog for Wales as a whole, but in order to do this effectively you ought to have a department of your own, with a competent civil service staff. This will help to give you the professional assistance you will need and avoid the risk of being regarded as a tiresome busybody who is always interfering with other people's business without having any business of your own.[12]

Without informing Griffiths, a few of his Welsh colleagues had written to the prime minister opposing a transfer of functions, on the grounds that this would be giving in to nationalist demands. Griffiths reacted angrily, and informed the prime minister that if no functions were transferred he would resign. In the event his view prevailed, but he still found that some of his Cabinet colleagues were not sympathetic to his demands, as they were under pressure

[9]   *Royal Commission on the Constitution, 1969–1973, Report*, vol. 1, October 1973 (Cmnd. 5460), 116.
[10]   NLW, J. Griffiths Papers, C7/4, *The Spectator*, 30 October 1964.
[11]   Labour Party, *Signposts to the New Wales* (Cardiff, 1963).
[12]   Griffiths, *Pages from Memory*, 166.

from their top civil servants to retain their Welsh sections.[13] Although functions were indeed transferred, the government had second thoughts about transferring all the responsibilities mentioned in the manifesto. Nevertheless, the essential point had been won, and now that the Welsh Office was in existence the transfer of additional responsibilities would undoubtedly be considered later.

THE SECRETARY OF STATE'S FUNCTIONS

The secretary of state's functions were not announced until 19 November, when the prime minister replied to a parliamentary question. In a long statement, Wilson explained that the secretary of state would have offices in Cardiff and London, and would take over responsibility for roads from the Ministry of Transport and practically all the executive functions of the Ministry of Housing and Local Government in Wales. The secretary of state would liaise closely with the first secretary of state, George Brown, in the field of regional planning and the Welsh Office would provide the chairman of the planning board for Wales. In addition, he would have oversight functions in the spheres of agriculture, education, health, transport, trade and labour, and would be assisted by a minister of state. The secretary of state would be putting Wales's case and applying pressure on other departments (particularly on the Board of Trade) to see that Wales got a 'fair crack of the whip'. It was envisaged that he would 'be a permanent deputation at the doors of the Board of Trade in London'.[14] James Griffiths was anxious that the Welsh Office should have a key role in promoting the Welsh economy, and in due course he appointed the minister of state, Goronwy Roberts, as chairman of the Economic Council. He thought that an elected council for Wales, which he was seriously considering at the time, might eventually take over the Economic Council's functions and might also be allocated executive powers in respect of economic planning.[15] For the Conservatives, Keith Joseph pointed out that the only additional powers transferred to the secretary of state, in addition to those relating to housing, local

---

[13]   *James Griffiths*, 45–7.
[14]   Parl. Deb., vol. 702, cols 623–4, 626–7.
[15]   Griffiths, *Pages from Memory*, 173–4.

government, and town and country planning, were those transferred from the Ministry of Transport.[16] That was so, but the
important difference was that, unlike the former minister for Welsh
Affairs, the secretary of state was now able to acquire additional
functions, so that by the time the first Conservative secretary of
state was appointed in 1970 the difference was quite marked. In the
Welsh Grand Committee in December 1964 Joseph argued that the
secretary of state would be in charge of a small department, and
that because his work was not essential to the functioning of other
ministries he would not 'have the same bargaining power' as the
minister for Welsh Affairs, who had also been a minister in charge of
a large department of state. Ness Edwards welcomed the appointment of a secretary of state able to devote all his time to Welsh
affairs as an attempt to make the civil service more accountable to
elected representatives. However, he regretted the decision to
transfer executive functions. In his view that was a mistake, because
what was needed was a minister above all departments who would
act as a coordinator. He had lost that argument within the Labour
Party in 1959, and the Conservatives, who had insisted that their
minister for Welsh Affairs was effective because he was the head of
a large department of state, had also rejected it. Edwards considered that the new Welsh Office would be judged on its ability to
achieve better government, coordination and accountability, and
particularly on its capacity to take initiatives. He wanted to see a
'dynamic' Welsh Office taking Wales into the next century.[17]

The secretary of state's oversight functions were defined by the
prime minister on 24 July 1965 as 'real powers to oversee the
activity of all Government Departments in Wales and to see that
they coordinate'; according to the Welsh Office itself in 1969 they
were discharged in a number of ways. In Whitehall there was coordination, because the secretary of state as a member of the
Cabinet participated in all policy decisions, and both he and other
Welsh Office ministers sat on ministerial committees to ensure that
Welsh interests were taken into consideration. They collaborated
with other departmental ministers on a day-to-day basis, and Welsh
Office officials were also members of Whitehall interdepartmental
committees. By contrast, coordination in Wales was achieved partly
through informal liaison with the regional offices. It was also

accomplished through the quarterly conference of heads of government offices in Wales, chaired by the permanent under-secretary of
state, and through the planning board, which consisted of senior
officials of departments involved in economic planning. The planning
board was chaired by the assistant under-secretary of state dealing
with economic affairs in the Welsh Office.[18] However, as Goronwy
Daniel, the permanent under-secretary of state, later explained, it
was very difficult to ensure interdepartmental cooperation when
departments did not have a Welsh office, because Wales, as far as they
were concerned, was not an administrative unit.[19]

Welsh Office ministers had thought at the outset that consultation
with the secretary of state was to be the rule and expressed the view
that other departments were 'expected to inform and consult the
Welsh Office on all matters relating to Wales'. It was argued that the
new arrangement would be far more dependable than simply relying
on 'the accident of personality'. Real consultation and coordination
would replace the previous arrangement, where there was intermittent
consultation and coordination.[20] However, eight years after the
creation of the office of secretary of state, Edward Rowlands, a
former under-secretary of state in the Welsh Office, maintained that
the 'effectiveness of oversight' still depended in part on the '"accident"
of personality, both official and political'. Much depended on the
cooperation of officials who were not responsible to the Welsh Office,
and who were reluctant to release information that could be, in J. A.
Cross's words 'embarrassing to their own Department'. Consequently,
it was still possible for decisions to be made prior to any consultation
with the Welsh Office itself. The Welsh Office was simply informed.
Since the application of oversight had been so 'uneven and patchy'
Rowlands suggested that only if a set of 'clearly defined procedures'
were formulated could the secretary of state exercise complete oversight over the work of other departments.[21] Giving evidence to the
Select Committee on Welsh Affairs established in 1979, Hywel Evans,
the permanent secretary of state admitted that the question of
consultation had still not been completely resolved. He stated that:

[18]   Commission on the Constitution, *Written Evidence 1: The Welsh Office* (1969), 13–14.
[19]   Sir Goronwy Daniel, 'The government in Wales', *Transactions of the Honourable Society of Cymmrodorion*, part 1 (1969), 125.
[20]   Parl. Deb., Welsh Grand Committee, 16 December 1964, cols 46–7.
[21]   E. Rowlands, 'The politics of regional administration: the establishment of the Welsh Office', *Public Administration*, 50 (1972), 337–8; J. A. Cross, 'The regional decentralisation of British Government departments', *Public Administration*, 48 (1970), 439.

The ideal condition would be that before anything was formulated at all we were fully associated with it. We are a lot of the time now but I would be misleading the Committee, and I do not believe you would believe me, sir, if I said it happened always.

Apparently, the secretary of state himself had not been given information by the British Steel Corporation and the secretary of state for Industry, and the Select Committee on Welsh Affairs expressed its concern that, as a territorial minister, the secretary of state was prone to be excluded from discussions on national affairs that had important implications for Wales. In its report published in July 1980, nearly sixteen years after the creation of the Welsh Office, the committee was able to make this comment: 'the close links at official level with relevant Whitehall Departments and the close and continuing liaison with nationalised industries in Wales are either illusory or operated in an incompetent fashion on one or both sides'. The committee recommended that mechanisms should be urgently devised to make sure that the secretary of state was aware of major issues crucial to Wales.[22]

In 1969 Goronwy Daniel explained that the Welsh Office administered general United Kingdom policies and, because it was necessary to ensure comparable standards throughout the country, it was possible to make only slight changes to meet specific Welsh needs.[23] Edward Rowlands argued later, in 1972, that only very limited executive action could be taken, because money that remained unspent under a particular heading could not be transferred to another. Legislation that applied to Wales as part of the United Kingdom continued to be sponsored by Whitehall ministries, though the Welsh Office also sponsored some legislation. After James Griffiths had accepted the principle of equal validity, in 1967 the Welsh Office sponsored the Welsh Language Act, incorporating the main recommendations of the Hughes Parry Report.[24] In the 1970s other legislation followed: in 1975 the Welsh Development Agency Act and the Community Land Act (jointly with the Department of the Environment); in 1976 the Development of Rural Wales Act; in 1977 the Water Charges Equalisation Act

[22]   House of Commons, First Report from the Committee on Welsh Affairs, Session 1979–80, *The Role of the Welsh Office and Associated Bodies in Developing Employment Opportunities in Wales, Report*, vol. I (30 July 1980), xxx, iii–iv.

[23]   Daniel, 'Government in Wales', 124.

[24]   Rowlands, 'Politics of regional administration', 342–3, 345–6.

(jointly with the Department of the Environment); and in 1976–8 the Scotland and Wales Bill and the Wales Act (both jointly with the Privy Council Office).[25]

At various times MPs demanded that the Welsh Office should be granted additional functions, but during the time when Goronwy Daniel was permanent under-secretary of state decisions to seek extra functions were taken only if the Welsh Office itself was confident that it could cope with the additional workload.[26] However, James Griffiths was requested by his private secretary, K. J. Pritchard, to press for additional powers at a meeting with the prime minister on 4 April 1966, just before his resignation as secretary of state. His attention was drawn to the fact that a Transfer of Functions Order was being prepared, and that responsibility for common land in Wales would be transferred to the Ministry of Agriculture and not, as it should be, to the Welsh Office. He was also asked to urge that responsibility for health, education, commons and agriculture, in that order, should be transferred to the Welsh Office.[27] Nothing materialized. The secretary of state assumed responsibility for health and agriculture (jointly with the Ministry of Agriculture, Fisheries and Food) in 1969, for education (primary and secondary) in 1970, for industrial development in 1975, and for agriculture (with similar powers to those exercised by the secretary of state for Scotland), and further and higher education, excluding the University of Wales, in 1978.[28] Edward Rowlands maintained that those functions that had been transferred before 1972 were 'painfully extracted from a reluctant Whitehall'. He wrote that:

the process by which he (Secretary of State) acquired additional functions has been haphazard; it has derived little from any Whitehall adherence to a concept of national administrative and political decentralisation; more from ad hoc adjustments and compromises extracted from the system by political pressure and manoeuvring.[29]

The later devolution campaign, between 1974 and 1979, was to facilitate the acquisition of functions by the Welsh Office. As

---

[25] Labour Party, *Campaign Handbook: Wales* (London, 1978), 5.
[26] Commission on the Constitution, *Minutes of Evidence 1: Wales* (1970), 12.
[27] NLW, J. Griffiths Papers, C7/42, note by K. J. Pritchard to J. G., 4 April 1966.
[28] Welsh Office, Transfer of Functions to the Secretary of State as regards Wales, 1964–80.
[29] Rowlands, 'Politics of regional administration', 334, 339.

secretary of state, John Morris took full advantage of the opportunity to increase its authority, so that even if the devolution proposals were rejected some benefits would have been accrued. His ultimate aim was that such functions would be transferred to an assembly.[30]

THE REJECTION OF AN ELECTED COUNCIL

As secretary of state, James Griffiths was soon able to exercise his influence and authority in the Cabinet. Local government was in urgent need of reform throughout the United Kingdom and, although Royal Commissions were to be established for England and Scotland, the Cabinet, including Richard Crossman as minister of Housing and Local Government, agreed with Griffiths that a Royal Commission for Wales was unnecessary. He had decided that, following the work undertaken by the Local Government Commission for Wales set up in 1958, all the essential information was available and therefore a Royal Commission would only result in delay.[31] When Griffiths announced his intention to go ahead with reorganization the approach was very different from that previously adopted. A meeting of the representatives of local authorities was convened, and a group of advisers representing councillors and officers from the different types of authorities was designated to work with an interdepartmental working party of officials.[32] The working party consisted of officials from the Welsh Office, the Welsh Board of Health, the Ministry of Health, the Education Office for Wales of the Department of Education and Science, the Home Office, and the Ministry of Housing and Local Government, together with Ivor Gowan, Professor of Political Science at the University College of Wales, Aberystwyth.[33] The merit of this proposal was that local authority representatives were directly involved in framing proposals. It was intended that local authorities would be able to choose from a number of alternatives, whilst the secretary of state himself would take the final decision.[34]

[30]   John Morris, review of David Foulkes, J, Barry Jones and R. A. Wilford (eds), *The Welsh Veto: The Wales Act 1978 and the Referendum* (Cardiff, 1983), in *Barn*, 242 (1983), 50.
[31]   *Local Government in Wales*, July 1967 (Cmnd. 3340), 1.
[32]   Special Correspondent, 'Local government in Wales', *Local Government Chronicle*, 22 January 1966, 129.
[33]   *Local Government in Wales*, 2.
[34]   'Local government in Wales', 129.

When Griffiths set up his working party, the executive committee of the Welsh Council of Labour, formerly the Welsh Regional Council of Labour, proposed to him that he should examine whether it was possible to establish an elected council to administer local government services 'where cooperation, coordination and amalgamation of financial strength' were essential for efficiency.[35] That the proposal was forwarded by the executive and passed by the Welsh Council of Labour's annual conference in May 1966 (before Labour lost Carmarthen to Plaid Cymru in a by-election in July) was due in no small measure to the influence of the newly appointed secretary of the Council, Emrys Jones, who had succeeded Cliff Prothero in February 1965. Both George Thomas and James Callaghan were opposed to the new idea.[36] The elected council proposed in the resolution was similar to that proposed in a document which had been considered by a Welsh Regional Council of Labour working party in September 1962, and to the one which Gwilym Prys Davies, a Pontypridd solicitor, had suggested in his pamphlet, *A Central Welsh Council*, published in 1963.[37] Earlier, in July 1962, a Welsh Parliamentary Labour Party working group had also supported an all-Wales council as a top tier of local government and suggested that it could be either indirectly or directly elected.[38] There was obviously a lack of unanimity on the subject. Cliff Prothero considered Prys Davies's plan for an elected council 'very nationalistic', but James Griffiths was very much in favour and had written a foreword to the pamphlet, in which he stated that the Local Government Commission for Wales should have considered the merits of an elected council for Wales. That shortcoming was now being addressed.[39] Griffiths was to raise the matter again in February 1964, prior to his appointment as secretary of state, during a debate on local government reorganization; he asked Keith Joseph to take into account the recommendation made in the

[35] Welsh Council of Labour, *Annual Report: Annual Meeting*, 21 May 1966, 6.

[36] *Report of the Annual Conference of the Welsh Council of Labour*, 21 May 1966, 5; interview, Gwilym Prys Davies, 4 July 1983.

[37] NLW, J. Griffiths Papers, C 6/8, memorandum on the reorganisation of local government in Wales prepared by the Welsh Council of Labour's Working Party on Local Government, September 1962, 2–3.

[38] Ibid., C 6/2, memorandum drawn up by the Welsh Labour Group Machinery of Government Panel: Reorganisation of Local Government, signed by J. G., 2 July 1962.

[39] Interview, Gwilym Prys Davies, 4 July 1983; Gwilym Prys Davies, *A Central Welsh Council* (Aberystwyth, 1963), 5.

Buchanan Report that it might be necessary to administer local government on a regional basis. He further asked the minister to consider the possibility of establishing an all-Wales body for certain functions.[40] Cliff Prothero later recalled how the executive of the Welsh Council of Labour approved what was effectively Prys Davies's proposal just a short time after his retirement as secretary, even though it had earlier rejected the idea.[41]

The local government working party set up by the secretary of state considered whether the structure as it was should be retained, but with fewer authorities, whether it should be replaced by a structure of all-purpose authorities, and whether a regional authority should be created. The majority of local authority advisers favoured the first alternative, a 'substantial minority' favoured the second, and opinion was evenly divided on the question of a regional authority.[42] For his part, Ivor Gowan maintained that there was 'a case, based upon a dispassionate analysis of political and administrative facts', for an elected council on the lines of the Greater London Council.[43] There is much to be said for the argument that this novel approach, adopted by James Griffiths, caused unnecessary delay. Griffiths clearly supported an elected council, and if officials had been told to work out a scheme in line with his views then it could have been submitted to the Cabinet before his retirement.[44] When he left office, the post that he had personally secured was firmly established and was to take on additional responsibilities, which in time would be transferred to a national assembly.

In the general election in March 1966, Labour's representation in Wales achieved an all-time record of thirty-two members; it recorded a vote of over 70 per cent in thirteen constituencies, and in three Monmouthshire constituencies (Abertillery, Ebbw Vale and Bedwellty) the vote was over 85 per cent.[45] As was to be expected, Labour also dominated the local authority scene, particularly in Glamorgan and Monmouthshire where the party's position was virtually impregnable. Representatives of miners, steelworkers and

---

[40]   Parl. Deb., vol. 690, col. 438.
[41]   Interview, Cliff Prothero, 19 December 1983.
[42]   *Local Government in Wales*, 2.
[43]   Ivor Gowan, *Government in Wales* (Cardiff, 1966), 16, 14.
[44]   Interview, Gwilym Prys Davies, 4 July 1983.
[45]   Jones, *Parliamentary Elections*, 141–6.

railwaymen invariably led the local authorities in both these counties. Perhaps the most prominent figure was Llewellyn Heycock of Glamorgan, though he was only one of a powerful group of Labour councillors in south Wales during the period. The party's impregnable position was the subject of a scathing attack by Roy Lewis, writing in 1969 after the shock by-election results. He said:

> In Wales, it is the Labour Party that represents the Establishment: still holding a large section of Welsh life immovably in its grip, dominating Trades Unions and local authorities notorious for their lack of vision, doling out patronage and sending its loyal and mediocre servants to Parliament instead of independent fighters, the Labour Party to-day represents an ageing, privileged class who have done well for themselves out of the poverty of the past.[46]

Cledwyn Hughes was appointed secretary of state on 6 April 1966 and, like his predecessor, he favoured an elected council, but when he presented his proposals to the Cabinet in 1967 he received little support. The secretary of state for Scotland, William Ross was much opposed, and argued that if the proposal for an elected council were implemented things would be difficult for him in Scotland.[47] The Cabinet was also aware that Welsh Labour MPs were evenly divided on the issue. On 30 June, when the proposal was under consideration, the *Western Mail* reported that twelve of these MPs had written to the prime minister and to Cledwyn Hughes urging a nominated body, while ten called for an elected council.[48] The furore that the proposal caused is fully recorded by Emyr Price. Apparently, nineteen Labour MPs sent a letter to Cledwyn Hughes and Harold Wilson opposing an elected Welsh council. In a letter to Richard Crossman in June, Ness Edwards expressed his delight that an elected council had been rejected. However, Edwards feared that Hughes would try to include in the White Paper a body that was partly elected and partly nominated. He saw such a hybrid development as a concession to nationalism and said so: 'Every concession to the "Nats" only increases their appetite.' Ironically, when Plaid Cymru seemed to be making a breakthrough in industrial south Wales in the 1960s, the by-elections in Rhondda West and Caerphilly were caused by the deaths of MPs who had throughout

---

[46] Roy Lewis, 'Wales joins the world', *Contemporary Review*, 214 (1969), 264.
[47] Lord Cledwyn, *Referendum*, 12.
[48] *Western Mail*, 30 June 1967.

their careers been very hostile to anything that bore a tinge of nationalism, namely Iorwerth Thomas and Ness Edwards. Cledwyn Hughes maintained that Labour MPs who do not speak Welsh have a 'big chip on their shoulders' and regard Welsh speakers as 'fellow-travelling Nationalists more often than not'.[49] The government set out its proposals in a White Paper published in July 1967. It had come to the conclusion that increasing the size of local government units and reducing their number would best remedy the defects in Wales. It rejected the proposal for an all-Wales directly elected council, on the grounds that if the administration of central government services were transferred changes would have to be made in legislation and in the administrative machinery nationally, and decisions would necessarily have to be taken on issues that could not be decided in the context of local government reorganization in Wales. It had been suggested that the most important local authority functions could be transferred to the council, but 'it would not be consistent to strengthen the local authorities for the better discharge of their functions and at the same time transfer the most important of these functions elsewhere'. Furthermore, responsibility for certain services would be divided, and that was seen as a disadvantage.

Instead, the government proposed that the Welsh Economic Council set up in 1965 should be superseded by a 'new all-Wales advisory and promotional body', to be known as the Welsh Council, with the following terms of reference:

> To provide a forum for the interchange of views and information on developments in the economic and cultural fields, and to advise on the implications for Wales of national policies.
>
> To assist in the formulation of plans for Wales having regard to the best use of resources, and to advise the Secretary of State for Wales on major land use and economic planning matters.
>
> To advise the Minister of Transport and the Secretary of State on transport policy and planning in Wales.
>
> To give advice on the national parks and countryside.
>
> To advise on the arts in Wales, particularly where arrangements need to be made on an all-Wales basis.
>
> To keep under review and help to promote the publicity and similar work for

---

[49] Emyr Price, *Yr Arglwydd Cledwyn* (Caernarfon, 1990), 52–3, 77.

encouraging industrial and tourist development in Wales done by the Development Corporation and the Tourist Board.

To encourage cooperation between the local authorities through schemes which would require the approval of the appropriate Ministers.[50]

In addition to having wider terms of reference than the Welsh Economic Council, the new Welsh Council would also include members drawn from statutory and promotional bodies.[51] The Council would elect its own chairman, its reports would be published, and it would be provided with a small number of assessors and a secretariat. The Royal Commissions appointed for England and Scotland had not reported, but it was pointed out in the White Paper, *Local Government in Wales*, that consideration would be given, in the light of their reports, to the possibility of strengthening the Council by conferring upon it 'additional powers and responsibilities and by making appropriate changes in its membership and constitution'.[52] Thus, James Griffiths's hope that the work of the Economic Council would eventually be transferred to an elected Welsh council did not become reality. Although Cledwyn Hughes failed to secure an elected council, he had nevertheless managed, as he was to claim later, to keep the 'door open to the principle of an elected body'.[53]

As expected, the White Paper was given a mixed reception by Welsh MPs. One member who was quite pleased with the decision not to proceed with an elected council was Leo Abse; he was of the view that Welsh interests could be protected only at Westminster.[54] In the House of Commons in July, Elystan Morgan, the new Labour MP for Cardiganshire, was the most vocal of critics, claiming that the council was a step back to the position that existed in 1949 when the Council for Wales and Monmouthshire had been set up. Morgan, a former Plaid Cymru candidate and vice-president, had come to the conclusion that a nominated council was a compromise between a complete rejection of any form of all-Wales machinery, on the one hand, and the creation of an elected council, on the other. Wales's case for an elected council, he claimed, rested not on

[50] *Local Government in Wales*, 6, 18, 21–2.
[51] Welsh Office, *Welsh Council, 1968–1971* (1971), 1.
[52] *Local Government in Wales*, 21–2.
[53] Lord Cledwyn, *Referendum*, 12.
[54] *Western Mail*, 12 July 1967.

regionalism but on nationhood, and as a nation Wales was entitled to have a particular structure of government. The creation of the Welsh Office had been justified on the basis that Wales was a nation; it had not been established as part of a comprehensive scheme for the whole country but, rather, was a specific arrangement for Wales. After Morgan had asked how many of the Council for Wales and Monmouthshire's reports had 'passed into obscurity, gathering respectable dust in some pigeon-hole in Whitehall', Eirene White, minister of state at the Welsh Office and the first woman to hold ministerial office in Wales, reminded him that the council had 'provided the basis and the stimulus' for many significant developments in Wales, including the Welsh Office itself. She reiterated the familiar argument that if it was advice that was required, then a nominated body, including members with experience and knowledge who were not prepared to stand for an elected body, was justified, and 'contempt' for a nominated body was 'entirely misplaced'. Eirene White conceded that nominated bodies with executive functions set up by central government were considered by ordinary people to be undemocratic, but she added that for some specialist bodies requiring 'a specialist element, as well as a popular element', election might not be appropriate. In her view an all-Wales authority should not be set up simply to take major powers from local authorities, but should be concerned primarily with powers devolved from central government, and that form of devolution should be discussed in the context of the United Kingdom. Although Eirene White was adamant that an all-Wales authority should not adversely affect local authorities, she did suggest that it could be responsible for those functions that required cooperation between local authorities, provided that they were represented.[55] In a debate in the Lords early in 1968, Baroness Phillips (Morgan Phillips's widow) for the government mentioned the possibility of an elected council undertaking the advisory, promotional and executive functions of nominated bodies, but she believed that certain questions needed very careful consideration.[56]

Following the publication of the White Paper, the nominated council was criticized by the *Western Mail* on 22 November on the grounds that it was a 'meaningless device' and 'would obviously

[55]   Parl. Deb., vol. 751, cols 611–14, 619–22.
[56]   Ibid., House of Lords, vol. 288, cols 713–14.

have no popular mandate and, equally obviously, no power'.[57] Later, on 9 January 1968, the newspaper referred to the nominated council as 'the half-baked nominated Council for Wales promised by Mr Cledwyn Hughes'.[58] Local authority opinion was divided on the matter, but the counties and county boroughs in favour of a nominated council represented a greater proportion of the population.[59] Both Cardiganshire and Caernarvonshire county councils refused to nominate members, claiming that if they did so they could not very well object to the principle of a non-elected council. Cardiganshire also called on all local authorities to boycott the council.[60] The decision to reject the proposal was regretted by the executive committee of the Welsh Council of Labour and the annual conference of the party in Wales in May 1968 carried a resolution, submitted by Callaghan's constituency of Cardiff South East, urging the government to reverse its decision and create an elected council, 'so bringing a new impetus to Welsh life and providing a central responsible forum for matters affecting Wales'.[61] Later, the executive committee came to the conclusion that because the Commission on Local Government in England was about to report, it would be better to await its proposals before going ahead with reorganization in Wales.[62] The executive had realized that there was a real possibility of a more radical scheme being adopted in England, whilst Wales would have to be content with the same basic structure as before.

Although Cledwyn Hughes had failed to secure an elected council, he had succeeded in publishing a White Paper, and in this he had gone very much against the wishes of Richard Crossman, the lord president and former minister of Housing and Local Government.[63] Crossman thought that publication in advance of the reports of the Royal Commissions in England and Scotland was sheer nonsense, and he said so in no uncertain terms.[64] Crossman seemed to be arguing in favour of uniformity of provision, whereas

[57]   *Western Mail*, 22 November 1967.
[58]   Ibid., 9 January 1968.
[59]   Parl. Deb., vol. 756, col. 258.
[60]   *Western Mail*, 19 January 1968; 11 January 1968.
[61]   Welsh Council of Labour, *Report to the Annual Meeting*, 24–5 May 1968, 7; *Report of the Annual Conference of the Welsh Council of Labour*, 24–5 May 1968, 7; *Western Mail*, 4 May 1968.
[62]   Welsh Council of Labour, *Report to the Annual Meeting*, 16–17 May 1969, 9.
[63]   Lord Cledwyn, *Referendum*, 11–12.
[64]   Richard Crossman, *The Diaries of a Cabinet Minister,* vol. II (London, 1976), 142.

to committed devolutionists like Cledwyn Hughes the argument was not a valid one. He was convinced that the provision in Wales should be appropriate to Wales, and that might mean differences between Wales and the rest of the United Kingdom. J. E. Trice, like Crossman, argued in 1970 that the White Paper had been a point-less exercise because the proposals would have had to be re-examined in the light of the proposals for England, to ensure that a uniform system was imposed on both England and Wales.[65] When the nominated council was being set up, the *Western Mail* commented, on 19 January, that Cledwyn Hughes, a man with 'a deep sympathy for Wales's regional aspirations', had been placed in charge of a ministry established to deal with uniquely Welsh prob-lems but had been prevented from implementing solutions that were uniquely Welsh.[66] On the other hand, there were those within the Welsh Parliamentary Labour Party who agreed with Edward Rowlands when he later argued that 'there was not necessarily a specific Welsh local government problem'.[67]

THE WELSH COUNCIL

The Welsh Council started work in 1968 and during its first three years it was able to claim some successes. The Council stressed that there was an urgent need for the M4 to be extended, and the government duly announced in April 1969 that the motorway would be given priority in the road-building programme. At the same time, the Council endorsed the view that Wales required its own financial institution, and a Commercial Bank of Wales was registered in February 1971; its proposal that the selective employ-ment tax should be reduced in development areas was subsequently adopted. The secretary of state's attention was drawn to the special problems of Pembrokeshire, as a result of the closure of defence establishments at Manorbier and Brawdy, and in March 1970 he announced that an alternative defence unit would be located at Brawdy. The pattern of public expenditure in Wales gave a high priority to items considered important by the Council, particularly

---

[65]   J. E. Trice, 'Welsh local government reform: an assessment of *ad hoc* administrative reform', *Public Law*, Autumn 1970, 292–3.

[66]   *Western Mail*, 19 January 1968.

[67]   Rowlands, 'Politics of regional administration', 350.

water supply and sewerage, roads and derelict land reclamation. The Council considered that it had a good working relationship with the secretary of state, who referred matters to it for consideration.[68] In May 1968 the minister of state referred to it for consideration the subject of land-use strategy in Wales, and in January 1970 the Council published a pilot exercise for Cardiganshire, Montgomeryshire and Radnorshire, entitled *Land Use Strategy: Pilot Report,* followed by a report in March 1971 entitled *A Strategy for Rural Wales.*[69] The Council in turn made recommendations to the secretary of state, and in order to do so it was given access to confidential documents. It was important, said the Council in its report for 1968–71, that its advice should be considered before the formulation of policy, and therefore its function could not be performed in public and could not be 'exercised without mutual trust'. 'Confidence', the Council said, was the 'lifeblood of the advisory function.' Another essential feature of this advisory function was that each question should be judged on its merits and that meant an 'objective, non-party approach'. The Council duly commissioned a piece of research through the Welsh Office 'in the field of regional social accounting', but it felt that its independence rested on the degree to which it could commission research and complete reports independent of the Welsh Office, and to that end both an independent secretariat and research unit were essential. The Council realized that its strength depended 'on being independent of Government and in being seen to be so'; whether it succeeded in that respect is doubtful.[70]

During its second three-year term, to 1974, the Council's work was undertaken by five panels: for industry and planning, environment and culture, communications, health and social services, and constitutional structure.[71] The government sought the views of the Council on the *Severnside Study Report* and on studies considering a possible Dee crossing, and it heeded the Council's advice on the development of Llantrisant.[72] At the end of the second term, members were asked by the secretary of state to continue to serve, but not for a fixed period because he wanted to be free to review the

[68]   Welsh Office, *Welsh Council, 1968–1971,* 1–2, 6, 9–10.
[69]   Welsh Council, *A Strategy for Rural Wales* (1971), 1.
[70]   Welsh Office, *Welsh Council, 1968–1971,* 10–11.
[71]   Ibid., *Welsh Council, 1971–1974* (1974), paras 3–4.
[72]   Parl. Deb., vol. 818, col. 1265.

situation, in the light of developments following the publication of the report of the Commission on the Constitution.[73] Eirene White, who as minister of state had defended the creation of the Welsh Council against critics, most notably Elystan Morgan, spoke out against advisory councils, now that the constraints of office had been removed. In her view, they were 'largely a waste of time' and were usually 'manipulated by the Civil Servants concerned'; they did not achieve much because 'Ministers and Civil Servants listen politely or read the report and then go on very much as they would have done in any case'.[74]

By-election shocks

The timing of a general election is crucial, and Richard Crossman was later to admit that Labour won the election in 1966 'by choosing the moment of worse inflation before the prices had really been felt to rise'.[75] The election was certainly well timed, because the government was returned with an overall majority of ninety-six seats. But soon after re-election its troubles began, and one crisis followed another. The period leading up to the crucial Carmarthen by-election in July, caused by the death of Megan Lloyd George, was a difficult one for the government. Almost immediately after the general election there was a seamen's strike; on 8 June Ray Gunter, the Welsh-born minister of Labour, warned the prime minister that if the Trades Union Congress could not mediate in the dispute the country would be facing 'the most serious industrial crisis for more than a generation'.[76] The Parliamentary Labour Party was bitterly divided over the issue of Vietnam, and the prime minister was reported in the *Western Mail* on 1 July to be 'fighting to retain his control over Labour MPs'.[77] Then, on 3 July, Frank Cousins, who had temporarily given up his post as general secretary of the Transport and General Workers' Union to enable him to join

[73]   Ibid., vol. 874, col. 210.

[74]   Baroness White, 'The Report of the Kilbrandon Commission on the Constitution', *Transactions of the Honourable Society of Cymmrodorion*, Sessions 1972 and 1973, 39–40.

[75]   R. H. S. Crossman, in 'The key to No. 10', BBC Radio 4 talk, 11 April 1971, quoted in David Butler and Dennis Kavanagh, *The British General Election of 1979* (London and Basingstoke, 1980), 347.

[76]   *Western Mail*, 8 June 1966; 9 June 1966.

[77]   Ibid., 1 July 1966.

the government as minister of Technology, resigned because he could not support the incomes policy.[78] Cousins led the opposition to the Prices and Incomes Bill, but after failing to rally trade union MPs behind him, he voted for the bill when it was given a second reading on 14 July. In the vote the government had a majority of 104.[79] During that same week, the pound took a hammering, slipping to £2.7868 against the dollar, and there were hints of a higher bank rate of 8 per cent to stop the decline.[80] James Callaghan announced that the ceiling on bank loans was to remain until the following March, which meant a much tighter credit squeeze, and the June trade figures announced during the week showed that the deficit was £55m, nearly twice that of £28m in May.[81] On 14 July, the very day of the Carmarthen by-election, the prime minister announced in the House of Commons that a statement outlining measures to be taken by the government was imminent. A rise in bank rate to 7 per cent had been announced earlier, and in order to cut back both private and public spending, banks' special deposits with the Bank of England were to be doubled.[82] This extraordinary chapter of crises experienced by Harold Wilson's government was the backdrop of a by-election in Carmarthen that was to open a new era in Welsh political history.

The Plaid Cymru candidate in Carmarthen, as in the recent general election, was Gwynfor Evans, the party's president. On several occasions he had been the parliamentary candidate in Merioneth, before contesting Carmarthen for the first time in 1964. In his address to the electors, Evans criticized Labour's agricultural policy; he emphasized the need for jobs, better communications and a just tax system; and he stressed the need to protect and develop Wales's water resources. He told the electors, 'Your hand can make history', and they responded in sufficient numbers to do precisely that.[83] Gwynfor Evans was elected with a majority of over 2,000. Emrys Jones, for the Welsh Council of Labour, suggested that Evans had benefited because the election had been fought on local issues; but although Evans had emphasized the need for jobs,

---

[78] Ibid., 4 July 1966.
[79] Ibid., 13 July 1966; 15 July 1966.
[80] Ibid., 12 July 1966.
[81] Ibid., 13 July 1966; 14 July 1966.
[82] Ibid., 15 July 1966.
[83] Gwynfor Evans's election communication, by-election, 1966.

unemployment in both the Carmarthen and Llandeilo travel-to-work areas was lower in June than it was in March.[84] In March the figures for Carmarthen and Llandeilo were 2.2 per cent and 3.5 per cent respectively, while in June they were 1.4 per cent and 2.5 per cent.[85] No collieries had been closed in the constituency since the general election, and since the closure of the railway line from Carmarthen to Aberystwyth in February 1965, Labour had won Cardiganshire and held Carmarthen.[86] The fact that a number of rural schools in the county were under threat of closure was an issue during the election campaign. This was so because the Labour-dominated Carmarthenshire Education Committee had just published a document, *Reorganisation of Primary Education in the Rural Areas*. If the proposals were implemented, seventeen schools would be closed and five others reorganized or closed. Gwilym Prys Davies, the Labour candidate, recalled later how amazed he had been that the proposals should have been released at that time. They were indeed 'political dynamite'. At the end of the day, only one school, St Clears Church in Wales School, was closed, which showed how impractical the scheme was, but the damage had been done.[87] That particular local issue played its part in deciding the election result, along with the events of that week, the unpopularity of the government's incomes policy among trade unionists and the seamen's strike. A protest vote against the government was likely to be in favour of Plaid Cymru, rather than of the Liberals, because in the previous general election Gwynfor Evans had increased his percentage vote at the expense of the Liberal candidate. In short, voters realized that the Liberals were losing ground and Evans was seen as the candidate most likely to defeat Labour.

In his election address, Evans said that those who had felt in the general election that the choice lay between the two parties likely to form the government were now free in the by-election to vote for Wales. Harold Wilson, Evans argued, had 362 MPs at his disposal so his need was 'less than that of our own land', and perhaps that point struck a chord with the electorate.[88] They may well have

[84]   *Western Mail*, 16 July 1966.
[85]   Information from Manpower Services Commission, Office for Wales.
[86]   Information from National Coal Board, South Wales Area; information from British Rail (Western), Cardiff Division.
[87]   Information from Director of Education, Dyfed County Council, 29 September 1983; Gwilym Prys Davies, *Llafur y Blynyddoedd* (Dinbych, 1991), 55.
[88]   Evans's election communication.

thought that only a revolt with a difference, a 'Welsh revolt', as
D. Watkin Powell has described it, could shake the government.[89] That
he was campaigning against the policies of a Labour government in
a by-election in a Labour-held seat was an advantage to Gwynfor
Evans. Circumstances, too, favoured him. He was a local man and a
member of the county council, an apt choice for this particular
constituency. It must be remembered, however, that although as
president of Plaid Cymru he had led a vigorous national campaign
against the drowning of the Tryweryn Valley in Merioneth, he had
failed to defeat the Labour candidate when he stood in that county
in 1959. Then, it had been a general election and his protests were
directed against the policies of a Conservative government. That
situation was very different from the one in Carmarthen. Whatever
the reasons for the shock result, it was ironic that the casualty of the
revolt was Gwilym Prys Davies, since no MP could have put the
Welsh case in parliament more effectively and with greater convic-
tion. He was a former member of Plaid Cymru and had been a
founder member of the Welsh Republican Movement that
stemmed from it in the late 1940s.[90] It was unfortunate for him that
he had not been selected by the Labour Party as its candidate in the
general election when it was known that Megan Lloyd George was
seriously ill, because he would almost certainly then have held the
seat. Meanwhile, at Westminster Gwynfor Evans was determined to
make an impact, and he took full advantage of every opportunity to
do so. During the period to October 1967 he asked hundreds of
questions on a wide range of topics and participated in several
debates on a variety of subjects.[91] Together with S. O. Davies, he
supported Emlyn Hooson (Liberal, Montgomeryshire) on 1 March
1967 in seeking 'to bring in a Bill to provide a scheme for the
domestic self-government of Wales'; nothing came of it.[92]

Following the result in Carmarthen, the *Western Mail* thought that
some good might flow from it. It opined that 'if Gwynfor Evans'
victory in Carmarthen can awaken Westminster to the basic needs
of Wales, the Principality will have cause for gratitude'.[93] But

[89] D. Watkin Powell, 'Carmarthen: before and after', *Contemporary Review*, 209 (October 1966), 182.
[90] Butt Philip, *Welsh Question*, 261.
[91] Parl. Deb., vol. 752, 349–53.
[92] Ibid., vol. 742, cols 417, 420.
[93] *Western Mail*, 16 July 1966.

Evans's victory had wider implications still. Some political commentators take the view that his triumph 'made Pollock possible; Pollock led to Hamilton' and the victory of the Scottish National Party candidate Winifred Ewing, because the nationalist parties were becoming credible and were no 'longer part of the lunatic fringe'.[94] When the Scottish National Party won Hamilton, Harold Wilson faced a real dilemma: 'Was it just a Poujadist protest, a short-lived reaction, or would it persist, with disastrous results in a general election?'[95]

From the early 1960s onwards, there was a marked growth in national consciousness in Wales. This was particularly evident in education. Since the late 1940s there had been moves to extend the use of the Welsh language as a medium of instruction at primary level. After the opening of the first Welsh-medium primary school, in Llanelli in 1947, dozens of others followed in different parts of Wales during the next two decades. Such was the increase, particularly in south-east Wales, where greater number of parents were anxious for their children to acquire knowledge of the language, that there were demands for Welsh-medium secondary schools. The first one, Ysgol Glan Clwyd, opened in Flintshire in 1956 and the same authority opened Ysgol Maes Garmon in 1961. In 1962 the Glamorgan Education Authority opened the first school in south Wales, Ysgol Rhydfelen. Inevitably, there were demands that pupils from these schools should be permitted to follow university and college courses through the medium of Welsh, and the University of Wales responded by appointing staff at Bangor and Aberystwyth to teach some subjects through the medium of Welsh. In 1962 Saunders Lewis, a founder member and a former president of Plaid Cymru, re-emerged on the political scene to effect a dramatic change of approach in respect of the language. In a BBC radio lecture, *Tynged yr Iaith* (Fate of the Language), he implored Welsh people 'to make it impossible to conduct local or central government business without the Welsh language'. He added: 'It is not a haphazard policy for isolated individuals . . . It is a policy for a movement, a movement rooted in those areas where Welsh is an everyday spoken language'. This led to the formation of *Cymdeithas yr Iaith Gymraeg* (Welsh Language Society) and the beginning of a

[94]   W. P. Grant and R. J. C. Preece, 'Welsh and Scottish nationalism', *Parliamentary Affairs*, 21, 3 (1968), 260.
[95]   Harold Wilson, *The Labour Government, 1964–70* (London, 1971), 569.

long campaign to extend the use of Welsh in everyday life. The society campaigned vigorously for bilingual summonses, car licences, birth certificates, Post Office forms and road signs, and in the 1970s for a Welsh-language television channel.[96] Although the society's methods did not win universal approval, it had a significant impact on the attitude of Welsh speakers towards their mother tongue, and there was a greater awareness of the need to retain the language and, with it, Wales's cultural identity. It was in this atmosphere that the historic Carmarthen by-election took place. Indeed, Gwynfor Evans's by-election victory gave this brand of Welshness political expression.

The next test for the government in Wales came in March 1967, following the death of Iorwerth Thomas, the member for Rhondda West. Unemployment in the Rhondda area was 5 per cent at the time of the election in March 1966, but by October it had crept up to 6.7 per cent (both the Cambrian Colliery in Clydach Vale and the Glenrhondda Colliery in Treherbert closed in September 1966); by February 1967 it had reached 9.1 per cent.[97] Thus, during the first year of the government's term in office the unemployment rate had virtually doubled. Vic Davies, the Plaid Cymru candidate and a non-Welsh speaker, made unemployment an issue in the by-election; in his election address he quoted the prime minister as saying that the highest tolerable level of unemployment was 2 per cent. He implored the electors on 9 March to 'Shock the Government into action', and they certainly did deliver a blow.[98] Labour's Alec Jones, a schoolmaster, held the seat, but compared with the general election and in spite of a higher poll the majority dropped from nearly 17,000 to just over 2,000.[99] Labour's troubles did not end there, because the deteriorating economic situation now forced the government to cut public spending. It had been hoped that increased spending on communications would eventually lead to lower levels of unemployment, but such a prospect faded when on 13 March, less than a week after the election, the government announced that the deteriorating economic situation necessitated a reduction of over £7m in the estimated expenditure on roads for 1967–8. The

[96] Davies, *History of Wales*, 648–50.
[97] Information from Manpower Services Commission; information from National Coal Board.
[98] Vic Davies's election communication, by-election, 1967.
[99] Jones, *Parliamentary Elections*, 147.

previous year the original estimate had already been reduced by
£5m.[100] Later in 1967, in November, the pound was devalued, and
petrol and, eventually, food prices were expected to rise.[101]
Unusually, in his first two years as secretary of the Welsh Council of
Labour, Emrys Jones had faced two by-elections. After interviewing
him, Cyril Aynsley of the *Daily Express* wrote on 1 March 1968 that
'The Labour Party is fortunate in having a man like Emrys Jones as
its regional organiser. He appreciates that the men of *Plaid Cymru*
are no longer Celtic mystics dreaming in the mists of an old
culture.' In the interview Jones said that the importance of the
nationalists should not be overrated, but having said that he did not
want to appear smug. He emphasized the fact that people had to be
reminded that a vote for the nationalists could result in a Tory
government. In a circular to all branches he had previously made 'a
brutal attack on the nationalists', maintaining that they wanted the
Labour government to fail in order to boost their membership. The
reporter concluded, 'Such bitterness of attack is indicative of the
Labour Party's anxiety'.[102]

This fascinating period, during which it seemed as if Welsh electors were being allowed regular opportunities to comment directly
on Harold Wilson's response to crises, received another twist with
the death of Ness Edwards, the member for Caerphilly. The third
Welsh by-election was set for 18 July 1968 and Labour's Fred Evans,
a local grammar school headmaster, was to be opposed by Plaid
Cymru's Phil Williams, a young local university lecturer. The
Caerphilly by-election could not have taken place at a worse time
for the government. At the beginning of the month, Ray Gunter
resigned from the Cabinet because of personal differences with the
prime minister, and a sterling crisis forced Monmouthshire-born
Roy Jenkins, the chancellor of the Exchequer, to seek international
support to the tune of over £830m.[103] Within hours of the Prices
and Incomes Act receiving the royal assent, Barbara Castle, the
secretary of state for Employment and Productivity, announced
that it would be used to extend the freeze (introduced the previous
December) on the £1 a week owing to municipal busmen, unless
they agreed to accept a productivity scheme. The government's

[100]   *Western Mail*, 14 March 1967.
[101]   Ibid., 20 November 1967.
[102]   *Daily Express*, 1 March 1968.
[103]   *Western Mail*, 1 July 1968; 9 July 1968.

decision had a significant impact in the Caerphilly constituency, where there was a municipal bus undertaking; on 10 July busmen's leaders in south Wales warned of strike action.[104] Moreover, since March 1966 sixteen collieries had been closed in south Wales, and miners were thoroughly disillusioned with Labour's policies. On top of this, the miners' nominee had not been selected to contest Caerphilly, and so miners at Bargoed Colliery refused to contribute to the Labour Party's fighting fund.[105] The pit-closure policy was being heavily criticized by the NUM, and its south Wales president, Glyn Williams, had earlier written a 'stinging' letter to Cledwyn Hughes, turning down an invitation to serve as a member of the Welsh Council. He was subsequently persuaded to change his mind by fellow NUM officials.[106] Unemployment in the Caerphilly area, which had been at 4.6 per cent in March 1966, was 8.7 per cent by June 1968. From May 1967 to July 1968 it never dropped below 8 per cent, and it reached 9.6 per cent and 9.8 per cent in August 1967 and January 1968 respectively.[107] In the period from September 1967 to September 1968 the average percentage rate of unemployment in development areas was higher in Wales than in Scotland. The average percentage rates had also been lower in the north and on Merseyside, areas that were not directly represented in the Cabinet by a secretary of state. The south-west was the only region with a higher average percentage rate of unemployment in development areas between September 1967 and September 1968.

In his election address, Phil Williams criticized the government for the high unemployment in the Welsh valleys and attributed it to the decline of coal.[108] In his message to Williams, Gwynfor Evans reiterated what he had said to the electors of Carmarthen, namely that a Plaid Cymru gain would force the government to 'think again about their bankrupt economic and political policies for Wales', whilst the election of a Labour MP would not change anything at all.[109] Nationalists invariably emphasized that if Wales managed its own resources, greater prosperity would result. Two days before the election the tobacco companies dealt another blow to workers when

[104]   Ibid., 11 July 1968.
[105]   Information from National Coal Board; *Western Mail*, 18 July 1968.
[106]   Interview, Glyn Williams, 19 December 1983.
[107]   Information from Manpower Services Commission.
[108]   Parl. Deb., vol. 770, cols 199–200; Phil Williams's election communication, by-election, 1968.
[109]   Phil Williams's election literature, by-election, 1968.

they raised tobacco and cigarette prices.[110] In fact, Labour won the by-election, but in a poll only slightly down on that of the general election, the majority crashed from over 21,000 to just below 2,000.[111] As in the Rhondda West by-election, Plaid Cymru brought in workers from all over Wales, and in the opinion of some Labour Party workers the threat was not taken seriously enough until it was too late. On the night of the count Fred Evans was booed and given a hostile reception by Plaid Cymru supporters, and Labour supporters who had left party stickers on their cars found them damaged. No doubt the treatment of Fred Evans influenced the attitude of the Caerphilly CLP towards devolution in the 1970s, although Fred Evans's views were anti-nationalist in any case.[112]

Plaid Cymru was obviously a serious threat to the Labour government, and its increasing importance as a political force played a part in influencing policy decisions. It is difficult to assess whether this influence was merely marginal or, as Gwynfor Evans maintained, significant. Evans cited the granting of a 'Welsh day' in parliament, the establishment of the Council for Wales and Monmouthshire and the creation of a minister for Welsh Affairs as examples of governments yielding to nationalist pressure, but Plaid Cymru was hardly a force on those occasions.[113] In the 1960s, Plaid Cymru may have had a more direct influence on policy, such as the decision to give the Welsh language equal status with English, although by then the pressure exerted by Cymdeithas yr Iaith could not be ignored. It should not be forgotten, too, that Cledwyn Hughes, a fervent supporter of the language, promoted the legislation. Several government offices were relocated in Wales, including the Royal Mint at Llantrisant. Whether the transfer was due to nationalist successes is a matter of conjecture, but it should be pointed out that the chancellor of the Exchequer from 1964 to 1967 was James Callaghan, a Cardiff MP, and it was his considerable influence in the Cabinet that swung the decision in favour of Llantrisant, much to the disappointment of William Ross, the secretary of state for Scotland.[114] Furthermore, the relocation of offices

[110]   *Western Mail*, 16 July 1968.
[111]   Jones, *Parliamentary Elections*, 147.
[112]   Interview, R. K. Blundell, 19 September 1983.
[113]   Gwynfor Evans, 'Hanes twf Plaid Cymru, 1925–1995', in Geraint H. Jenkins (ed.), *Cof Cenedl 10: Ysgrifau ar Hanes Cymru* (Llandysul, 1995), 162–3, 171, 174.
[114]   Kenneth O. Morgan, *Callaghan, A Life* (Oxford, 1997), 283–4.

in the regions was an essential strand of the government's policy to reduce unemployment.

The swing to Plaid Cymru in the Rhondda West and Caerphilly constituencies meant that, against his own wishes, James Griffiths was requested by the party to stay on in Llanelli, because the government feared another by-election.[115] It was ironic that of all MPs, the one who had done most to change the state of Wales could not risk giving up his seat. Political observers take the view that after the measures of July 1966 there was no recovery for Labour.[116] A government that included so many Welsh members and a secretary of state for Wales had failed to satisfy expectations, and voters registered their protest by supporting Plaid Cymru candidates in the by-elections.[117] Plaid Cymru was favourably placed to exploit the situation because the Carmarthen by-election had shown that it could win, and that therefore a vote for the party was no longer necessarily a wasted vote. Carmarthen was very largely a rural and Welsh-speaking constituency, but what had really heralded the new status of Plaid Cymru was its ability to pick up votes in the largely Anglicized and traditionally Labour mining valleys. The vital question was whether these nationalist turnouts in the valleys were protest votes or an expression of support for the idea that Wales should be given a new constitutional status. Clearly, Labour was in trouble nationally, but were Welsh electors doing anything more than criticizing the government's failure to address problems facing both Welsh and similar communities in other parts of the United Kingdom? Michael Hechter claims that central government's failure led to demands by disadvantaged groups, such as those in Scotland and Wales, for 'localized' decision-making 'so that their special problems might become appreciated and therefore taken into account in the allocation process'.[118]

Following the Caerphilly by-election, James Griffiths, now in his late seventies and, with S. O. Davies, the doyen of Welsh Labour politicians, realized that a change was taking place in Welsh politics and that Labour was in danger of losing the initiative. For the first

---

[115]   NLW, J. Griffiths Papers, E1/12, reflections on the General Election, June 1970, 9.

[116]   David Butler and Dennis Kavanagh, *The British General Election of October, 1974* (London and Basingstoke, 1975), 7.

[117]   Morgan, 'Welsh nationalism', 170.

[118]   Michael Hechter, *Internal Colonialism: The Celtic Fringe in British National Development, 1536–1966* (Berkeley and Los Angeles, 1975), 310.

time Plaid Cymru was making an impact in valley seats where Labour had been the dominant party for nearly half a century. In October 1968 Griffiths prepared an article, *The Political Situation in Wales*, in which he wrote: 'What is imperative is that we regain the initiative in Welsh political life. We must not be driven on the defensive, and a negative attitude on the constitutional issues will have serious consequences for our electoral prospects.' In an earlier speech at Llandybïe on 27 September he proposed the creation of national councils for Wales, Scotland and the regions of England. In Wales the Welsh Council should be transformed into an elected council, and take on the functions administered by nominated bodies and responsibilities from central government that could be administered more effectively by such a council. He was quite adamant that the way forward was to press for changes that were achievable at that particular time. He repeated these views in a debate in parliament on 15 October, but unfortunately he again did not elaborate when making the suggestion that there should be some devolution from the centre.[119] It is interesting to note that Griffiths, who had always claimed that the Welsh nation should be given political recognition, now stressed also the need for democratic accountability not only in Wales, but in Scotland and the regions of England as well. Devolutionists like Emrys Jones were later to emphasize, when putting their case, that there was a need to democratize institutions throughout the United Kingdom. Greater democracy, not narrow nationalism, was the impetus behind their demands.

THE COMMISSION ON THE CONSTITUTION

Ethnic nationalism had long been thought of as a European phenomenon, associated with countries like France, Spain and Belgium, rather than as a United Kingdom phenomenon. The Labour government was now faced with nationalist threats in Wales and Scotland. Labour found itself in a difficult situation. It did not want to embark on a course of action only to discover later that the threat was not a significant one; at the same time, ideas of ethnicity

---

[119] NLW, J. Griffiths Papers, C3/18, article by J. Griffiths entitled, 'The political situation in Wales', October 1968; C4/103, J. Griffiths at Llandybïe, 27 September 1968; Parl. Deb., vol. 770, col. 277.

and decentralization were fashionable amongst liberal intellectuals and it did not want to give the impression that the matter was not being taken seriously. Elystan Morgan, who had earlier supported Liberal moves to establish parliaments in Scotland and Wales, was now an under-secretary of state at the Home Office.[120] He thought that a Royal Commission should be appointed and discussed the idea with John Morris, the minister of Defence (Equipment), before submitting a paper to James Callaghan, the home secretary.[121] Callaghan discussed the matter with Cledwyn Hughes, now minister of Agriculture, Fisheries and Food, who urged him to go ahead with the proposal, because he thought that a Royal Commission's report would be more influential than departmental papers.[122] Harold Wilson, who had turned down Elystan Morgan's requests for a Royal Commission in July and December 1967, was impressed by the idea, and gave Callaghan full credit for formulating it.[123] The government probably took the view that a Royal Commission would take years to report, and if the economic position improved in the meantime nationalism would be a less threatening force and no action would be necessary.[124] Richard Crossman, writing later, thought that it was 'the stalest idea one can think of'. Passing judgement on George Thomas, who had succeeded Cledwyn Hughes as secretary of state, and William Ross, the secretary of state for Scotland, he noted that, 'These two have been bought over very easily, because they are anti-nationalist and this is a way of doing nothing'.[125] The government may also have been encouraged by the findings of some opinion polls. Although two polls conducted by Opinion Research Centre in November 1967 and September 1968 had indicated that around 60 per cent of those questioned favoured some form of parliament for Wales, two other polls, conducted in May by Market Information Services and by NOP Market Research in September 1968, recorded support of only 39 per cent and 49 per cent respectively. The poll conducted by Market Information Services also found that only 22 per cent considered that the rise in nationalist feeling was likely to last.

[120]   *Western Mail*, 21 February 1968.
[121]   Morris, review of *The Welsh Veto*, 49.
[122]   Lord Cledwyn, *Referendum*, 12.
[123]   Parl. Deb., vol. 750, col. 293; vol. 756, col. 49; Wilson, *Labour Government, 1964-70*, 725.
[124]   *Western Mail*, 1 November 1973.
[125]   Richard Crossman, *The Diaries of a Cabinet Minister*, vol. III (London, 1977), 193, 235.

Before the government made known its decision, Emrys Jones emphasized the party's commitment: 'Labour believes in devolution in the machinery of government and in providing increasing facilities for discussions on Welsh affairs in Wales.'[126] Subsequent events were to prove that he was far more committed than was his own party in parliament and in the country. In the autumn of 1968 the government announced its intention. Speaking in the debate on devolution at the Labour Party conference, James Callaghan stated that the prime minister had authorized him to say that the government was working on the problem 'as to how far and how best the facts and the alternatives' could be established, and he therefore asked that the resolution should be remitted; this was accepted by the conference.[127] There quickly followed an announcement in the Queen's Speech on 30 October that consultations would begin on the appointment of a Commission on the Constitution, to 'consider what changes may be needed in the central institutions of Government in relation to the several countries, nations and regions of the United Kingdom'.[128] The Commission's function was to 'be concerned with devolution, which is the delegation of central government powers without the relinquishment of sovereignty'.[129] Although the Conservative Party was strictly unionist, some of its MPs were sympathetic to the devolution of government. Geraint Morgan (Denbigh) was not opposed to regional government, provided the people supported it. In the meantime, he advocated a further transfer of powers to the Welsh Office, which was to happen under subsequent Conservative governments.[130]

A statement prepared for the Labour Party's home policy subcommittee in December 1968 recognized that nationalism was a problem and that there was a need for more effective propaganda and organization to confront it. The possibility of submitting evidence to the Commission on the Constitution was also mentioned.[131] Eventually, it was agreed that evidence should be submitted, and in Wales a study group, whose members were chosen by Emrys Jones, assisted the Labour Party's executive

---

126   *Western Mail*, 26 September 1968.
127   *Labour Party Annual Report*, 1968, 185–6.
128   Parl. Deb., vol. 772, col. 9.
129   *Royal Commission on the Constitution, 1969–1973*, 165.
130   *Western Mail*, 1 October 1968.
131   LPA, Home Policy Subcommittee, Re. 389/December 1968.

committee. This group provided information and draft proposals for discussion.[132] J. Barry Jones recalled how by April 1969 the study group had 'produced a draft proposal of a quasi-federal nature, suggesting a Welsh senate of 72 seats with certain legislative powers, particularly in domestic and welfare matters'. To George Thomas the proposal was anathema, and he was even opposed to an elected council – as indeed were a considerable number of other Labour MPs.[133] As J. Barry Jones and Michael Keating explain, 'In the face of such hostility the Welsh Executive progressively modified the proposed evidence in order to accommodate the various fears and prejudices of different groups within the Party'.[134] Emrys Jones confirmed later that George Thomas and Eirene White attempted to persuade him to accept a nominated body, but he insisted that the proposed council should be directly elected.[135] In her address as retiring chair of the Labour Party conference in 1969, Eirene White said that, following the report of the Royal Commission on the Constitution, there should be changes in the government of Wales which would enable people to make decisions that affected 'the local quality and colour of life'. She thought that 'some genuine devolution, including some financial decentralisation', was essential. The Treasury's control of minor matters could not be justified and, she added, 'Whitehall does not really always know best and people should be trusted at a lower level to make more decisions for themselves'.[136] She was obviously in favour of change, but it seems that this did not encompass an elected council.

Emrys Jones was a decidedly key figure at this point and remained so throughout the whole devolution debate. He was able, resolute and showed courage in standing up to Welsh Office ministers and Labour MPs. Indeed, if it had not been for him the party in Wales would not have submitted evidence at all to the Commission.[137] He was the antithesis of the traditional Labour secretary in that he played a major role in framing policy. The party centrally was becoming increasingly concerned because the Scots and the Welsh were adopting different standpoints with regard to

[132] Welsh Council of Labour, *Report to the Annual Meeting*, 15–16 May 1970, 6.
[133] Jones, 'Development of the devolution debate', 23.
[134] Jones and Keating, 'British Labour Party as a centralising force', 17.
[135] Interview, Emrys Jones, 29 March 1983.
[136] *Report of the Annual Conference of the Labour Party*, 1969, 145–6.
[137] Interviews: John Morris, 16 November 1999; K. S. Hopkins, 13 April 1983; Gwilym Prys Davies, 4 July 1983.

devolution. The Scots did not want to have anything to do with it, whilst the Welsh were proposing the establishment of a 'new and fairly powerful Welsh Council'. The party was also very anxious that the evidence submitted from Scotland and Wales, even if different, should be founded on the same principles.[138] In December 1969 the National Executive Committee received the views of the Welsh Parliamentary Labour Party. The MPs opposed any transfer of ministerial functions to a Welsh assembly, and maintained that the transfer of responsibility for Welsh matters with accountability from Westminster to an assembly would conflict with the sovereignty of parliament. Ministers were responsible to MPs, the people's elected representatives, and an assembly would only duplicate matters. Nevertheless, a national council with its functions clearly defined might be the answer to the demand for greater democratic control over nominated bodies; but Labour councillors would certainly oppose the transfer of local government functions.[139] Ifor Davies, a former under-secretary of state at the Welsh Office, who opposed the Labour government's devolution proposals in the 1970s, drew up a memorandum which he asserted expressed the views of many members of the Welsh Parliamentary Labour Party. It claimed that these MPs thought that existing machinery at Westminster could be made more effective and that in itself would result in greater accountability. The work of the Welsh Grand Committee should be extended, further opportunities for Welsh questions explored and a Welsh Select Committee established. The MPs stressed that any submission should not be 'too definitive'.[140] Davies's attitude was an enigma. As a Welsh speaker and prominent nonconformist, he might seem to have been a natural supporter of devolution. However, he was a former county councillor, and the perceived threat to local government – and further reorganization – played a part in his thinking. Moreover, in the 1970s his fellow MPs in neighbouring constituencies in the new county of West Glamorgan, with the exception of John Morris, were opposed to devolution.

In January 1970, following discussions between representatives of the executive committee and a subcommittee of the NEC, the

---

[138]   LPA, evidence to the Commission on the Constitution, Re. 540/November 1969.

[139]   Ibid., memorandum on devolution in Wales presented to the NEC by the Welsh Group of Labour MPs, 1969.

[140]   UWS, Fred Evans Papers, A3, memorandum by Ifor Davies.

evidence from the Labour Party in Wales was submitted to the Commission on the Constitution. In addition, Emrys Jones and Gwyn Morgan, the assistant general secretary of the Labour Party, gave oral evidence to the Commission on 26 January 1970.[141] Although this evidence fell short of the proposals submitted by the study group in the previous April, the party went further than had been the case five years earlier still. In Kenneth O. Morgan's words, 'the Labour Party had at last begun to break free from the shackles of Sidney and Beatrice Webb and to acknowledge the value of decentralized power being accorded to small local communities'.[142] When preparing its evidence, the Labour Party in Wales had taken into consideration a number of factors, such as reform of local government, the need to extend democratic control over nominated bodies and to scrutinize government administration, and also the need to provide machinery to enable central government to devolve responsibilities that could be executed in Wales.[143] The Commission on the Constitution was not concerned with local government reform, yet the Labour Party in Wales advocated an all-Wales authority with 'its roots in local government'. As Emrys Jones was giving his oral evidence, the chairman of the Commission had to remind him that they were not considering local government.[144] On 4 February, Anthony Crosland, secretary of state for Local Government and Regional Planning, confirmed in the House of Commons that the appointment of the Commission on the Constitution would not prevent the reform of local government from going ahead, and that the Commission itself was concerned with 'transfers from the centre to the provinces not from local government to the provinces', which the government accepted were not suitable for the administration of local government functions.[145] The Commission on the Constitution likewise stated:

> We have no doubt that the main intention behind our appointment was that we should investigate the case for transferring or devolving responsibility for the exercise of government functions from Parliament and the central

[141]   Welsh Council of Labour, *Report to the Annual Meeting*, 15–16 May 1970, 6–7.
[142]   Kenneth O. Morgan, 'Welsh politics. Cymru Fydd to Crowther', in R. Brinley Jones (ed.), *Anatomy of Wales* (Peterson-super-Ely, 1972), 135.
[143]   *Evidence of the Labour Party in Wales to the Commission on the Constitution*, 12.
[144]   Commission on the Constitution, *Minutes of Evidence 5: Wales*, 1972, 23, 26.
[145]   Parl. Deb., vol. 795, col. 441.

government to new institutions of government in the various countries and regions of the United Kingdom . . .[146]

In its evidence, the Labour Party in Wales stated categorically that there was 'a natural sense of Welsh identity' and 'an innate consciousness that the Welsh nation exists and can contribute effectively to its own self-government'. That did not mean that it accepted the demand for a sovereign Welsh parliament.[147] Rather, it meant that there was a Welsh identity and that Wales was regarded as a unit for administrative purposes. Not all Welsh Labour MPs shared this view. Later, in December 1976, Leo Abse in the debate on the Scotland and Wales Bill declared that he did not see Wales as a unit for government administration. In his view, even if there was a case for regional government, that could mean linking parts of south Wales with Bristol to form a Severnside authority and parts of north Wales with Merseyside.[148] He was advancing a view that had been totally rejected by both major political parties, and the creation of the Welsh Office in 1964 and developments since had certainly strengthened a sense of Welsh identity. Not only did the Labour Party in Wales emphasize that there was a Welsh identity, but it also admitted that not enough time was being given to Welsh matters. When questioned by a member of the Commission on the Constitution as to whether the Westminster government of the day gave enough attention to Welsh matters, Gwyn Morgan replied, 'No, it is not the view of the Welsh Council of Labour that sufficient time has been given, throughout the history of Westminster Government.'[149] Some Welsh Labour MPs would have regarded that reply as nationalistic, to say the least. Interestingly, James Griffiths, when he met the Commission on the Constitution, supported a Welsh national council, and was prepared to go further and accept a subordinate parliament if the Commission were to recommend a federal constitution.[150]

[146] *Royal Commission on the Constitution, 1969–1973*, 5–6.
[147] *Evidence of the Labour Party in Wales to the Commission on the Constitution*, 10–11.
[148] Parl. Deb., vol. 922, col. 1791.
[149] Commission on the Constitution, *Minutes of Evidence 5*, para. 97.
[150] NLW, J. Griffiths Papers, C3/23, notes by J. Griffiths for his meeting with the Commission on the Constitution, February 1970.

In its manifesto for the 1970 general election, *Now Britain's strong let's make it great to live in*, Labour promised that 'an elected council for Wales with extended powers' would be established, as had been promised in its evidence to the Commission on the Constitution.[151] Labour lost the election and in the process lost five seats in Wales. Throughout the principality there were some significant new faces, including for Labour Neil Kinnock (Bedwellty), Brynmor John (Pontypridd), Caerwyn Roderick (Brecon and Radnor) and Denzil Davies (Llanelli), and for the Conservatives Michael Roberts (Cardiff North), Wyn Roberts (Conway), Anthony Meyer (Flint West) and Nicholas Edwards (Pembroke). In Brecon and Radnor, and in Llanelli, Caerwyn Roderick and Denzil Davies succeeded Tudor Watkins and James Griffiths respectively. Gwynoro Jones's victory for Labour in Carmarthen was at the expense of Gwynfor Evans, but perhaps the biggest surprise was at Merthyr Tydfil, where S. O. Davies, the veteran socialist of the Parliament for Wales Campaign, who had refused to retire, stood as an Independent Socialist candidate and was elected with a majority of over 7,000. He held the seat until his sudden death in 1972, when Edward Rowlands, who had previously been the member for Cardiff North, regained Merthyr Tydfil for the Labour Party.[152] With Labour having lost the election, there was a possibility that the party would become less committed to an elected council. Although the Labour Party in Wales remained committed to it, there was a danger that the Welsh Parliamentary Labour Party would be swayed by the persuasive arguments of MPs who, above all, wanted to preserve their own positions, and who saw any form of elected body as a threat to their own authority and a concession to nationalism. James Griffiths may have had this in mind when he wrote, immediately after the election, 'What I am anxious to ensure is that Labour remains in Wales the voice of constructive change. We have tended to live on our inheritance.'[153] Labour had been the major political force in Wales since the 1920s and Griffiths realized that such dominance could lead to resistance to change. Coming at the end of his long parliamentary career, this warning was to be one of Griffiths's

[151]   Labour Party, *Now Britain's strong let's make it great to live in* (London, 1970), 21.
[152]   Jones, *Parliamentary Elections*, 148–54.
[153]   NLW, J. Griffiths Papers, E1/12, reflections on the general election, June 1970, 21.

last contributions to the debate on the devolution of government. It was a warning that a radical party could not afford to ignore; if it did so, then inevitably it would hasten its decline.

As the newly elected Conservative government proceeded to draw up its plans for the reform of local government, the Labour Party in Wales maintained that reform should be delayed until the Commission on the Constitution had reported. Peter Thomas (now MP for Hendon South), the secretary of state for Wales, speaking in the Welsh Grand Committee in July 1971, saw no reason why reform should be delayed, especially since Lord Crowther, the chairman of the Commission, had assured him that he had no objection to proposals for local government reform being drawn up in advance of the Commission's report. Labour MPs, however, agreed with the party in Wales that reform of local government should await the report. Alan Williams was of the view that some of the extra tier's functions might well come from local government, and Brynmor John spoke of a body taking functions from central government, from local government and from nominated bodies, adding 'If that is what Lord Crowther suggests, democracy itself will be the winner'. He was later reminded by David Gibson Watt, the minister of state at the Welsh Office, of the Commission on the Constitution's terms of reference, which did not include consideration of local government. Peter Thomas admitted that a small number of local authorities had suggested that legislation should be delayed, but a strong body of opinion requested an end to uncertainty. He quoted the comments he had received from the Labour-controlled Monmouthshire County Council:

> The County Council has carefully considered such views but does not support the same and urges the speedy implementation of reorganisation proposals because it believes that the Commission's recommendations can only have a marginal effect on local government, as it was set up to examine the scope of devolution of central government functions and not to review local government. The last Government emphasised that the existence of the Commission was not a bar to immediate action on local government reorganisation and this is the view of the present Administration.[154]

The Conservatives went ahead without much delay, and when their plans for the reorganization of local government were announced, the reaction in parts of Wales was particularly hostile. The proposal

---

[154] Parl. Deb., Welsh Grand Committee, 13 July 1971, cols 71, 29, 48–9, 104, 6.

to split Glamorgan into three counties, namely West Glamorgan, Mid Glamorgan and South Glamorgan, was opposed by the Labour-dominated authority, by the Labour Party in Wales and by Labour MPs, and practically all the Welsh authorities supported the county council in its efforts to have the proposal changed.[155] The county council's local government committee urged the authority to 'ban all contact by its officials or members with the Welsh Office or any other Government department which is based on the assumption of a three-way split of the county'.[156] A Glamorgan 'Two not Three' committee was set up in order to oppose the proposals for the county, and the voices of Professor Brinley Thomas, of the University College, Cardiff and the singer Heather Jones were heard putting the county's case on tapes played in clubs, public houses and meetings.[157] Emrys Jones, for the Labour Party in Wales, declared that a Labour government would be asked to revert to the original proposal of two counties, as outlined in the Conservative government's consultative document.[158] Labour MPs claimed that even Conservatives deplored the decision to create a county of South Glamorgan, since the authority would be dominated by the city of Cardiff.[159] In fact, the same was true as far as West Glamorgan was concerned, because the representatives of the borough of Swansea would comprise nearly half the total membership of the authority.[160] In an amendment to the Local Government Bill, Labour proposed that Glamorgan should be split into two counties, and a petition against the three-way split, signed by 125,000 people, was handed to the prime minister by George Thomas. A delegation comprising representatives of all political parties and of sixteen local authorities from the county travelled to London to put the county's case.[161] Even church leaders, such as the bishop of Llandaff, voiced their objections to the government's proposal. Bishop Eryl S. Thomas argued perceptively that he was 'not convinced that Mid Glamorgan will have all the resources and land available for effecting such necessary improvements as easily as could be done in an administrative area with greater resources and with a more natural focal centre'.[162] In

---

[155] *Western Mail*, 21 January 1972.
[156] Ibid., 16 February 1972.
[157] Ibid., 8 February 1972.
[158] Ibid., 16 March 1972.
[159] Ibid., 21 January 1972.
[160] Ibid., 26 January 1972.
[161] Ibid., 15 March 1972; 2 March 1972.
[162] Ibid., 15 February 1972.

west Wales, too, the proposal to amalgamate Pembrokeshire, Cardiganshire and Carmarthenshire was unwelcome. As in West and South Glamorgan the new Dyfed authority would be dominated by one area: Carmarthenshire would have forty-one councillors, Pembrokeshire twenty-three and Cardiganshire fifteen. In Pembrokeshire, a seat held by the Conservatives, a Keep Pembrokeshire campaign coordinated opposition to the government's proposals. The campaign to keep the county out of Dyfed included 'motor cavalcades, protest meetings, a petition and a lobby of MPs at Westminster'. In mid Wales, Montgomeryshire County Council and Breconshire County Council opposed the proposal to amalgamate the two counties with Radnorshire to create the county of Powys.[163] Despite all these protests, however, the government was able to push through its proposals, and the reorganization of local government in Wales took effect from 1 April 1974.

By now George Thomas had accepted the need for an elected council to administer the work of nominated bodies.[164] When the Local Government Bill was being discussed in Standing Committee D on 16 March 1972, his amendment was that 'There shall be established from the first day of April 1976 an elected Council for Wales'. He explained that there was a need on the part of MPs 'to anticipate Crowther'; the amendment was submitted in anticipation of the findings of the Commission on the Constitution and was therefore not relevant to the current debate. It proposed a council to administer the functions of nominated bodies, as recommended by the Welsh Parliamentary Labour Party in the memorandum forwarded to the NEC in December 1969. As David Gibson Watt pointed out, the only local government body taken over would be the Welsh Joint Education Committee.[165] Meanwhile, the executive of the Labour Party in Wales had again written to the Commission on the Constitution expressing concern that it had not requested the government to delay consideration of the reorganization of local government. In its reply, the Commission reiterated Lord Crowther's earlier statement that local government reorganization did not come within its terms of reference and could go ahead.[166]

[163]   Ibid., 2 February 1972; *Y Cymro*, 10 November 1971.
[164]   *Wales: Cymru Radical*, 7 May 1971, 1.
[165]   House of Commons Standing Committee D, 16 March 1972, cols 2888–9, 2904.
[166]   Labour Party Wales news release, 26 October 1973, extracts from a letter sent to the Commission on the Constitution.

Emrys Jones maintained, however, that an elected council should have 'its base in local government, taking over such functions as control of police, fire and ambulance services, and certain specialist social services from local authorities'. He insisted that the council should be part of local government and claimed that a regional authority between local and central government would be like 'a jellyfish on a bed of nails'.[167] In May 1973 the Welsh Parliamentary Labour Party restated its support for an elected national council for Wales, but emphasized again that the 'influence and jurisdiction of the County and District Councils would also require special recognition'.[168] Then, at a meeting on 6 November, following the publication of the Commission on the Constitution's report, the party 'welcomed the establishment of an all-Wales elected assembly with real powers as the best means of exercising closer democratic control over the distinctive features of Welsh life'.[169] Michael Foot later recalled that Cledwyn Hughes was the 'dominant voice' at that meeting.[170] In a speech at Aberystwyth on 30 November, George Thomas explained that the aim was the 'democratisation of Government services': making bodies such as the health and water boards answerable to the electorate. On 2 December he told party workers in north Wales that the Labour Party would 'lose all credibility' with the electorate if it went back on its policy of an 'elected executive assembly for Wales'.[171] Whilst the Labour Party in Wales had throughout included local government functions among those to be administered by an elected council, the Welsh Parliamentary Labour Party for its part had consistently supported an elected council that would administer the functions of nominated bodies. It is interesting to note that Eirene White, who had originally opposed an elected council, was prepared, following the publication of the Commission on the Constitution's report, to accept what she termed a 'modified' form of the scheme B that had been proposed. She thought that an elected assembly could have some involvement in the legislative process. It could discuss bills having a particular impact on Wales at a first-reading stage and private bills relating to

[167] *Western Mail*, 24 March 1972.
[168] UWS, Fred Evans Papers, A8, statement recommending an elected assembly for Wales, 1973, 1–2.
[169] *Western Mail*, 7 November 1973.
[170] Interview, Michael Foot, 18 July 1984.
[171] *Western Mail*, 1 December 1973; 3 December 1973.

Wales at the Committee stage, and pass by-laws. She conceded that there would 'be a place for separate legislation in such matters as language, if this were needed, where real rather than imaginary differences pertain'. Some 'internal revenue or loans for special schemes or projects' could be raised, and this was important because 'it would provide for some freedom of initiative'.[172] Having retired as a MP, she was prepared to go much further than were her former colleagues in the Welsh Parliamentary Labour Party.

Following the euphoria of the 1960s, the 1970 general election was a disappointing one for Plaid Cymru; though it contested all of the Welsh seats for the first time, it polled just 11.5 per cent of the votes cast and lost two-thirds of its deposits.[173] The party not only lost the seat in Carmarthen but also lost the ground gained in the Rhondda West and Caerphilly constituencies, although in Aberdare it managed to poll 30 per cent of the votes cast. In north Wales the party's best result was in Caernarvonshire, where its candidate received a vote amounting to 33.4 per cent.[174] The nationalists failed to maintain the momentum of the 1960s, and that was partly due to disillusioned Labour voters returning to the fold, as was to be expected in a general election. Meanwhile, other voters who had switched to the nationalists in order to embarrass the Labour government were less inclined to do so in a general election. In by-elections the nationalists had been able to highlight Welsh issues and swamp particular constituencies with canvassers. That was not possible in a general election, when the issues were predominantly United Kingdom issues and when scarce resources could not be concentrated in one or two constituencies. The nationalists' disappointing performance in the 1970 general election naturally resulted in the Labour Party taking the view that in Wales the tide was turning, and it was content to await further developments.[175] The political scene in Wales, with Labour in opposition, was much more stable than it had been in the 1960s.

During the period 1964 to 1973 devolution emerged as a major issue within the Labour Party in Wales. The creation of the office of secretary of state with limited functions led to further demands, and

[172] Baroness White, 'Report of the Kilbrandon Commission', 41–6.
[173] David Butler and Michael Pinto Duschinsky, *The British General Election of 1970* (London and Basingstoke, 1971), 402.
[174] Jones, *Parliamentary Elections*, 148–54.
[175] Private information.

additional functions were subsequently transferred by Labour and
Conservative governments. When proposals for the reorganization
of local government were being formulated, both governments
continued to reject an elected council. Following a series of by-elections during a period of almost unprecedented financial and
industrial crises, when voters disillusioned with its performance
turned to the nationalists, the Labour government responded by
setting up a Royal Commission on the Constitution. In doing so,
Labour was probably playing for time and to an extent such a
strategy worked, for following the Commission's report there was a
brief interlude of inactivity. This period of stability, however, was to
come to a dramatic end in February 1974, when Edward Heath
called a general election that was to have profound consequences
for Wales, not least in enabling the nationalists to make another
breakthrough at Labour's expense.

V

THE UNWANTED TIER OF GOVERNMENT, 1974–1979

LABOUR GRASPS THE NETTLE

Although the Commission on the Constitution had now reported, Labour's national manifesto, *Let us work together. Labour's way out of the crisis,* for the February 1974 general election made no reference to devolution, and only 7 per cent of Labour candidates made any reference to devolution or decentralization in their addresses.[1] Meanwhile, the party's Welsh manifesto, *Labour's Policies for a Brighter Future for Wales,* promised an elected council 'with function, power and finance to enable it to be an effective democratic force in the life of Wales'.[2] The discrepancy between the two manifestos was raised in the *New Statesman* on 16 January 1976 by Eric Heffer (Labour, Liverpool Walton), who argued that because decisions on issues were taken at regional conferences it did not necessarily mean that they became national policy for the party.[3] After the election Labour was the largest party, with 301 seats, and was able to form a government, albeit a minority one. Edward Heath had called an early election because of the miners' strike, and the overall result meant that there was still a somewhat unstable political situation. In the election the nationalist vote in Wales dropped from 11.5 per cent in 1970 to 10.7 per cent, but the nationalists in Scotland and Wales gained four seats from Labour and four from the Conservatives.[4] Plaid Cymru candidates, Dafydd Elis Thomas and Dafydd Wigley, won Merioneth and Caernarvonshire from Labour, but Gwynfor Evans failed by just three votes to regain Carmarthen. Wigley defeated Goronwy Roberts, who over a period of nearly twenty-nine years as a MP had steadfastly advocated changes that would give Wales as a nation greater recognition in government. In

[1]   Labour Party, *Let us work together. Labour's way out of the crisis* (London, February 1974); David Butler and Dennis Kavanagh, *The British General Election of February 1974* (London and Basingstoke, 1974), 62.
[2]   Labour Party, *Labour's Policies for a Brighter Future for Wales* (Cardiff, February 1974).
[3]   *New Statesman*, 16 January 1976, 69.
[4]   Butler and Kavanagh, *British General Election of February 1974*, 260; *idem, British General Election of October 1974*, 33.

Cardiganshire another Labour incumbent, Elystan Morgan, was defeated by the Liberal Geraint Howells, whilst Ioan Evans, the former Labour MP for Birmingham Yardley and a native of Llanelli, was returned in Aberdare.[5] Support for devolution among Welsh Labour MPs was weaker than it had been in the late 1960s and early 1970s. The Labour Party faced a real dilemma, with another general election likely just months away. If the support for opposition parties was merely temporary, the seats lost might be won back, but if it was of a more permanent nature and growing, then other seats could be in jeopardy.

Harold Wilson's new secretary of state was John Morris, a Welsh speaker and a committed devolutionist. To Morris, a native of Cardiganshire, a county with a radical tradition, the need to make government more democratic and accountable was a priority, but he was equally conscious that the Welsh nation needed further constitutional recognition, and a Welsh assembly was a means of achieving that end.[6] This desire to give Wales enhanced political status had never been a majority view in the Labour Party in Wales, but individuals had long pressed for such recognition, and not without some success. Urging support for devolution at the Labour Party Annual Conference in 1968, John Morris maintained that the conference should 'ensure that we as a radical socialist movement lead the way to ensure that our machinery of government is updated to satisfy the aspirations of a people'. In his view, the machinery of government should reflect that Wales was a nation.[7] Significantly, the post of secretary of state had not been restored to George Thomas, whose opposition to devolution was well known and whose responses to Welsh-language matters had made him unpopular in nationalist and Welsh-speaking circles. No doubt (in Kenneth O. Morgan's words) his 'fierce suspicions of the nationalist movement (perhaps reinforced by his inability to speak much Welsh)' had 'made the gap between the Labour Party and the new nationalist mood in Wales somewhat wider'.[8] Thomas later revealed that his views on devolution had been an embarrassment to the prime minister and he claimed that plotters had 'quietly but insidiously destroyed' his chances of returning to the government.

[5] Jones, *Parliamentary Elections,* 155–61.
[6] Interview, John Morris, 16 November 1999.
[7] *Labour Party Annual Report,* 1968, 182.
[8] Morgan, 'Welsh politics', 134–5.

Interestingly enough, William Ross, who shared this antagonism towards devolution, was nevertheless made secretary of state for Scotland.[9] James Callaghan was a senior member of the government as foreign secretary, but he was not enthusiastic about devolution, whilst Michael Foot, the secretary of state for Employment, had never been involved with the subject. They were joined in the government by Alan Williams, who was a minister of state, and by Barry Jones (Flint East), Edward Rowlands and Brynmor John, who were appointed under-secretaries. It was reported before the election that Williams and Rowlands, like George Thomas, were 'worried about an elected Welsh assembly clashing with the Westminster Parliament'. If Rowlands did have reservations, he put them to one side and supported Labour's policy, with which he became closely involved. As a Welsh Office minister, he was appointed an assistant to Edward Short in the Cabinet's devolution unit, and the intention was, he said, 'to bring about a constitutional reform of major significance'.[10]

Immediately after the election, the prime minister made it known that he had appointed a constitutional adviser, Lord Crowther-Hunt, to advise those ministers engaged in discussion of the Commission on the Constitution's proposals. In the Queen's Speech, on 12 March, the government announced that discussions would be initiated in Scotland and Wales on the Commission's report and that proposals would be brought forward for consideration.[11] The Labour Party in Wales had already, in January 1970, made known its views as to the type of assembly it favoured. In its evidence to the Commission on the Constitution, it had rejected an assembly with legislative functions, on the grounds that it would result in 'wasteful duplication and inevitable confusion'.[12] By 1974 the matter seemed not as straightforward. Speaking in Skewen in January 1974, John Morris said that an assembly could fit into the legislative process. This caused some concern in Labour Party circles because it was envisaged that such an assembly would be given legislative powers; in the view of the *Western Mail*, 'We agree that it is not a little unreal to envisage a body charged with

[9]   Viscount Tonypandy, *George Thomas, Mr. Speaker* (London, 1985), 127, 129.
[10]   Butler and Sloman, *British Political Facts*, 55–8; *Western Mail*, 26 February 1974; 22 October 1974.
[11]   Parl. Deb., vol. 870, col. 83.
[12]   *Evidence of the Labour Party in Wales to the Commission on the Constitution*, 12.

implementing policy on a wide front having no say in the determination of that policy.' This newspaper, with Yorkshireman Duncan
Gardiner as its editor, would give the government's devolution
proposals its support from 1974 onwards. Apparently, John Morris's
speech particularly angered Welsh Labour MPs.[13] In May, the South
Wales Area Conference of the National Union of Mineworkers
approved a motion in favour of an assembly with 'law-making
powers', and the motion was subsequently carried later in the
month at the conference of the Wales Trade Union Council.[14] The
Wales TUC henceforth played a prominent part in the devolution
debate, and Dai Francis, its chairman in 1974, was also the secretary
of the South Wales Area of the NUM. The motion was then
submitted to the annual conference of the Labour Party in Wales,
which on 17 May, under the skilful direction of Emrys Jones,
decided to defer a decision on the matter to a special conference to
be held after the government had published its consultative document.[15] Ron Hayward, the general secretary of the Labour Party,
made it quite plain that the NUM, supported by the Wales TUC,
could not speak on behalf of Labour in Wales. In his speech he
stressed that 'The voice of Labour in Wales are the decisions
reached at this Welsh conference. No other organisation that is affiliated to the Labour Party can speak for you authoritatively on
political matters.' On the following Monday, the *Western Mail*
suggested that:

> Clearly for the more conservative elements in the party who are frightened
> stiff by the thought of creating focuses of political power outside the London
> borough of Westminster, the sight of the Wales TUC voting unanimously at
> its first congress in favour of a legislative assembly must have been somewhat
> alarming.[16]

The special conference was held at Llandrindod Wells on 22 June
and, in an attempt to avoid a rift within the party, the executive
presented a policy document, *Devolution and Democracy*. The document differed from the earlier one prepared for the annual
conference, and entitled *Devolution*, in stating that the assembly
would have 'power to participate in policy decisions of Government-

---

[13]   *Western Mail*, 18 January 1974; interview, Gwilym Prys Davies, 4 July 1983.
[14]   *Western Mail*, 2 May 1974.
[15]   Ibid., 18 May 1974.
[16]   Ibid., 20 May 1974.

owned commercial and industrial undertakings in Wales'.[17] The statement was an attempt to satisfy the demands of the Wales TUC and was in line with the views of Gwilym Prys Davies, the defeated Labour candidate in Carmarthen in 1966, who was now a newly appointed adviser to the secretary of state.[18] Indeed, he was also acting as an unofficial adviser to Emrys Jones.[19] After the publication of the report of the Commission on the Constitution, Prys Davies declared that the essential question was 'whether an assembly, however constituted, would have the power really to influence the economic life of Wales'. He explained that unless an assembly had the 'power to ensure that any reorganisation strategy put forward by the British Steel Corporation was compatible' with its own economic plan for Wales, the people would have the 'shadow and not the substance of devolution'.[20] The special conference gave overwhelming approval to the policy document, *Devolution and Democracy*, and incidentally Ioan Evans, who was later to oppose the government's policy, also supported it.[21]

When John Morris appointed Gwilym Prys Davies as his adviser, Welsh Labour MPs had expressed misgivings.[22] Some members of the Labour Party in Wales executive were rather suspicious of his earlier association with Plaid Cymru and separatism. That criticism was unfair because Prys Davies, as chairman of the Welsh Hospitals Board from 1968 to 1974, was only too aware of the lack of accountability.[23] In November 1973 the Welsh Parliamentary Labour Party confirmed the decision of December 1969, but MPs felt that on devolution Prys Davies was prepared to go much further.[24] Shortly after his appointment, eight Labour MPs replied to a questionnaire sent to all Welsh MPs, arguing that an assembly should have executive functions and that none of the secretary of state's functions should be transferred.[25] These replies confirmed that Welsh Labour MPs were thinking in terms of an elected council to undertake the work of nominated bodies. The MPs were

[17]   Labour Party in Wales, *Devolution and Democracy* (Cardiff, June 1974).
[18]   *Western Mail*, 3 May 1974.
[19]   Interview, K. S. Hopkins, 13 April 1983.
[20]   *Western Mail*, 1 November 1973.
[21]   Interview, J. Vaughan Jones, 3 August 1982.
[22]   *Western Mail*, 3 May 1974.
[23]   Interview, K. S. Hopkins, 13 April 1983.
[24]   Parl. Deb., vol. 922, col. 1603.
[25]   *Western Mail*, 27 May 1974.

clearly at odds with the Labour Party in Wales, whose views were summarized by Emrys Jones in a letter to the *Western Mail* on 26 July. In it he said that the aim was the creation of a directly elected council with 'real authority and the capacity for growth', as 'part of a radical change' in the machinery of government in the United Kingdom. Central government would 'legislate broadly', leaving a range of decision-making powers to the council, which would also participate 'in the decision-making process of central government', with particular reference to economic policy as it affected Wales.[26]

The Conservative Party in Wales, unlike the other major parties, did not submit evidence to the Commission on the Constitution, thereby confirming the perception that it was essentially an 'English' party. The *Western Mail* reminded its readers that when the Young Conservatives became interested in the issue the party had 'remained bored and uninterested'. Now the party showed just sufficient interest to reject a Welsh assembly, but it did join in the debate and the newspaper's comment on this action was: 'We might have applauded the action had his [Peter Thomas, the shadow secretary of state] first contribution to the debate not been a basket of red herrings trawled from the shallows of the speeches that preceded his announcement.' The Conservative Party supported the transfer of additional powers to the Welsh Office and proposed that the existing Welsh Council should have a majority of indirectly elected members, drawn from the local authorities. Peter Thomas, explaining the changes in respect of the Welsh Council, said that 'It should have the power to debate publicly all matters affecting Wales, to examine Bills relating to Wales, to invite Ministers and Welsh Office officials to attend and also request reports from nominated bodies dealing with health, water, recreation and the like.' The party also proposed the creation of a parliamentary select committee of MPs from Welsh constituencies, with authority to investigate the entire range of Welsh administration. Another proposal was that Wales should receive a block grant and that the Welsh Office should decide how it should be allocated. A further proposal was that a generous share of the revenues from Celtic Sea oil should be given to Wales through a development agency. The *Western Mail* was very critical of the Tories' proposals, saying that they were not prepared to support a democratic institution for fear

---

[26] Ibid., 26 July 1974.

of what would be decided. This, it claimed, was 'a slur on the political maturity of the people of Wales'.[27]

Meanwhile, at the close of the Scottish Conservative Party conference in Ayr, Edward Heath proposed an indirectly elected assembly, with its members drawn from local authorities. The assembly would discuss some parts of legislation dealing exclusively with Scotland. It would also advise the Scottish Office as to how the Scottish share of the United Kingdom budget should be spent. Although a future elected assembly was not ruled out, the Conservatives had retreated from earlier commitments. In 1968 Edward Heath had 'committed the party to legislative devolution for Scotland', and in 1970 Alec Douglas-Home's Scottish Party committee had proposed a 'directly elected Scottish assembly'.[28] Responding to the latest proposals, the SNP Chairman Malcolm Wolfe judged, 'The half-baked proposals are impractical and would do nothing to meet the needs and aspirations of the Scots'.[29]

In June the two parties which wanted to see major changes in the machinery of government made known their views. The Liberals, who had forced the government to debate the report of the Royal Commission on the Constitution in March, wanted a parliament in Wales with legislative powers, and they said that they would not support any proposals unless they included proportional representation. Plaid Cymru too wanted a legislative assembly, and they knew that further nationalist gains in Scotland and Wales would enable them to press their claims.[30]

The government was contemplating calling an autumn election, in which it hoped to increase its representation and to win back seats from the nationalists in Scotland and Wales. Consequently, both the National Executive Committee and the government were busily preparing separate policy statements on devolution. In September the NEC issued its statement, entitled *Bringing Power Back to the People*. This proposed assemblies for Scotland and Wales, and also recognized that it had 'an equal commitment to democratic accountability of government and equality of political rights

[27]   Ibid., 17 June 1974; 31 July 1974.
[28]   Ibid., 20 May 1974; Denis Balsom and Ian McAllister, 'The Scottish and Welsh devolution referenda of 1979: constitutional change and popular choice', *Parliamentary Affairs*, 32, 4 (Autumn 1979), 403.
[29]   *Western Mail*, 20 May 1974.
[30]   Ibid., 22 June 1974.

in the English regions'. The Labour Party in the north-west had expressed the view that establishing assemblies in Scotland and Wales while ignoring 'the opportunities for devolution in other regions in the UK would be wrong'. The NEC proposed that the Welsh assembly should be responsible for some Welsh Office functions and for the responsibilities of nominated bodies, but that it should not take powers from local government. The transfer to the assembly of executive powers in respect of trade and industry would enable it to make decisions in the light of its own needs 'in the promotion of employment and industrial regeneration'. The proposed Welsh Development Agency would also be responsible to such an assembly.[31] Although the government had announced that discussions should commence, the Cabinet was far from convinced that devolution was necessary and some ministers, as Barbara Castle later disclosed, had strong reservations.[32] The government's proposals were announced immediately after those of the NEC, and just in time to be included in the national manifesto for the forthcoming general election. Like the NEC, the government proposed an assembly and not an elected council, as had been proposed in the Welsh manifesto for the February election.[33] The government's new response was attributed to the political situation in Scotland. On 9 July the *Scotsman* predicted that as many as thirteen Labour seats would fall to the Scottish National Party, and it quoted a Labour Party study document to the effect that 'we are facing a potentially explosive political situation in Scotland, particularly if the Labour Party fails to take a lead on the issue of Scottish government'.[34] In the party's Welsh manifesto, *Wales will win with Labour*, the assembly's role was specified in detail:

> Labour will establish a directly elected Welsh Assembly with responsibility for a wide range of functions, for instance Housing, Health, Education, Economic and Environmental Planning, and Water, currently performed by Central Government and undemocratic nominated bodies. It will have real powers in the field of economic and industrial development. The Assembly will receive a block budget from the Treasury, and will decide its own spending priorities, having to choose between many competing claims. The

[31] Labour Party, *Bringing Power Back to the People* (London, September 1974), 3–5, 9; *idem*, Devolution Working Group Res. 134, July 1974.
[32] Barbara Castle, *The Castle Diaries, 1974–76* (London, 1980), 173.
[33] Labour Party, *Labour Party Manifesto* (London, October 1974), 21.
[34] *Scotsman*, 9 July 1974.

Assembly will have a wide range of decision making, including certain powers of the Secretary of State with respect to delegated legislation, within a broad framework of Central Government legislation, in the formulation of which the Assembly will have a substantial impact.

The manifesto did not envisage that local government functions would be transferred to an assembly.[35] Despite the threat posed by the nationalists, devolution was still not a burning issue within the Labour Party nationally, and it is revealing that only 10 per cent of candidates made any reference to it in their election addresses.[36]

In the general election, the government was re-elected, though with an overall majority of only three seats.[37] Gwynfor Evans, with 45.1 per cent of the vote, recaptured Carmarthen for Plaid Cymru, and Donald Anderson, the former Labour MP for Monmouth, was elected for Swansea East. In Caernarvonshire and Merioneth, Plaid Cymru MPs, Dafydd Wigley and Dafydd Elis Thomas, not only retained their seats, but also increased their shares of the vote, to 42.5 per cent and 42 per cent respectively.[38] Plaid Cymru's percentage of the total Welsh vote remained virtually unchanged, at 10.8 per cent.[39] In Scotland, the Scottish National Party captured four seats from the Conservatives to bring their total to eleven, and although the party had fewer MPs than the Conservatives, it had a higher percentage of the Scottish vote and thus emerged as the second party to Labour.[40] Of the ten constituencies where the nationalists had near misses (losing by a majority of under 6 per cent), seven were held by Labour.[41] The increased support for the nationalists, particularly in Scotland, and the small Labour majority ensured that devolution remained an issue and could not be quietly forgotten.

The minister responsible for the devolution legislation was the lord president, Edward Short. In February 1975 the Welsh Parliamentary Labour Party expressed to him its anxieties that the government was committed to proposals beyond those agreed in 1969.[42] A week later, on 1 March, it was reported in the *Western Mail* that Welsh Labour backbenchers were actively lobbying behind the

[35]   Labour Party, *Wales will win with Labour* (Cardiff, October 1974).
[36]   Butler and Kavanagh, *British General Election of October 1974*, 235.
[37]   Idem, *British General Election of 1979*, 18.
[38]   Jones, *Parliamentary Elections*, 162–8.
[39]   Butler and Kavanagh, *British General Election of October 1974*, 351.
[40]   *The Times Guide to the House of Commons, October 1974* (London, 1974), 287.
[41]   Butler and Kavanagh, *The British General Election of October 1974*, 325.
[42]   *Western Mail*, 26 February 1975.

scenes against these proposals.[43] In an interview in the *Sunday Times* on 2 November 1975 before the proposals were announced, Short defended them, on the grounds that the government had merely accepted a pattern that had emerged from discussions in both countries.[44] He explained later that he would have gone further and offered Wales a legislative assembly. The decision to opt for executive devolution instead meant that civil servants would have to search for functions and there were not enough to give the assembly a role. There was a limit to what could be devolved to an executive assembly, and people might have thought such an assembly not worth supporting.[45] This latter view was shared by trade union officials, who believed that the Labour Party in Wales had fudged the issue and that what eventually emerged was the lowest common denominator.[46] Prominent Labour local authority leaders, perhaps because they were fearful of their own positions, also supported legislative functions so that the assembly could respond to the country's particular needs. Prior to his death in August 1975, James Griffiths had also supported the need for parity with Scotland. In a letter to *The Times* on 26 October 1974, he wrote, 'I would offer one counsel to my comrades – do not make the differing powers between the two Celtic Assemblies too marked . . . A slight on Wales, however unintentional, can only play into the hands of the Welsh Nationalists.'[47] On 29 October the *Western Mail* quoted from an article in *The Times* by Lord Chalfont, a native of Monmouthshire, who maintained that Wales and Scotland were treated differently because of the strength of support for the SNP. Consequently, 'Wales was left outflanked, still identified with more modest aspirations'.[48] We now know that rather than being too modest, they were perhaps too ambitious, and even Gwilym Prys Davies, who supported an executive assembly, conceded after the rejection of the Wales Act in the referendum that the decision should have been for an elected council, trusting a future generation to build on its foundation.[49]

[43]   Ibid., 1 March 1975.
[44]   *Sunday Times*, 2 November 1975.
[45]   Interview, Edward Short, 19 December 1984.
[46]   Interview, Keith Jones, 18 March 1985.
[47]   *The Times*, 26 October 1974.
[48]   *Western Mail*, 29 October 1974.
[49]   Interview, Gwilym Prys Davies, 4 July 1983.

Labour MPs again made their position quite clear at a meeting with the executive of the Labour Party in Wales on 4 November 1975. The Welsh Parliamentary Labour Party confirmed the policy statement that had been agreed in 1973.[50] When the government's proposals were announced, they were opposed by some Welsh Labour MPs, who claimed that the proposals went beyond what had been accepted in the policy statement. Neil Kinnock, who, with Leo Abse and certain other Welsh Labour MPs, led the offensive against the government's proposals, challenged Edward Short in January 1976 to point out where an undertaking had been made to give the assembly powers to raise revenue; Abse stated that the decision of November 1973 was for an elected council to supervise nominated bodies only.[51] The devolution debates gave Kinnock a higher profile than would normally be afforded to a backbench MP, and that, no doubt, helped him to win a seat on the NEC in 1978, alongside Frank Allaun, Tony Benn, Barbara Castle, Eric Heffer, Joan Lestor and Dennis Skinner.[52] Gwynfor Evans maintained that Neil Kinnock was the major beneficiary of the devolution campaign, because he probably would not have become leader of the Labour Party 'but for the ability he displayed leading the destruction of the decentralist measure'.[53] The so-called rebel MPs had earlier been supported by Heffer, who claimed in an article in the *New Statesman* on 19 December 1975 that what was at stake was not whether there was to be devolution, as agreed by Welsh Labour MPs in 1973, but whether there was to be a disunited kingdom.[54] The MPs were also only too aware of the situation within the Cabinet. Like the secretary of state, Edward Short was really committed to the policy and showed determination in executing it, despite the opposition of hostile ministers.[55] So many ministers did not really believe in the policy and merely supported it as a means of countering the nationalists' threat; this was also true of Labour MPs. As he admitted later, Short was aware that the climate had not really changed. There had never been much enthusiasm for devolution within the Labour Party, whatever the views of some individual

[50]   Welsh Council of Labour, *Report to the Annual Meeting*, 14–15 May 1976, 16.
[51]   Parl. Deb., vol. 903, cols 400–1, 461–2.
[52]   Interview, Emrys Jones, 29 March 1983.
[53]   Gwynfor Evans, *The Fight for Welsh Freedom* (Talybont, 2000), 157.
[54]   Eric Heffer, 'Devolution and the Labour Party', *New Statesman*, 19 December 1975, 778.
[55]   Interview, Michael Foot, 18 July 1984.

MPs.[56] Ministers were also influenced by their officials who, in Barbara Castle's words, were 'deeply alarmed at the whole business'.[57] A very strange situation was beginning to develop, in which many MPs openly criticized the government's policy, even though it was a manifesto commitment.

AN EXECUTIVE ASSEMBLY

The secretary of state's pronouncements in February 1975 on the powers to be transferred, just prior to the Welsh Parliamentary Labour Party's meeting with Edward Short, gave further grounds for concern to those MPs worried that the proposals would go too far. Westminster, he said, would be 'yielding enormous powers of policy-making and implementation' to the assembly and what was being considered would 'necessarily have far-reaching consequences for the United Kingdom'. In that parliamentary debate on 4 February, John Morris suggested *senedd* as a Welsh translation of assembly, and that immediately sent the alarm bells ringing among a group of Welsh Labour MPs. He later admitted that at that moment he could sense a change of mood in the chamber.[58] Interestingly, when there was so much opposition on the Labour benches, George Thomson, the EEC's Commissioner for Regional Policy and a former Labour minister, supported the policy. He claimed that it was the decentralization of power that had made West Germany so strong economically.[59] Following the publication in November 1975 of the White Paper, *Our Changing Democracy: Devolution to Scotland and Wales,* John Morris in January 1976 talked about extensive functions being devolved, and on 13 December the prime minister, James Callaghan, explained that the Scotland and Wales Bill would 'provide a wide measure of self-government for Scotland and Wales', which could hardly have been regarded as helpful by those who genuinely believed in devolution but rejected separatism.[60] About the same time, on 16 December, Edward Heath, the former Conservative leader, talked about giving Wales

---

[56]   Interview, Edward Short, 19 December 1984.
[57]   Castle, *Castle Diaries,* 497.
[58]   Parl. Deb., vol. 885, cols 1178, 1176; Morris, review of *The Welsh Veto,* 50.
[59]   *Western Mail,* 21 May 1975.
[60]   Parl. Deb., vol. 903, col. 609; vol. 922, col. 991.

'the greater freedom of self-government'.[61] The Liberals, on the other hand, reacted differently, and, in Jeremy Thorpe's words, the White Paper represented 'the very least which the Government believes it can get away with to satisfy what it believes is a transitory upsurge of nationalist emotion in Scotland and Wales'.[62]

As the Scotland and Wales Bill was being debated on 15 December, John Morris explained that only a small proportion of subordinate instruments made by him were being examined, but that a larger number would be considered once an assembly was established. In those areas where it would have executive and policy-making powers, the assembly's scrutiny of issues would be much closer than the scrutiny exercised by ministers and the House of Commons. The secretary of state considered that issues should be decided by elected representatives rather than by a minister, and Conservatives were convinced that he saw the Labour-dominated assembly as a shield to protect Wales from a future Conservative government at Westminster.[63] That may well have been in the secretary of state's mind, but even he could not have foreseen the Conservative hegemony from 1979 to 1997. A major function for the assembly would be in deciding priorities, and Edward Short had agreed on 3 February 1975 that differing standards would result, but that standards should not become 'too depressed in any one direction'.[64] Expenditure on devolved services in 1974–5 would have been £850m and the block grant £650m, so that deciding priorities, said Harold Wilson on 13 January 1976, represented a high degree of economic, social and political power for members of the assembly. Opponents like Neil Kinnock maintained that there would be little scope to decide on priorities because almost all the finances allocated to the assembly would have to be earmarked. John Morris, however, was convinced that the assembly would be more sensitive to Welsh needs.[65] This claim, Tam Dalyell (Labour, West Lothian) argued later, was 'by implication a damning indictment' of the secretary of state himself.[66] The secretary of state perhaps overstated the improvement in decision-making that could be expected, especially since on 21 March 1974 Denzil Davies, his

[61] Ibid., vol. 922, col. 1782.
[62] *The Times*, 28 November 1975.
[63] Parl. Deb., vol. 922, cols 1570–1.
[64] Ibid., vol. 885, col. 967.
[65] Ibid., vol. 903, cols 224, 293, 612.
[66] Ibid., vol. 947, col. 471.

parliamentary private secretary, admitted that functions were to be transferred to an assembly 'not because the decisions or the end results might be different, but because the people of Wales could then see how the decisions were arrived at in a democratic manner'.[67] While the proposals aroused the hostility of the hard-liners from south-east Wales who thought that the government had gone too far, they were equally unacceptable to many within the Labour movement who demanded an assembly with legislative powers. Therefore, from the outset the proposals had few friends.

The government also announced how the services to be devolved were to be financed and where the assembly was to be housed. The devolved services were to be financed by a block fund, assessed according to need and voted by parliament.[68] Harold Wilson later remarked how the Treasury had seen it as a 'most revolutionary change'.[69] An initial proposal whereby the assembly would be permitted – if it so desired – to levy a surcharge on rates had been dropped.[70] Critics then stated that such a body without revenue-raising powers would be an irresponsible body, since it would not have to face the unpopularity that is associated with the raising of finance.[71] Allowing the assembly to levy a tax would have given it some independence, but EEC regulations did not permit a sales tax and the Treasury did not consider the introduction of a local income tax feasible. Furthermore, the government was only too aware that other regions would demand comparable treatment.[72] If the assembly were to operate from a date immediately following the passing of legislation, the government would have to move quickly to ensure that a suitable building was available. The original choice in August 1975 was the Temple of Peace and Health in Cardiff, and the estimated cost of alteration quoted in June 1976 was £1.7m.[73] Opponents of the proposals, such as Leo Abse and Neil Kinnock, challenged the right of the secretary of state to negotiate for assembly buildings when the assembly had not been approved by parliament, and the decision to do so without submitting the proposal for parliament's examination was termed 'bureaucratic'

[67] Ibid., vol. 870, col. 1441.
[68] *Devolution to Scotland and Wales: Supplementary Statement*, August 1976 (Cmnd. 6585), 7.
[69] Harold Wilson, *Final Term: The Labour Government, 1974–1976* (London, 1979), 48.
[70] *Devolution to Scotland and Wales: Supplementary Statement*, 7.
[71] Parl. Deb., vol. 947, col. 350.
[72] Interview, Michael Foot, 31 March 1984.
[73] Parl. Deb., vol. 897, col. 168; vol. 914, col. 35.

and 'autocratic'.[74] On 26 October 1976 it was announced that, after spending £24,000 on the Temple of Peace and Health, the government had decided to accommodate the assembly in the Exchange Building in Cardiff Bay. Although the capital costs of the Exchange Building were higher, because of lower running costs and greater availability of accommodation the total costs of the two projects were similar. The lease could be terminated after ten years, and the adaptation costs would be £60,000 in 1976–7 and £2.4m in 1977–8.[75] In 1979 it was estimated that the conversion would have cost £3.5m. After £42,000 had been spent on preliminary renovation and repair work completed in 1977, no further costs were incurred.[76]

THE CLAMOUR FOR A REFERENDUM

Long before the government published its detailed proposals, in *Our Changing Democracy: Devolution to Scotland and Wales*, in 1975, there were demands for a referendum. It seems that Labour's commitment to a referendum on membership of the EEC provided the impetus for such a demand. In the Welsh affairs debate on 21 March 1974, Wyn Roberts maintained that 'any major change in Welsh membership of the United Kingdom should be put to the Welsh people'.[77] Demands for a referendum were subsequently made at the annual conference of the Labour Party in Wales in May 1974. At the special conference which followed in June, Emrys Jones rejected a referendum, on the grounds that as a radical party Labour should lead the way and not wait until the demand for devolution was overwhelming. In contrast, the Caerphilly constituency delegates argued that the debate on a call for a referendum at the May conference had been adjourned to the special conference, and they walked out when they were not permitted to put the issue to a vote.[78] The Labour Party in Wales's executive committee agreed to consider the referendum issue, but when it did so the idea was unanimously rejected.[79] On 12 July the general management committee of the Caerphilly

[74]   Ibid., vol. 916, cols 12–13.
[75]   Ibid., vol. 918, cols 948, 946; vol. 923, col. 616.
[76]   Ibid., vol. 963, col. 749.
[77]   Ibid., vol. 870, col. 1430.
[78]   *Western Mail*, 24 June 1974.
[79]   Welsh Council of Labour, *Report to the Annual Meeting*, 9–10 May 1975, 37.

Constituency Labour Party approved the delegates' action and agreed that a telegram should be sent to the secretary of state demanding a referendum. The telegram requested 'that before any, repeat any, government decisions are finalised or implemented on a Welsh Elected Council, that a full Referendum be made among all, repeat all, the people of Wales'.[80] From then on, the Caerphilly Constituency Labour Party, and particularly its secretary, R. K. Blundell, spearheaded a demand for a referendum on the devolution proposals. A campaign was launched to gain support, and following the publication of the White Paper, *Democracy and Devolution: Proposals for Scotland and Wales*, in November, a circular was sent to all Welsh constituency Labour parties on 30 November in which the Caerphilly CLP argued that the Labour Party in Wales had 'not afforded adequate facilities for members of the Constituency Parties in Wales to consider this broad aspect of a Welsh Assembly'. Constituencies were asked to support a referendum and to express their views by notifying MPs, councillors and the Labour Party in Wales, and by writing to Edward Rowlands, under-secretary of state at the Welsh Office, and to the press.[81] Blundell had earlier, on 31 October, claimed in a letter to *The Times* that 'many anxieties would be allayed by the whole-hearted acceptance of the principle that the ultimate decision will be given to the people'.[82] A very unusual situation was now developing: a constituency party was beginning to mount a challenge to the Labour Party in Wales that would gain momentum and prove successful. Why, then, did the Caerphilly CLP adopt such a combative stance? There was a long tradition in the constituency of opposing any form of devolution. Ness Edwards, its former MP, had always been a fierce opponent of nationalism, but there were other factors too. The Caerphilly CLP knew that the Welsh CLPs were divided on the issue, that there was little support among rank and file members and that some Welsh Labour MPs, including its own, were extremely hostile to the proposal. In addition, in Caerphilly they had a very energetic secretary in R. K. Blundell, who was able to advance the constituency's views effectively and successfully. The result of the Caerphilly by-election, which made devolution a more pressing issue within the Labour Party, actually consolidated the opposition to it within the constituency. As Cledwyn Hughes recalled later, a hostile

[80] R. K. Blundell Papers, Caerphilly CLP, GMC, 12 July 1974.
[81] Ibid., Caerphilly CLP circular, 30 November 1974.
[82] *The Times*, 30 October 1974.

reaction from Labour Party members resulted when Plaid Cymru made inroads into the Labour vote.[83]

In a White Paper issued in February 1975, the government explained that a referendum was to be held on membership of the EEC because the issue had implications 'for the political relationship between the United Kingdom and the other Member Governments of the Community, and for the constitutional position of Parliament'.[84] Opponents of the devolution proposals argued in a debate on 3 February that these proposals were comparable to the issue of continued membership of the EEC. The government rejected that argument, on the grounds that devolution was a domestic matter and that the assembly would be subordinate to the jurisdiction of parliament. After Neil Kinnock maintained that the Welsh people had not been directly consulted, the minister of state at the Privy Council Office, Gerry Fowler, reminded him that the people of Wales and of the United Kingdom had been consulted at the previous general election. In that February debate, Gwynfor Evans, when asked by Donald Anderson whether or not he supported a referendum, replied in the affirmative.[85] On 14 March the executive of the Labour Party in Wales issued a news release declaring that it was unanimously opposed to a referendum, and this suggested that the party was taking the referendum demand very seriously.[86] The Caerphilly CLP kept up the pressure, and R. K. Blundell was asked to protest to Emrys Jones

> at the manoeuvres which seemed to be designed to prevent any Referendum on the finalised proposals for a Welsh assembly being permitted and despairing of CLPs' opinion being given any weight in the face of NUM demand for a Welsh Parliament with full legislative powers.[87]

His letter was also sent to other interested constituency Labour parties and to the press. In a further letter to Emrys Jones, on 24 October, the CLP objected to the way in which devolution was promoted and again emphasized that there had not been adequate discussion at local level. It stated that the commitment had come about as a result of manoeuvres by a few Labour Party leaders in

[83]   Interview, Cledwyn Hughes, 29 March 1983.
[84]   *Referendum on United Kingdom Membership of the European Community*, February 1975 (Cmnd. 5925), 2.
[85]   Parl. Deb., vol. 885, cols 965, 1070–1, 1005.
[86]   Labour Party Wales, news release, 14 March 1975.
[87]   R. K. Blundell Papers, Caerphilly CLP, EC, 25 April 1975.

south Wales. Adequate time was needed to examine government proposals, and the CLP declared that it 'would therefore, strenuously resist any further "bull-dozer" tactics being used to curtail the time available for "grass roots" discussion', adding, 'We feel that the use of this time limit tactic in the recent past has contributed to the unsatisfactory situation which exists today'. A copy of this letter was sent to Harold Wilson, to the general secretary of the Labour Party and to the secretary of the Welsh Parliamentary Labour Party, and in a covering letter the CLP stated that it had 'decided on this unusual course of action because of anxiety that the normal channels of communication within the Labour Party may not have succeeded in conveying the intensity of feelings on this issue which exists amongst Party members and supporters in South Wales'.[88] Regional meetings had been held to enable party members to air their views on the devolution proposals, but only a few had attended each meeting. Perhaps not enough time had been given for discussion of the proposals at local level, but it has to be admitted also that CLPs are prone to failing to engage in serious discussion of policy. This has been endemic in CLPs, particularly in Wales. The striking difference this time was that the matter of concern was an aspect of Labour Party policy which applied exclusively to Wales and affected several vested interests.

The referendum call was fast gaining ground in the Labour Party in Wales, and in October 1975 West Flintshire Constituency Labour Party and the Labour groups on the Clwyd and Mid Glamorgan county councils joined forces with Caerphilly Constituency Labour Party, although the Ogmore Constituency Labour Party and the Mid Glamorgan County Labour Party unanimously supported the government's policy. Brecon and Radnor CLP also supported it, but East Flintshire CLP was opposed.[89] Despite the demands, in November Edward Short was not considering a referendum, whereas Emrys Jones thought that although one was very unlikely he did not rule it out altogether; there was not expected to be a free vote because devolution was party policy, and the whole party was expected to support it.[90] On 12 November, just before the publication of *Our Changing Democracy: Devolution to Scotland and Wales*, Fred Evans placed an early-day motion on the order paper calling for a

[88]   Ibid., Caerphilly CLP letter to Emrys Jones, 24 October 1975.
[89]   Private information.
[90]   *Sunday Times*, 2 November 1975; *Western Mail*, 6 November 1975.

referendum; it was supported by Neil Kinnock and Donald Anderson and attracted sixty signatures.[91] Earlier, on 31 July, Anderson had warned the government that it had a potential revolt among its own MPs on its hands. Describing the situation, he said that 'It would be unfortunate if the Government, like generals, looked over their shoulders and found that the troops were not following'.[92] It is worth recording that in February 1969 Fred Evans, a leading advocate of a referendum, Ifor Davies and Ioan Evans had opposed the second reading of the Scotland and Wales (Referenda) Bill introduced by the Liberals.[93] While some Labour MPs were actively promoting the referendum cause, Conservative MPs Michael Roberts and Nicholas Edwards were opposed to it.[94] By December Fred Evans was confident that he would succeed in his demand for a referendum, and R. K. Blundell wondered whether the Welsh were 'being dragged along by the apron strings of Scotland where the Nats. seem to have put the frighteners well and truly on the Labour Party'. Initially, however, Wales was in advance of Scotland, because the Welsh Council of Labour had proposed an elected council back in the 1960s. Blundell also wondered whether the support for a referendum could be pushed 'to the extent of demanding a separate White Paper and separate legislation for Wales as distinct from Scotland'.[95]

From the beginning, John Morris took an uncompromising stand on the referendum issue. On the day that *Our Changing Democracy: Devolution to Scotland and Wales* was published he expressed the view that referenda were 'completely alien to our tradition of parliamentary government', and chided those MPs who wanted their powers retained at Westminster and yet, by advocating a referendum, were prepared to renounce those very powers.[96] The MPs may have been prepared to renounce their powers, but by doing so over this particular issue they were in all probability ensuring their eventual retention. The secretary of state seemed to have all the answers when, in January 1976, he defended the government's attitude and emphasized that the proposals were a manifesto commitment and

[91]   Parl. Deb., vol. 899, col. 1600.
[92]   Ibid., vol. 896, col. 2195.
[93]   Ibid., vol. 777, cols 1829–30.
[94]   *Western Mail*, 18 November 1975; 16 December 1975.
[95]   R. K. Blundell Papers, Caerphilly CLP letter to J. Marek, 6 December 1975.
[96]   *Western Mail*, 28 November 1975.

that he was the guardian of that manifesto.[97] He reminded his constituents that the party conference had rejected a demand for a referendum and, very much aware that it was an instrument deployed to retain the status quo, he added, 'it is a path that any radical or progressive movement would tread at its peril ... It is frequently easier to muster a vote against a proposal than for it. Every prejudice, every vested interest is exploited.'[98] Speaking in the House of Commons on 15 January, he listed a number of practical difficulties, such as what questions would be asked, would the referendum be confined to Scotland and Wales, and how would the results be interpreted if there were no clear majority. While Cledwyn Hughes and Roy Hughes (Labour, Newport) supported him in the debate, he did not get much support from backbenchers.[99] The Labour Party in Wales, in an attempt to halt the referendum campaign, somewhat exaggerated the implications, maintaining that in future other radical changes, such as the extension of public ownership and the abolition of the eleven-plus examination, would have 'to overcome this new hurdle before being put into effect'.[100]

The day following the publication of *Our Changing Democracy: Devolution to Scotland and Wales*, R. K. Blundell announced that a Referendum Action Campaign had been launched to coordinate activities in support of a referendum. The campaign adopted the slogan 'When they say devolution you say referendum', and Blundell, as secretary, wrote to individuals and organizations seeking support.[101] By January, Mid Glamorgan, West Glamorgan, Gwent, Clwyd, Dyfed and Powys county councils and Swansea Borough Council had requested a referendum.[102] Within the Labour movement, demands for a referendum came from the general secretary of the Construction Workers' Union, the Rhondda Constituency Labour Party, Aberystwyth Labour Party and the Swansea Labour Association.[103] The last sent a telegram to the prime minister, Harold Wilson, and a telegram objecting to the assembly was also sent to the prime minister by the Abertillery Constituency Labour

[97] Ibid., 6 January 1976.
[98] Labour Party Wales, news release, 5 January 1976.
[99] Parl. Deb., vol. 903, cols 607, 703, 463.
[100] Labour Party, Welsh Office, *Speakers' Notes on Devolution* (Cardiff, January 1976), 12.
[101] R. K. Blundell Papers, Caerphilly CLP, EC, 28 November 1975; interview, R. K. Blundell, 19 September 1983.
[102] Parl. Deb., vol. 903, col. 902; *Western Mail*, 28 November 1975; 17 January 1976.
[103] *Western Mail*, 27 January 1976; 16 December 1975; Parl. Deb., vol. 903, col. 902.

Party.[104] The Caerphilly Constituency Labour Party knew that every opportunity had to be exploited, and so the executive committee agreed on 19 December that in order to maximize support for the demand for a referendum, all Welsh constituency Labour parties should be requested to submit an identically worded resolution to the annual conference in Swansea in May 1976. Support for such a move was forthcoming from the Neath Constituency Labour Party and from the Swansea Labour Association.[105] The resolution read: 'This Conference instructs the executive committee to take every step necessary to secure a referendum amongst all the electorate in Wales on the *finalised proposals* for a Welsh Assembly.'[106] However, there was little chance of the motion being passed because by then the general council of the Wales TUC had decided to oppose any moves to secure a referendum on the government's proposals.[107] Meanwhile, Conservative spokesmen Nicholas Edwards and Michael Roberts were still not convinced that a referendum was the answer.[108] However, the advocates of a referendum received a boost on 21 January when the *Western Mail*, in its editorial, declared: 'we now believe, in spite of our initial opposition to the idea, that it is becoming harder for the Government to continue to ignore the demands for a Welsh referendum'.[109] The secretary of state and the prime minister remained unmoved.[110] On 19 March the *Western Mail* stated that:

> the setting-up of Welsh and Scottish assemblies, will affect the lives of every single one of us and we now believe that it is right that the Government should discover whether its proposals are in line with a fair percentage of public opinion. We now believe, in short, that there should be a referendum.[111]

The Referendum Action Campaign claimed this change of heart as its first victory. Meanwhile, the advocates of a referendum had been denounced in a document issued by the Labour Party in Wales and which Neil Kinnock described as a 'deliberate bullying tactic'.[112] At

---

104 Private information.
105 Ibid.
106 R. K. Blundell Papers, Caerphilly CLP circular, 6 February 1976.
107 *Western Mail*, 27 January 1976.
108 Parl. Deb., vol. 903, cols 594, 642.
109 *Western Mail*, 21 January 1976.
110 Parl. Deb., vol. 906, col. 1; vol. 907, col. 241.
111 *Western Mail*, 19 March 1976.
112 Ibid., 11 March 1976.

this stage, a compromise might have been possible. In a conciliatory speech in the Welsh Grand Committee on 7 April, Leo Abse asserted that 'Most of us do not want a referendum. What we want is a measure of consensus acceptable to the elected Members for the whole of Wales.' He emphasized that a constitutional change could not be reversed; he did not rule out a move towards devolution, provided it was by 'modest steps'. He suggested measures that could overcome some of the deficiencies that had already been highlighted. A select committee of the House of Commons could be set up to examine civil servants and exercise a measure of control over them. Subcommittees could examine secondary legislation, and a central council of Wales, consisting of elected representatives from local government, could supervise the work of nominated bodies.[113] The alternatives advanced by Abse and other opponents of the bill did not include a directly elected body, and they were to be reminded later by the secretary of state that they had not shown 'Wales the courtesy of working out any democratic alternatives'. Prophetically, he added, 'Devolution will not go away'.[114] According to a *Western Mail* survey of constituency Labour parties taken just before the annual conference of the Labour Party in Wales in May, fifteen constituency parties supported a referendum, twelve were opposed, and nine were undecided.[115] Six resolutions demanding a referendum were submitted to the conference and the composite resolution (submitted by the Caerphilly Constituency Labour Party) was defeated. The conference carried a resolution opposing a referendum on devolution.[116]

By this stage, James Callaghan had become prime minister, and Michael Foot, who had given Edward Short excellent support in the Cabinet, assumed responsibility for devolution as lord president.[117] Callaghan was not an enthusiastic supporter of devolution, but he 'understood the political necessity' to get the legislation on to the statute book.[118] Foot supported devolution not only because it was party policy, but also because he believed in it. The active members of his constituency party in Ebbw Vale were also committed to it.

[113]   Parl. Deb., Welsh Grand Committee, 7 April 1976, cols 76–9.
[114]   *South Wales Echo*, 1 March 1978.
[115]   *Western Mail*, 13 May 1976.
[116]   *Report of the Annual Conference of the Labour Party in Wales*, 14–15 May 1976, 27, 23.
[117]   Interview, Edward Short, 19 December 1984.
[118]   Interview, Michael Foot, 18 July 1984.

Ron Evans, his agent, was closely involved with Emrys Jones and had always been in favour of devolution.[119] In the House of Commons, following the annual conference of the Labour Party in Wales, Foot declared that there would be no referendum and that the general elections in February and October 1974 had been a good test of public opinion in Wales. It would also be difficult to present proposals for devolution to the electorate in the form of a referendum and, in his opinion, the House of Commons was the place to make the decision on how the devolution programme was to proceed.[120] Speaking later, in the debate at the Labour Party conference, he said that a referendum which held up the proposals would be 'justly seen, as a device for escaping from the commitment', and the government was not prepared to give up that commitment. Furthermore, he added, if the government went back on its pledge, its legislative programme would be placed in jeopardy. He went on, 'In order to carry through all we pass at this Conference we must sustain a Labour Government. We must ensure here and now that that Labour Government is kept there.'[121] By then, of course, Labour had lost its overall majority of three seats.[122] Although Foot insisted that the government considered that parliament was competent to pass the proposals without a referendum, he conceded that if, during the Scotland and Wales Bill's passage through parliament, there were proposals that did not delay the bill and the operation of the act, they would be considered. The fact that the government was prepared to contemplate a referendum in certain circumstances was a victory for the pro-referendum lobby. The conference proceeded to pass the resolution, seconded by Ron Evans; Ebbw Vale CLP urged 'the Government to carry out its full manifesto commitment on democratic devolution to Wales and Scotland without any resort to a referendum or any other delaying device'.[123]

Following the Labour Party conference, *The Times* of 1 November was able to reveal that the government was planning a referendum in order to get the Scotland and Wales Bill through the House of Commons. It was anticipated that the government's problems would begin when the bill got to the committee stage and a timetable

---

[119]   Interview, Michael Foot, 18 July and 31 March 1984.
[120]   Parl. Deb., vol. 912, cols 276–7.
[121]   *Labour Party Annual Report*, 1976, 202–3.
[122]   Butler and Kavanagh, *British General Election of 1979*, 19.
[123]   *Labour Party Annual Report*, 1976, 202–3, 196, 198, 210.

would have to be imposed.[124] Whether the government had already decided on a referendum or not, ministers were under increasing pressure in the House of Commons from Leo Abse and Donald Anderson to insert a clause in the bill ensuring that its provisions were subject to the approval of the people of Wales. Abse declared that a failure to do so would mean that he would not support the government, even if there were a six-line whip. Meanwhile, Anderson tried to do a deal with the government. If a referendum clause were inserted, he promised that he and his friends would reconsider their position on the second reading and would adopt a more constructive approach in the following session's debates. He predicted that unless a referendum were conceded, one would be forced on the government by 'cross-party cooperation'.[125] Conservative and Labour MPs did cooperate to oppose the government's devolution proposals. Ian Grist (Cardiff North) was one of three joint secretaries of the Union Flag Group, a backbench group in the Conservative Party whose members chatted informally with dissident Labour MPs.[126] During the debate on the address on 30 November, Michael Foot reiterated what he had said at the Labour Party conference: the government was prepared to consider proposals for a referendum in Scotland and Wales as long as they did not delay the bill's passage in parliament. If, after agreeing to the proposals, the House thought that there should be a referendum, then the government would be prepared to listen. Although Conservative front-bench spokesman Francis Pym agreed that a referendum at some stage could be a valuable guide to the House, Nicholas Edwards insisted that Conservatives had a duty to defeat the bill and only if that failed should a referendum be demanded.[127] The executive of the Labour Party in Wales, however, held out against any compromise and its research officer, J. Vaughan Jones, declared on 10 December: 'The only poll that counts is at the ballot box in a general election.' The Wales TUC added its support, stating that a referendum would be 'both divisive and inconclusive'.[128]

[124] *The Times*, 1 November 1976.
[125] Parl. Deb., vol. 918, cols 1754, 1773.
[126] Interview, Ian Grist, 31 July 1984.
[127] Parl. Deb., vol. 921, cols 828–9, 818; *Western Mail*, 1 December 1976.
[128] *Western Mail*, 11 December 1976.

During the second reading of the Scotland and Wales Bill, in December, the prime minister conceded that the volume of support for referenda impressed the government. It was considering the question, but no conclusion had been reached: it would be influenced by what was said in the debate. The government would make its views known to enable the House to discuss the question during the committee stage; he hoped, having given those assurances, that the bill would be given a second reading. If the government agreed that there should be referenda, it would put down an amendment; if not, it would ensure that time would be provided so that the matter could 'be thrashed out properly with the full information before the House'. Leo Abse's amendment calling for a referendum had gained the support of at least seventy Labour members and twenty Conservative members, and support for a referendum also came from former prime minister, Harold Wilson, and the former Labour Cabinet minister, Douglas Jay. Edward Heath now believed that there should be a referendum and Nicholas Edwards had also come to the same conclusion. During the debate, statements were made which questioned the sovereignty of parliament. Donald Anderson said that 'for a major constitutional change such as this . . . one needs an endorsement greater than that provided by this House', and Wyn Roberts commented that the demand for a referendum was 'based on a distrust of the present proposals and of the judgement of this House'. On the other hand, John P. Mackintosh (Labour, Berwick and East Lothian) pointed out that inviting the electorate to contradict a decision of the House would only reduce parliament's standing, and Cledwyn Hughes warned that referenda would weaken the authority of parliament far more than would assemblies in Wales and Scotland. While the government was prepared to consider a referendum as long as the bill was not impeded, members like Alan Glyn (Conservative, Windsor and Maidenhead) thought that a referendum should be held before any more time was wasted on the bill. Contrariwise, Hugh Jenkins (Labour, Putney) considered that if a referendum were to be held it should take place three years after the assemblies had been established, and experience had shown that the decision then would be to maintain the status quo.[129] The pressure for a referendum came

[129]   Parl. Deb., vol. 922, cols 979–81, 974, 1008, 1594, 1779, 1578, 1421, 1633, 1607, 1649, 1413, 1418, 1353.

from all sides of the House, and after a meeting of the Labour group of anti-devolution MPs on 15 December, Eric Moonman (Labour, Basildon) warned, 'unless Mr Foot tonight is able to go beyond what the Prime Minister said, then the numbers on the Labour side who will abstain or vote against will be fairly substantial'.[130] By 16 December, Leo Abse's amendment had attracted 151 signatures, and the prime minister, in reply to a question, stated that the government's decision would be made known at the commencement of the day's debate. It was clear that a referendum had been conceded. Later that day, John Smith, minister of state at the Privy Council Office, announced that referenda would be held in Scotland and Wales before the act came into effect, and that a new clause would be brought forward during the committee stage for the House's consideration. Abse's demand had been granted in full, and it was his opinion that by conceding a referendum, the government had recognized that it had no mandate to pass the bill.[131] Writing in the *Spectator* on 24 January 1979, immediately before the referendum, he attributed his success not only to the support given to the amendment by Labour and Conservative backbenchers, but also to the presence of a 'fifth column of anti-devolutionists in the Cabinet'.[132] Meanwhile, the government thought that by granting a referendum it had at least saved the bill, but there was more trouble ahead.

One man who must have been bitterly disappointed at the outcome was John Morris: as the self-appointed guardian of the manifesto he had steadfastly rejected a referendum, only now to have one imposed upon him. After an obvious personal defeat, his comment was: 'I did not regard our proposals as tablets from Moses. We were prepared to listen and respond to constructive criticism and comment. This we have done.'[133] That was his answer to his critics, but he did not resign, although opponents and a few among the supporters of devolution thought that it was the only course open to him after such a setback. On the other hand, if he had resigned the Labour rebels would have gained a notable victory, and given the very difficult situation in which the government was placed, the secretary of state's resignation would have added to its

---

[130] *Western Mail*, 16 December 1976.
[131] Parl. Deb., vol. 922, cols 1725–7, 1736–7, 1794.
[132] Leo Abse, 'Exploiting the natives', *Spectator*, 24 January 1979, 9.
[133] *Western Mail*, 17 December 1976.

problems. Furthermore, the secretary of state was personally committed to the policy and he knew that his departure would have left the pro-devolution cause much weakened.

For their part, the Conservatives were intent on excluding Wales from the Scotland and Wales Bill and they tabled an amendment to that effect during the committee stage. Addressing himself to the amendment, Peter Rees (Conservative, Dover and Deal) maintained that the responsibility for considering devolution rested with parliament.[134] On the Labour side, Neil Kinnock defended his action in handing back responsibility to the people, on the grounds that a referendum gave voters a chance to pass direct judgement on the proposals.[135] He said that he was prepared, as a matter of expediency, to support the government against the Conservative amendment to take Wales out of the bill, in order to give the Welsh people an opportunity to reject the bill. Without a referendum, 'the ghost of devolution would still exist in Wales'; a referendum would ensure that no more was heard of it. For him, taking Wales out of the bill would mean throwing out 'the referendum baby with the bathwater'. The Welsh Counties Committee took a similar view and dissociated itself from the decision of the Association of County Councils to support the Conservative amendment. Leo Abse said that he was not prepared to vote with the government in order to reject the amendment because such action could be interpreted as support for a bill that he 'abhorred'.[136] The amendment was duly defeated by a majority of twenty-four.

The original proposal was that the referendum should be mandatory; it was then modified to be a consultative referendum because the government considered that the House of Commons should take the final decision.[137] J. Enoch Powell, now Ulster Unionist MP for South Down, refused to accept that a consultative referendum was different from a mandatory one, for in practice it was just as mandatory and just 'as much an arrogation or usurpation of the sovereignty of the House of Commons'. It was adopted, he said, because the Labour Party was unable to settle its internal conflicts and it provided both sides with a means of escape.[138] That was a

---

[134]   Parl. Deb., vol. 924, cols 99, 181.
[135]   Ibid., vol. 925, col. 255.
[136]   Ibid., vol. 924, cols 150, 101–2, 147, 136, 220.
[137]   Ibid., vol. 925, col. 1691; vol. 926, col. 275.
[138]   Ibid., vol. 926 cols 377, 376.

fair comment on the situation. The Labour Party was hopelessly divided on devolution, and ministers realized that unless a referendum were conceded the House of Commons would not pass the proposals. If they were not passed, the nationalists would withdraw their support for the government, and so its entire legislative programme would be in peril.

GOVERNMENT EXPEDIENTS

Opponents of the Scotland and Wales Bill anticipated that a timetable motion would be introduced, and so in the summer of 1976, before the bill was presented, seventy Labour MPs, led by Tam Dalyell, warned the government that they would not support such a motion.[139] On 22 February 1977, two months after the referendum had been conceded, the government was forced by the bill's slow progress to introduce a timetable motion to ensure that the major proposals would be discussed. In order to secure support, John Smith gave assurances that there would be opportunities to make amendments to the bill in committee and that it could even be rejected on the third reading.[140] MPs reminded Michael Foot that during the debate on the European Communities Bill on 2 May 1972 he had denounced the timetable as 'the last resort of a Government who know that they cannot get the full-hearted consent of Parliament but are determined to have their way in any case', and that he had accused the Conservative government of showing 'full-hearted contempt for the democratic processes of this country; full-hearted contempt for the normal legislative processes of this House of Commons'.[141] Replying, Foot defended his stand on that previous occasion on the grounds that the European Communities Bill was unparalleled, in that it deprived the House of Commons of its sovereign powers. He further reminded the House that he had on occasion argued that timetables had been introduced to enable the House to reach a decision.[142] Since 1974 timetable motions had been debated in connection with the following bills: Finance; Industry; Petroleum and Submarine

---

[139] *The Economist*, 3 July 1976, 18.
[140] Parl. Deb., vol. 926, cols 1355–6.
[141] Ibid., vol. 926, col. 1285; vol. 836, col. 234.
[142] Ibid., vol. 926, col. 1286.

Pipelines; Aircraft and Shipbuilding Industries; Health Services; Dock Work Regulations; Rent (Agriculture); and Education.[143] Those measures were passed with the support of minority parties which wanted to see the devolution proposals enacted. Prior to 1976, the nationalists could have made things difficult for the government; after 1976 their votes were crucial. When the government was being threatened, they gave it their support and Gwynfor Evans had discussions with Foot to ensure that there was cooperation.[144] Foot added that more time was being allocated for discussion of the bill than was allocated to the European Communities Bill and more time than for any other bill since the 1930s. Whilst opponents of the clause on allocation of time maintained that they were being denied the opportunity of reshaping the bill, its supporters claimed that the sole objective of those Labour members who intended voting against the clause was to see the bill halted.[145] In order to gain the support of some at least of those members who intended voting against the clause, Michael Foot went round different groups in the House of Commons and tried to accommodate their anxieties, while emphasizing that devolution was a manifesto commitment.[146] The government did not make the timetable motion an issue of confidence, because it feared that the vote on it might be lost, but 'all kinds of pressures and stratagems' were used to persuade dissident Labour MPs to change their minds.[147] Hours before the crucial vote, a joint deputation from the Labour Party in Wales executive and the Wales TUC met the Welsh Parliamentary Labour Party to impress upon members the importance of supporting government policy.[148] The deputation met with little success because of the six MPs defying the government, only Ifor Davies voted for the timetable motion and it was defeated by twenty-nine votes. In the division, Plaid Cymru MPs Gwynfor Evans, Dafydd Elis Thomas and Dafydd Wigley supported the government, as did the Liberals Emlyn Hooson and Geraint Howells. The remaining eleven Liberals voted against the government.[149] A month after the defeat of the timetable motion, the government concluded a pact with the

---

[143]   Information from Public Information Office, House of Commons, 31 October 1984.
[144]   Interview, Michael Foot, 18 July 1984.
[145]   Parl. Deb., vol. 926, cols 1242, 1325, 1262.
[146]   Interview, Michael Foot, 31 March 1984.
[147]   Private information; Parl. Deb., vol. 925, col. 1738.
[148]   Labour Party Wales, *Report to the Annual Meeting*, 27–8 May 1977, 20.
[149]   Parl. Deb., vol. 926, cols 1361–6.

Liberal Party, because if further progress was to be made Liberal support was essential; yet some Labour MPs would have to be won over, too. That pact remained in force until July 1978.[150] Writing later about the Labour dissidents who had voted against the timetable motion, James Callaghan said, 'I never succeeded in getting any left-wing purist to explain why he should have a dispensation to ignore Conference decisions while he denied the Government, with its greater responsibilities, the right ever to do so.'[151] Dissidents are normally disciplined, but with the government in such a precarious situation action against them would only have caused further problems for party managers.

The defeat of the timetable motion came virtually at the end of James Callaghan's first year as prime minister. It had been a most difficult period for him. There had been a decline in living standards, as wage increases failed to match the increase in prices, and unemployment stood at 5.5 per cent of the labour force in the fourth quarter of 1976 and the first quarter of 1977. Compared with the first quarter of 1974, the unemployment figure had more than doubled. The one consolation for Callaghan was that the number of working days lost in stoppages in 1976 was considerably lower than in 1974 and 1975. The balance of payments continued to be in deficit and reached £511m in the third quarter of 1976, while in December Denis Healey, the chancellor of the Exchequer, announced drastic cuts in planned public spending and excise tax increases. Immediately after the Lib-Lab pact had been concluded, the government suffered further setbacks when two more seats were lost, at Stechford and Ashfield.[152]

Following their success in securing a referendum and in defeating the timetable motion, opponents of the bill endeavoured to secure separate bills for Scotland and Wales. There had been earlier attempts to do so, in 1975. On 24 November 1975, John Morris turned down Caerwyn Roderick's request for two bills, and a similar demand at a meeting of the Welsh Parliamentary Labour Party on 3 December was also rejected.[153] The secretary of state had been most anxious to keep in step with Scotland in every

---

[150] 'Ending of Labour-Liberal co-operation agreement', *Keesing's Contemporary Archives*, 21 July 1978, 29098; private information.
[151] James Callaghan, *Time and Chance* (London, 1987), 450.
[152] Butler and Kavanagh, *British General Election of 1979*, 19–20, 24–5.
[153] Parl. Deb., vol. 901, col. 465; *Western Mail*, 4 December 1975.

respect, short of legislative devolution, and he was later to admit that it was quite an achievement that the government had been persuaded to include two dissimilar measures in the one bill.[154] In the Grand Committee on 7 April 1976, Leo Abse appealed to the secretary of state to insist that there should be a separate bill for Wales, with a long title that would 'allow the widest canvass of views'. Abse was sure that if such a course of action were followed, John Morris would 'find a remarkable degree of good will on all sides in trying to bring the matter to a fair conclusion' and a referendum could be avoided.[155] The government did not respond and the campaign to obtain a separate bill continued. Michael Foot interpreted the demand as an attempt to prevent the implementation of the devolution proposals for Wales, and he claimed that if there were two bills some would argue that precedence should be given to the Scottish bill.[156] The Scottish proposals were more important to the government, and Welsh ministers realized that they stood a better chance of getting the Welsh proposals through by 'clinging hard to the kilts of the oil sheikhs', in Leo Abse's words.[157] Government spokesmen insisted throughout that both sets of proposals should be included in one bill, but the defeat of the timetable motion compelled the government to rethink its strategy. By then, as J. Kerr maintained, the 'sap' had been 'steadily drained away from the Scotland and Wales Bill' by the 'nit-pickers' who had 'set about their destructive labours like so many deathwatch beetles'.[158] At a meeting in June with Michael Foot, representatives of the executive committee of the Labour Party in Wales opposed the proposal for two bills, which was favoured by the Scottish representatives.[159] Foot was able to assure them that no decision had been taken, but on 26 July he announced in the House of Commons that the government thought 'that the House would welcome the separate consideration of dissimilar proposals'.[160] The Labour Party in Wales's immediate response was that the government's proposal was 'yet another mistaken concession' to those whose sole aim was

---

[154]   Morris, review of *The Welsh Veto*, 50.
[155]   Parl. Deb., Welsh Grand Committee, 7 April 1976, col. 79.
[156]   Ibid., vol. 912, col. 274; vol. 924, col. 221.
[157]   Ibid., vol. 924, col. 113.
[158]   J. Kerr, 'The failure of the Scotland and Wales Bill: no will, no way', *Scottish Government Yearbook*, 1978, 114.
[159]   *Labour Party Wales Annual Report*, 1978, 14.
[160]   Parl. Deb., vol. 936, col. 313.

to prevent the policy being implemented. Granting a referendum had been a mistake because opponents 'continued their efforts to wreck the Government's proposals' after it had been granted. The party thought that the concessions had not only failed to overcome opposition, but had 'created an atmosphere of uncertainty and doubt over the whole devolution policy'.[161] The government proceeded to draft a separate bill, and the Wales Bill was presented on 4 November 1977. Plaid Cymru and the Liberals supported it, although both considered it inadequate, but by then the devolution policy had effectively been lost.[162]

During the second reading of the Wales Bill, in November 1977, the government reaffirmed its view that a consultative referendum would be held after the bill had passed through all its stages in parliament; it was considered important that the public should know what they were voting for.[163] In the debates on the Wales Bill, the points made in the debates on the Scotland and Wales Bill were tediously repeated. Although the referendum was to be purely advisory and the assembly was to have no legislative functions, the opponents of the government's proposals were not satisfied with a referendum that would be decided by a simple majority of the electors taking part. The referendum result on EEC membership had rested on a simple majority, and the White Paper *Referendum on United Kingdom Membership of the European Community* had stated that conditions were 'usually intended to make it impossible for constitutional changes to be introduced too easily or by a minority of the electorate'.[164] That was certainly the motive behind the move to insert a threshold requirement of 40 per cent during the committee stage of the Wales Bill in April 1978. The government was at pains to explain that it was very much opposed to the concept and would recommend that it should not be adopted. However, it considered that the House should be given the opportunity of expressing a view and was therefore prepared, if necessary, to move the amendment.[165] The House approved the amendment and the clause was inserted. Plaid Cymru did not support the threshold, and Gwynfor

---

[161] Labour Party Wales, news release, 26 July 1977.
[162] Parl. Deb., vol. 938, col. 163; vol. 939, cols 405, 410, 417–18.
[163] Ibid., vol. 939, col. 364.
[164] *Referendum on United Kingdom Membership of the European Community*, 4.
[165] Parl. Deb., vol. 948, col. 457.

Evans realized that once it was conceded the government's heart was no longer in the bill.[166]

On 6 November the government announced that the referendum would be held on 1 March 1979.[167] John Morris explained that this was the earliest suitable date after the new register came into effect, thus enabling the maximum number of electors to participate. Leo Abse and Welsh Conservatives criticized the choice of St David's Day. Abse said that it was a day that had 'unpleasant chauvinistic overtones, a chauvinism so alien to the whole international mood and spirit of the Welsh Labour movement'. To Nicholas Edwards it was an attempt 'to create a wave of patriotic enthusiasm to build up an Arms Park atmosphere', and 'to play the joker of patriotism and, with it, to trump reasoned argument'. John Morris took the opportunity to clarify the position regarding the 40 per cent threshold requirement. He explained that 'the strict determination' of what constituted 40 per cent of the electorate was important in determining whether an order repealing the act should be laid, but that it would not determine the fate of the act because it would be parliament's and the government's responsibility to 'exercise a judgement' based on the referendum result. The question of what was a significant threshold would have to be decided by parliament, and Donald Anderson (who did not support the threshold) and Nicholas Edwards agreed that 35 per cent for and 25 per cent against would be a sufficient vote. Michael Roberts concurred that if there were a substantial majority in favour, even though the 40 per cent vote were not quite reached, the House would decide that the will of the Welsh people had been clearly stated and it would act accordingly.[168]

Although the government had been forced to make several concessions to its opponents, if the main grounds that it had originally put forward in support of its proposals were valid ones, they should surely still apply. Government ministers claimed from the outset that there was a feeling of alienation in certain parts of the country which were remote from London, and that there was 'a deep underlying desire' in Wales for changes in the structure of government.[169] On the other hand, it was possible that the government's

[166]   Ibid., vol. 949, cols 258, 1073.
[167]   Ibid., vol. 957, col. 484.
[168]   Ibid., vol. 958, cols 1338, 1358, 1385–6, 1340–1, 1352–3, 1363.
[169]   Ibid., vol. 885, cols 969, 1185.

opponents were right and that these were arguments that could not be sustained.

ENGLISH HOSTILITY AND THE WIDER DEBATE

The government's failure to formulate proposals for England aroused the hostility of some English MPs, and they were supported by economic planning councils and by local authorities in the regions. In March 1974 Richard Wainwright (Liberal, Colne Valley) maintained that a situation could not be tolerated where some parts had representation in assemblies and parliament and others had representation in parliament only. In reply, the government argued that it had been decided to proceed with Scotland and Wales because the issues there were more pressing.[170] In June 1974 the executive of the Labour Party in Wales stressed, in a statement, *Devolution and Democracy*, prepared for the special conference at Llandrindod Wells, that a Welsh council should be part of a radical transformation in government procedure throughout the United Kingdom. Wales was merely to lead the way.[171] This was also underlined in the National Executive Committee's document *Bringing Power Back to the People*, issued in the following September.[172] At that time, Emrys Jones went further when he said that the creation of assemblies in Scotland and Wales and the regions of England would precede the reform of the House of Lords and that the assemblies could nominate members to sit in the reformed chamber, thus establishing a link between central and regional government.[173] In February 1975, T. W. Urwin (Labour, Houghton-le-Spring) expressed the concern of MPs from the English regions. They feared that their areas would lose out to the Scots and the Welsh, who would be able to take decisions that could be damaging to other regions' interests. Urwin declared that the northern region, with the highest percentage of unemployment, did not intend to remain silent on the question of devolution.[174] This fierce opposition from northern MPs arose principally because Scotland had its

---

[170] Ibid., vol. 870, cols 1090, 1197.
[171] Labour Party in Wales, *Devolution and Democracy*.
[172] Labour Party, *Bringing Power Back to the People*, 5.
[173] *Western Mail*, 27 September 1974.
[174] Parl. Deb., vol. 885, cols 1195, 1197.

own development agency, whereas their own region had no such body. Some northern MPs ignored the wishes of their constituency parties because they were only too aware that the government's survival depended on their support.[175] The questions of regional government and the extension of democracy in England were never taken seriously enough by the Labour government, and its failure to indicate clearly in *Our Changing Democracy: Devolution to Scotland and Wales* that the proposed changes in respect of Wales and Scotland would be followed by similar changes in the regions of England was regretted in a statement issued on 20 February 1976 by the executive committee of the Labour Party in Wales.[176] Indeed, this failure before publication of the White Paper was one of the causes of the opposition from MPs representing some English constituencies. Commenting earlier, on 26 January, on the government's proposals, the *Western Mail* thought that they 'would have had an easier ride had the Government published its Green Paper on regional government in England at the same time'; it then added prophetically, 'The fact that it did not do so may yet prove to have been a grave tactical error'.[177]

Speaking in Liverpool, on 17 September 1976, the former prime minister, Harold Wilson, declared:

> In the Parliamentary Party there is deep concern among a substantial number of Labour MPs, a natural concern, that the provision of additional resources to aid the economic and social regeneration of both Scotland and Wales may prove to be at the expense of hard-hit areas in various parts of England. These anxieties must be taken seriously.

In his view the answer was to provide a real measure of devolution of responsibilities from Whitehall to the regions of England. The creation of such regional authorities would perhaps necessitate the removal of one local government tier. He thought that there should be a national debate on his proposal, but if democracy was to be strengthened the devolution legislation should be passed.[178] At the Labour Party conference in October, Michael Foot repeated the assurance that had been given earlier, in August. He said that fulfilling the promise to give assemblies to Scotland and Wales did

[175] Interviews: Edward Short, 19 December 1984; Michael Foot, 31 March 1984.
[176] Labour Party Wales, comments of the Executive Committee on *Our Changing Democracy: Devolution to Scotland and Wales* (Cmnd. 6348), 20 February 1976.
[177] *Western Mail*, 26 January 1976.
[178] *Liverpool Daily Post*, 18 September 1976.

not mean that regional policies and assistance to other areas were to be abandoned. At the conference a resolution against the devolution of economic powers to Scotland and Wales without guarantees of similar financial provision for the regions of England, including a development agency for the north, was defeated on a card vote. A delegate from the north-east, seconding the motion, maintained that the north-east was in a worse predicament than Scotland or Wales and that the gap was increasing all the time. The Celts had their development agencies, but Lord Ryder's promise that the area would get its fair proportion of investment was not adequate for the Labour electors in the north-east. He predicted that once the bill reached 'the floor of the House, its unfairness, its divisiveness, its dangers and its fundamentally reactionary nature' would be so glaring that Labour members would 'consign it to the historical dustbin'.[179] Harold Wilson later confirmed that the creation of the Scottish and Welsh development agencies had increased the anxieties of MPs representing English constituencies, and he added:

> They would have been still more worried had they heard – or since read – the evidence of the SDA given in Edinburgh to the Committee of Inquiry into Financial Institutions in December 1977 and that of the WDA in February 1978, recording the extent of their activities.

On 31 March 1979 the SDA's assets were £126.740 m and those of the WDA £105 m.[180]

Trouble was looming for the government, as was clear during the debate on the address in November, when one MP explained that his loyalty had to be to his constituents.[181] The government clearly needed to show that some provision for England would follow and so, belatedly, in 1976, it issued a consultative document entitled *Devolution: The English Dimension*. Some of its arguments advanced against regional councils in England were equally applicable to the form of devolution proposed for Wales. Those arguments were that a considerable number of staff would be required, that ministers' abilities to 'maintain national policies on devolved subjects' would be reduced, that the scope of MPs' work would be restricted and that a block grant would make the 'Government's task of economic

---

[179] Parl. Deb., vol. 916, col. 1464; *Labour Party Annual Report*, 1976, 202, 194, 196.

[180] Wilson, *Final Term*, 49; information from Scottish Development Agency and Welsh Development Agency.

[181] Parl. Deb., vol. 921, col. 799.

management more difficult'. It was claimed, too, that there would have to be public support 'for the acceptance of potentially differing policies and standards'. Furthermore, the revised local government structure and new structures for the administration of the health, water and police services were in the 'process of settling down', and if one set of changes was followed by another 'the point may come at which the penalties of the process of change outweigh the advantages which it is hoped ultimately to achieve'. Reorganization would also confuse the average elector and 'he would feel more remote from the affairs of a local government body administering services over a much wider area'.[182] Writing in 1977, in the *Political Quarterly*, Lewis Gunn made the following observation on the document: 'In other words, all the problems identified by critics of Welsh and Scottish devolution which were played down by the Government are here played up in order to block such needless and disruptive innovations in England. The anti-devolution case could not be in better hands.'[183]

Two former ministers considered the document to be wholly unsatisfactory. Lord Crowther-Hunt, the former constitutional adviser to the government, maintained in *The Times* on 21 December that the document was misleading, because devolution to Scotland and Wales would have a greater effect on England than the document led people to believe; while Gerry Fowler, the former minister of state at the Privy Council Office, described it on 13 December as a 'wet and windy' document. He claimed that until a decision was taken regarding England, the situation in Scotland and Wales would be unsatisfactory because the assemblies could not be given powers to raise taxes.[184] Although critical of the document, Fowler was and remained a keen advocate of devolution all round. Writing in 1984, he explained that his views on devolution, which he had stated on thirteen occasions in Wales during the referendum campaign, remained unchanged: 'They stem from the belief that we need a national/regional tier of Government *throughout the U.K.*: too much is centralised.'[185]

[182] *Devolution: The English Dimension*, 1976, 13, 17–19.

[183] Lewis Gunn, 'Devolution: a Scottish view', *Political Quarterly*, 48, 2 (April–June 1977), 139.

[184] Lord Crowther-Hunt, 'Will England come off third best on devolution day?', *The Times*, 21 December 1976; Parl. Deb., vol. 922, cols 1079, 1081.

[185] Information from G. T. Fowler, 21 December 1984.

MPs from the English regions continued to voice their objections to the proposals, and during the debate on the timetable motion on 22 February 1977 Colin Phipps (Labour, Dudley West) said quite bluntly that if there were to be devolution it had to be devolution all round. Arthur Blenkinsop (Labour, South Shields) was one MP who took a different view from that of his colleagues in the north-east. The people there would not escape from their difficulties by opposing devolution to Scotland and Wales, and it was up to them to demand a 'development agency or some regional development of the National Enterprise Board' – and in the long term an elected assembly.[186] The rebellion of northern MPs against the timetable motion secured a number of concessions for the region: the head-quarters of British Shipbuilders were located in the northern region; the Central Electricity Generating Board, on the government's instructions, placed an order for a power station with a northern firm, C. A. Parsons; in the second quarter of 1977 the 'proportion of regional relevant public expenditure per head' in the north was the highest in the United Kingdom; and in November 'substantial inner-city aid' was given to Newcastle and Gateshead.[187] On 8 November 1977 Eric Varley, the secretary of state for Industry announced a greater role for the regional boards of the National Enterprise Board to deal with the problems in the north-east, Merseyside and the north-west. It was immediately said that the creation of the regional boards was an inducement to secure the support of MPs from those areas for the Scotland Bill.[188] On 15 November Nicholas Budgen (Conservative, Wolverhampton South West) described the proposal for regional offices of the National Enterprise Board in the north-west and the north-east as a 'crude and obvious form of bribery of those two regions'.[189] As Roger Guthrie and Iain McLean point out, the 'list of concessions, symbolic and concrete, accruing to the Northern Region since the guillotine rebellion demonstrates the potential value of "exit" (that is, the withholding of support in the division lobbies) as a strategic weapon to regional groups of MPs'.[190] The government was asked

---

[186] Parl. Deb., vol. 926, cols 1340, 1330.
[187] Roger Guthrie and Iain McLean, 'Another part of the periphery: reactions to devolution in an English development area', *Parliamentary Affairs*, 31, 2 (Spring 1978), 198–9.
[188] Parl. Deb., vol. 938, cols 527, 598.
[189] Ibid., vol. 939, col. 484.
[190] Guthrie and McLean, 'Another part of the periphery', 198–9.

to consider the possibility of establishing a West Midlands agency.[191] It was also argued that people in the West Midlands had seen work withdrawn from the area and industrial development certificates refused, in order that employment might go to the people of Scotland and Wales. MPs pointed out that the favoured treatment of Wales was the result of the loud 'bark' of its Labour MPs, and that on the basis of need Wales was already receiving a higher level of support than their areas, for example, in the level of rate-support grant.[192] The Welsh Development Agency and the Development Board for Rural Wales were seen as threats to the prosperous areas close to the Welsh border, and Nicholas Budgen demanded that the secretary of state for Wales, who was responsible to the United Kingdom parliament, should exercise their functions.[193]

The economic planning councils were also opposed to the Scottish and Welsh proposals. In January 1976 the Northern Economic Planning Council pointed out that although Scotland and Wales had their development agencies, the National Enterprise Board would operate in both countries as well as in England.[194] The North-West Economic Planning Council considered that all functions other than those not exercised by central government should be the responsibility of local authorities, because there was no room for a form of regional government between central and local government.[195] The Council's views were forwarded to the Department of the Environment on 28 January 1976. There was concern, too, in the traditionally prosperous West Midlands. The chairman of the West Midlands Economic Planning Council, writing to the minister for Planning and Local Government in February 1976, explained how the Council's views had hardened since 1974. The Council was opposed to assemblies and the retention of full Scottish and Welsh representation at Westminster, which would give Scotland and Wales a louder voice than was justified, and he emphasized that 'United Kingdom economic policy should reflect the economic needs of the English regions, no less than those of Scotland and Wales'. It was feared that assemblies, together with

---

[191]   Parl. Deb., vol. 938, col. 585.
[192]   Ibid., vol. 939, cols 672–3, 704.
[193]   Ibid., vol. 949, cols 337–9.
[194]   Northern Economic Planning Council, views on *Our Changing Democracy*, 28 January 1976, 2.
[195]   North-West Economic Planning Council to the Department of the Environment, giving the Council's view on *Our Changing Democracy*, 28 January 1976, 1.

over-representation at Westminster, would increase the tendency to divert resources from the more prosperous areas to Scotland and Wales. The Council's anxieties were exacerbated by the economic decline of the West Midlands, and unless care was taken the English regions would 'find themselves forced to organise defensively, to press their own political and economic interests against those of their neighbours'.[196] In its evidence submitted in January 1970 to the Commission on the Constitution, the Labour Party in Wales had admitted that firms would not have been attracted 'had it not been for the policy which combined disincentives in congested industrial areas with attractions in development areas'.[197] The West Midlands Economic Planning Council felt that such policies had already damaged its economy and that the damage was likely to be more extensive if the devolution proposals were approved. In its observations on *Devolution: The English Dimension*, the Yorkshire and Humberside Economic Planning Council claimed that the proposals would adversely affect the economy of the region, and that the break-up of the United Kingdom could follow. There was no need for devolution of a similar nature in the region, and requirements could be met by nominated advisory bodies, similar to the economic planning councils but with more influence over the distribution of resources between regions. The Council feared that Scotland and Wales, with their secretaries of state, assemblies and generous allocation of MPs, would get a larger share of national resources than their entitlement. It considered that the two regions were at the time receiving a higher proportion of financial aid than was their due, and it was unhappy about the effects on English regions of the Water Charges Equalisation Bill, which would give advantages to Wales. The Council conceded that although there was no demand for English assemblies, there was more support for bringing health and water authorities under some form of democratic control.[198]

Local authorities in the regions also voiced their objections to the devolution proposals. Tyne and Wear County Council, which had been Labour-controlled since its inception in 1974, passed a resolution

[196] Chairman, West Midlands Economic Planning Council to John Silkin, Minister for Planning and Local Government, 19 February 1976, 1–2, 4.

[197] *Evidence of the Labour Party in Wales to the Commission on the Constitution*, 8.

[198] Yorkshire and Humberside Economic Planning Council, draft views on *Devolution: The English Dimension*, 1–3, 7.

on 27 November 1975, the very day that *Our Changing Democracy: Devolution to Scotland and Wales* was issued; this resolution deplored any proposals to extend power to Scotland since that would 'adversely affect the economy of the English regions and would inevitably lead to the break-up of the United Kingdom and to separatism'. A similar motion was passed in January 1977, and at a seminar organized by the Council on 7 January the leader of the Council declared: 'devolution has got to be based on equal treatment and I mean equal treatment for the English regions, for Scotland and for Wales'. The participants at the seminar included Tam Dalyell, George Lawson, director of the Scotland is British campaign and a former MP for Motherwell, T. W. Urwin, W .H. Sefton, the leader of Merseyside County Council, and Stanley Yapp, the leader of West Midlands County Council.[199] Merseyside County Council also organized a seminar on 4 March 1977 at which the speakers included Tam Dalyell and Eric Heffer; its conclusions were sent by letter to the prime minister. At the seminar it was agreed that devolution for Scotland and Wales should not be discussed by parliament until its implications for England had been worked out and that the promotion of a bill for Scotland and Wales would be divisive.[200] Merseyside County Council, at a further meeting on 24 June 1977, reaffirmed its views on devolution. It considered that the proposals would prevent the restoration of powers to local authorities and it resolved to initiate a dialogue to achieve decentralization throughout the United Kingdom.[201]

The fact that no proposals were formulated for the regions of England confirmed to opponents that the bills were inspired by the upsurge in nationalism. Writing after the referendum, in the *Spectator* on 10 March, Vernon Bogdanor agreed that 'the Scotland and Wales Acts were born, not out of a principled belief in the dispersal of power from Whitehall, but from expediency'.[202] For some Labour MPs, like Ioan Evans, nationalism was an 'evil' force, while Leo Abse argued that the Scotland and Wales Bill was particularly evil because it would 'inflame and encourage . . . the menace

---

[199] Tyne and Wear County Council, *Devolution: The Case Against. Is This a United Kingdom?*, document produced following a seminar on 7 January 1977, 2, 4.

[200] Merseyside County Council, *Devolution: The Prospects*, report of a one-day seminar held on 4 March 1977, 10.

[201] Ibid., Devolution CSS/128/77, report of the County Solicitor and Secretary to the Merseyside County Council Policy, Planning and Resources Committee, 9 December 1977.

[202] Vernon Bogdanor, 'The defeat of devolution', *Spectator*, 10 March 1979, 13.

of nationalism'.[203] Unfortunately, Abse failed to see that there was a
rational argument for the reform of the machinery of government.
To him devolution was merely an attempt to appease nationalists.[204]
Cledwyn Hughes, speaking in May 1978 during the Wales Bill's
final stages through the House of Commons, maintained that the
proposals did not violate the tenets of socialism, as some declared.[205]
He referred to the views of Arthur Henderson, a former chairman
of the Parliamentary Labour Party, who in 1918 had written: 'It is,
therefore, a perfectly natural development of Labour policy that a
comprehensive scheme of separate legislative assemblies for
Scotland, Wales, and even England – as well as for Ireland – is put
forward as an integral part of its general programme of reconstruction'. In Henderson's view, there was 'no necessary antagonism
between the international spirit and the sentiment of nationality'.[206]
Sixty years later, Walter Padley, a former chairman of the Labour
Party, expressed the same view in the Welsh affairs debate. He
argued that 'The demand for Home Rule for Scotland and Home
Rule for Wales, to which the Bill is a modest step, is not inconsistent
with internationalism in either Europe or in the whole world'.[207]

Shortly after the February 1974 general election, John Morris
argued that it was important that the elected body set up should be
'a developing instrument, its powers being shaped in the light of
experience and the democratic needs and aspirations of the people
of Wales'.[208] That reference to 'a developing instrument' alarmed
MPs, and in November 1975, prior to the publication of the White
Paper, they expressed fears that devolution would merely be a first
stage on the way to independence.[209] This view was shared by
Frank Chapple, general secretary of the EETPU, who stated at the
Labour Party conference in October 1976: 'It (the bill) will be the
biggest stimulus to nationalism that there has ever been and I do not
think anything can stop this nation from sliding into the disastrous
separatism that will result.'[210] Like Chapple, Wyn Roberts maintained, during the second reading of the Wales Bill in November

[203] Parl. Deb., vol. 922, cols 1341, 1791.
[204] Ibid., vol. 959, col. 396.
[205] Ibid., vol. 949, col. 1034.
[206] Arthur Henderson, 'Home rule all round', *Welsh Outlook*, 5 (1918), 184–5.
[207] Parl. Deb., vol. 949, col. 1044.
[208] Ibid., vol. 870, col. 1365.
[209] Ibid., vol. 899, col. 1612; vol. 903, col. 652.
[210] *Labour Party Annual Report*, 1976, 201.

1977, that the proposals gave 'the biggest fillip to nationalism and separatism' that they had received for a long time.[211] Plaid Cymru MPs supported the bill, even though they considered it inadequate, and to its opponents – like Nicholas Edwards – that was conclusive proof that the nationalists hoped it would be a first step to home rule.[212] The government tried hard but unsuccessfully to combat these arguments. Edward Rowlands, a Foreign Office minister, had assured Labour supporters early in 1976 that it was 'no part of the lead being given by the Labour movement in Wales to propose devolution as a first stage towards home rule', but many felt that this would be the inevitable consequence.[213] During the second reading of the Scotland and Wales Bill, in December 1976, John Smith for the government, acknowledged that it rested on the assumption that both countries wished to preserve the union, and 'on an assumption of basic political maturity, wisdom, skill and moderation both in Scotland and Wales and at Westminster'. In the debate, Nicholas Edwards for the Opposition claimed that there would be conflict between the assembly and parliament, because the assembly, unlike local authorities, would claim to speak for a nation, and would therefore be in a position to challenge parliament's authority, particularly when such an assembly was expected to execute the policies of a government of a different political hue. In arguing that there would be constant clashes and conflicts if the bill were passed, Edwards (in Douglas Jay's words) 'greatly exaggerated the horrors' that would result.[214]

On 3 February 1975, before the detailed proposals were announced, Neil Kinnock maintained that proposals that could jeopardize the unity of the United Kingdom had to be resisted. For him, a single parliament for the United Kingdom could do more for working people than an assembly in Cardiff. Kinnock time and time again emphasized class interests and saw himself as the emancipator of the working classes. In his view, their emancipation was more likely to be achieved when working-class people across the United Kingdom stood together against 'any bully, any Executive, any foreign Power, any bureaucratic arrangement be it in Brussels

---

[211]   Parl. Deb., vol. 939, col. 437.
[212]   Ibid., vol. 948, col. 1222.
[213]   *Western Mail*, 3 April 1976.
[214]   Parl. Deb., vol. 922, cols 1753, 1580–1, 1589.

or Washington'. In a letter to the *Western Mail* on 1 December 1976, he wrote:

> If EEC membership or the devolution proposals gave advantage to the working class of my constituency, of Wales or of Britain, I would support either or both of them. But they don't and consistency with the whole idea of representation persuades me that I should oppose both.[215]

Kinnock's view that essentially he was in parliament to promote the interests of a particular class was becoming increasingly irrelevant. Writing at the end of the decade, Vernon Bogdanor, quoting Suzanne Berger, made the point that in western Europe, and in Britain in particular, 'The weakening of old class and corporatist ideologies had created a political space in which new ideas and explanations of the world have a better chance of survival'.[216] At the time that Kinnock was expressing his concern for the unity of the United Kingdom, some Conservatives did not see devolution as a threat to that unity. Malcolm Rifkind (Edinburgh Pentlands) thought that the unity of the United Kingdom could be reconciled with devolution. He therefore supported it.[217] Nearly two years later, during the second reading of the Scotland and Wales Bill, Edward Heath said that he supported devolution in order to maintain the union.[218] Yet Labour members who represented English constituencies, such as Ted Leadbitter (Hartlepool), continued to express their concern that the proposals would weaken the unity of the United Kingdom and considered it their duty to defend that unity.[219] The government was just as committed to the unity of the kingdom, but it took the view that by allowing a Scottish and a Welsh dimension to emerge in the constitutional structure within the context of the United Kingdom that unity would be strengthened, rather than weakened.[220] Indeed, advocates of more radical reform – like Tom Nairn (whose work represented a 'Marxist reflection on the United Kingdom') – thought that English members had no reason to be concerned, because the proposals were designed to maintain the old order. They were, said Nairn, 'at heart ways of

---

[215] Ibid., vol. 885, col. 1031; *Western Mail*, 1 December 1976.
[216] Suzanne Berger, 'Bretons and Jacobins', in Milton J. Esman (ed.), *Ethnic Conflict in the Modern World* (Cornell, 1977), 175, quoted by Bogdanor, *Devolution*, 7.
[217] Parl. Deb., vol. 885, cols 1032, 1059.
[218] Ibid., vol. 922, col. 1776.
[219] Ibid., vol. 924, cols 485–6.
[220] Ibid., vol. 926, col. 1360.

preserving the old state – minor alterations to conserve the antique essence of English hegemony. There was no real belief in a new partnership of peoples.'[221] The only party advocating such a radical reform was the Liberal Party. D. N. MacIver, writing later, in 1982, shared Nairn's view. He maintained that most reforms of the machinery of government have 'been an attempt to accommodate the needs of central administration to ethno-regional political demands while still maintaining the balance in favour of the former'.[222] This reluctance to yield centralist power has been a characteristic of the British state in modern times, as successive secretaries of state for Wales quickly learned. Cledwyn Hughes later acknowledged that 'governments of whatever colour, and the Civil Service, have stood firm against any tendency towards devolution for Wales'.[223]

THE MAJOR ISSUES

Executive devolution was seen as a threat to local government, and that led to intense debate both inside and outside parliament. Local authority leaders in Wales were all too aware of the stand of the Labour Party since the mid 1960s, and they now feared the worst. In the 1960s they had been divided on the issue of an all-Wales authority when the party had suggested to the secretary of state that an elected council should be established as a top tier of local government. Again, in 1970, when the Labour Party in Wales, in its evidence to the Commission on the Constitution, stated that an elected council should be firmly rooted in local government, both the Welsh Counties Committee and the Association of Welsh Local Authorities went out of their way to state in their evidence that while they supported an elected council, they opposed any loss of functions by local authorities.[224] After parliament passed the bill for the reorganization of local government in 1972, Labour leaders accepted that a second reorganization within a short space of time was not possible. Speaking in February 1973 at the Labour Party local government conference, Harold Wilson reiterated what

---

[221] Tom Nairn, *The Break-Up of Britain: Crisis and Neo-Nationalism* (London, 1977), 62–3.
[222] D. N. MacIver, 'Ethnic identity in the modern state', in Colin H. Williams (ed.), *National Separatism* (Cardiff, 1982), 303–4.
[223] Lord Cledwyn, *Wales Yesterday and Tomorrow* (Bro Colwyn, 1995), 9.
[224] Commission on the Constitution, *Written Evidence 7: Wales* (1972), 68, 2, 5.

Labour spokesmen had said in the conference of the previous year, namely, that 'the next Labour Government would not throw the whole of local government into the melting-pot with all the disruption and unsettlement that would create'.[225] In a speech to the Association of District Councils, Peter Shore said that 'Reorganisation is a fact and I do not have any proposals to undo it; after one major operation I doubt if the patient is yet strong enough to undergo another'. The party had stated, however, that it reserved the right to make amendments to the Act where these might be required.[226] In Wales, Emrys Jones had not said categorically that local government would not be reorganized. After the Commission on the Constitution published its report in October 1973, he commented that an elected council would probably not mean a reorganization of local government, but 'sooner or later the two would have to be "married together"'.[227] In its Welsh manifesto for the February general election of 1974, the Labour Party adhered to the view taken earlier by Peter Shore, and declared that it reserved the right to amend parts of the local government legislation, particularly in relation to south Wales.[228] By June the executive committee of the Labour Party in Wales had accepted in its statement *Devolution and Democracy*, which was endorsed by the special conference, that it was not practical for local government tier to be reorganized again.[229] The local authorities were much relieved that the party had accepted the local government changes as a fait accompli, and in July the Welsh Counties Committee and the Council of the Principality, representing the district councils, issued statements supporting an elected council. The former stipulated that it should control 'all regional outposts of central government', and the latter that it should control nominated bodies and should not administer local government functions.[230] Therefore, at that stage the Labour Party in Wales was not at odds with the local authority associations. In its Welsh manifesto for the October general election, *Wales will win with Labour*, the party stated categorically that 'We do not envisage that the Assembly will be given any of the existing functions carried out by Local Authorities in Wales'.[231] Just before the October election, the

---

[225] Harold Wilson, 'Democracy in local affairs', *Edinburgh Series of Policy Speeches*, 2 (1973), 4.
[226] Wilson, *Final Term*, 195.
[227] *Western Mail*, 30 October 1973.
[228] Y Blaid Lafur, *Polisïau Llafur ar gyfer dyfodol gwell i Gymru* (Caerdydd, Chwefror 1974).
[229] Labour Party in Wales, *Devolution and Democracy*.
[230] *Western Mail*, 11 July 1974; 20 July 1974.
[231] Labour Party, *Wales will win with Labour*.

National Executive Committee in *Bringing Power Back to the People*, also concluded that to take powers away from local government would undermine the aims of bringing power closer to the people.[232] That was also the view of the Labour government, and early in 1975, Edward Short and Gerry Fowler, the two ministers in charge of devolution, reaffirmed that the assembly would not be taking powers away from local authorities and that there was no intention of reorganizing local government in the foreseeable future.[233] That remained the government's view as late as April 1976, when John Morris explained in the Welsh Grand Committee that the aim was 'the democratisation of an existing level'.[234]

In the meantime, the Labour Party in Wales had changed its attitude. It announced in January 1976 that a review of local government was being conducted so that proposals could be formulated to create a better structure of local government as soon as the assembly was established.[235] Then, in February, Denzil Davies, the secretary of state's parliamentary private secretary, claimed that once a fourth tier was created there would be sufficient reason for the reorganization of the much-criticized local government structure.[236] Alwyn Roberts and Alun Jones (chief executive of Gwynedd), writing in July in the *County Councils Gazette*, saw his remarks as 'dangling the carrot of reorganisation' before a people who were not enthusiastic supporters of an elected assembly.[237] In the Welsh Grand Committee in April, John Morris was urged by Cledwyn Hughes to give further thought to the reform of local government, and in May the Labour Party in Wales's annual conference passed the following resolution: 'Conference calls on the Government to make a firm commitment to restructure Local Government in Wales, merging County and District Councils into single tier multi-purpose Authorities, as a matter of urgency.'[238] Immediately there was a change in government policy. On 25 May Michael Foot announced that another approach would have to be taken to the

[232] Labour Party, *Bringing Power Back to the People*, 9.
[233] Parl. Deb., vol. 885, cols 29, 1076.
[234] Ibid., Welsh Grand Committee, 7 April 1976, col. 8.
[235] Labour Party, Welsh Office, *Speaker's Notes on Devolution*, 11.
[236] *Western Mail*, 14 February 1976.
[237] Alwyn Roberts and Alun Jones, 'Devolution and local government', supplement to the *County Councils Gazette*, July 1976, 1.
[238] Parl. Deb., Welsh Grand Committee, 7 April 1976, cols 25–6; *Report of the Annual Conference of the Labour Party in Wales*, 14–15 May 1976, 23.

subject.[239] The opposition of local authorities and their staffs could be expected. Restructuring would not be a return to the pre-1974 situation, and it would take several years to plan, thus creating a further period of uncertainty after one of change. Alwyn Roberts and Alun Jones concluded that 'There is a point at which debate must be closed and change allowed time to settle and seek to justify itself. We believe that this point has been reached in local government in Wales.'[240] In *Devolution to Scotland and Wales: Supplementary Statement*, which was issued in August, the government announced its revised plans. It would 'ask the Assembly to consider and report, after appropriate consultations, on future local government structure in Wales in the context of the Assembly's own new responsibilities for the whole of Wales'.[241] Jack Brooks, James Callaghan's agent and the leader of South Glamorgan County Council, thought that the government in its new devolution statement had responded swiftly to 'grassroots opinion in Wales'.[242] It had certainly acceded in part to the demand of the executive committee of the Labour Party in Wales when it declared that the structure of local government should be re-examined. The Labour Party in Wales issued a press release on 3 August 1976 in which it stated:

> We welcome the Government's recognition that there is a need for another look at the structure of Local Government in Wales and their decision to ask the Assembly to consider and report on this question. We reaffirm our view that the Government itself should make a firm commitment to restructure Local Government in Wales as a matter of urgency.[243]

On the day that this statement was issued Michael Foot made the remark that the proposal for an assembly would 'provide the opportunity for making proposals for the drastic changes in local authorities', which must have sent a chill down the spine of the leaders of Labour-controlled authorities in south Wales.[244] These councillors exercised considerable power and because they had a vested interest in maintaining the status quo, they joined forces with

---

[239] Parl. Deb., vol. 912, col. 282.
[240] Roberts and Jones, 'Devolution and local government', 8.
[241] *Devolution to Scotland and Wales: Supplementary Statement*, 8.
[242] *Western Mail*, 4 August 1976.
[243] Labour Party Wales news release, 3 August 1976, on *Devolution to Scotland and Wales: Supplementary Statement*.
[244] Parl. Deb., vol. 916, cols 1462–3.

those MPs who opposed an elected assembly. Indeed, it could be said that they were the people who really counted in the Labour Party in Wales.

Speaking in December, during the second reading of the Scotland and Wales Bill, John Morris explained that the bill did not propose to take away responsibilities from local authorities, but opponents nonetheless feared that local authority functions were threatened.[245] Michael Foot stated on 18 January 1977 that in his view local government would be reorganized 'under the aegis of the Welsh assembly'.[246] By May the executive of the Labour Party in Wales had reached its conclusions on the structure of local government, and its annual conference approved a resolution that the assembly should be the top tier of local government, with a single tier of all-purpose authorities beneath it.[247] The Association of County Councils opposed the clause in the Wales Bill that required the assembly to review the structure of local government, and its views were circulated to over 100 MPs before the second-reading debate on 15 November 1977.[248] The clause embodied the only mandatory duty placed on the assembly, leading critics to declare in July 1978 (during the Wales Bill's final passage through the House of Commons) that it was 'an attempt to buy popularity for an unpopular Bill by attacking something else believed to be unpopular'.[249] The prime minister, James Callaghan, seemed to confirm this to be so. Speaking in Swansea on 21 February 1979, during the referendum campaign, he said that the extensive dissatisfaction with the reorganization of local government was an additional reason for supporting the Act in the referendum.[250] There is no doubt that the government had made a fatal mistake when it decided that the Welsh assembly should be mandated to review the structure of local government.

Since the 1960s there had been dissatisfaction within the Labour Party in Wales with the nominated bodies that functioned between central and local government; in its evidence to the Commission on the Constitution, the party had suggested that the work undertaken

[245] Ibid., vol. 922, cols 1568, 1417, 1583.
[246] Ibid., vol. 924, col. 226.
[247] *Report of the Annual Conference of the Labour Party Wales*, 27–8 May 1977, 20.
[248] Association of County Councils, Executive Council Minutes, February 1978, 323.
[249] Parl. Deb., vol. 954, col. 619.
[250] Labour Party, news release, 21 February 1979, 5.

by such bodies should be the responsibility of an elected council. The Welsh Parliamentary Labour Party agreed with the party in Wales that an elected council should replace the nominated bodies. In its policy statement, *Bringing Power Back to the People*, issued in September 1974, the National Executive Committee pointed out that in effect there was a form of 'regional government without regional democracy'.[251] Labour's Welsh manifesto for the October general election, *Wales will win with Labour*, claimed that with the assembly assuming functions exercised by civil servants and nominated bodies democracy would be strengthened and the 'anti-democratic trend' reversed.[252] As the secretary of state assumed more functions, the number of appointments made by him to nominated bodies had increased. In 1975 he made 628 appointments to nominated bodies, including 117 made jointly with other ministers.[253] The Labour Party in Wales criticized nominated bodies because their existence enabled a Conservative secretary of state to place his own nominees on key boards and committees, even though in Wales his party had been rejected at the polls. At the annual conference of the Labour Party in Wales in 1976, the following resolution was carried:

> Conference, however, insists that the responsibilities of ALL the present nominated bodies must be brought under the democratic control of the Assembly, including the Welsh Development Agency and the Rural Development Board, and all such organisations that have impact on our industrial and economic life.[254]

The government responded to the conference's demand, and in *Devolution to Scotland and Wales: Supplementary Statement* issued in August it strengthened the role of the assembly by giving it power, subject to the secretary of state's approval, to subsume the functions of nominated bodies operating in Wales in devolved areas. The initiative would be with the assembly and not with the secretary of state, as was previously intended.[255] John Morris explained in May 1978 that this meant that nominated bodies remotely controlled by parliament through the secretary of state would henceforward be controlled directly by the people's elected representatives. Alec Jones, under-secretary of state at the Welsh Office, also explained

---

[251] Labour Party, *Bringing Power Back to the People*, 2.
[252] Labour Party, *Wales will win with Labour*.
[253] Parl. Deb., vol. 902, col. 417.
[254] *Report of the Annual Conference of the Labour Party in Wales*, 14–15 May 1976, 23.
[255] *Devolution to Scotland and Wales: Supplementary Statement*, 9.

186   DEVOLUTION IN WALES: CLAIMS AND RESPONSES

that if the assembly decided to subsume the Welsh Development
Agency and the Development Board for Rural Wales, not only
would it have to seek the approval of the secretary of state, but their
respective functions would have to be exercised within the guide-
lines laid down by parliament. Both bodies would be financed from
the block grant, but the assembly would determine the amounts to
be allocated. The assembly therefore was to be given some powers
in economic matters, as demanded by the Labour Party in Wales
backed by the Wales TUC, but opponents considered that such
powers should remain with the secretary of state, who was responsible to parliament.[256] Ironically, Anthony Meyer, a Conservative,
supported the move to achieve greater democratic control over
nominated bodies, but Labour critics of the government's proposals
– like Tam Dalyell – questioned whether politicians would have the
expertise to run certain committees.[257] Assembly members would
be able to do so because they would have at their disposal the full
range of civil service expertise.

The government's case for the democratization of nominated
bodies was a sound one, but it was difficult to justify a remedy for
part of the United Kingdom and not for other regions. Emrys Jones
was as aware as anyone that the issue was a United Kingdom issue.
He wanted the changes proposed for Scotland and Wales implemented in the regions of England, where the democratic deficit was
just as prevalent. He made this point consistently from the very
beginning. Following the decision to promote separate bills for
Scotland and Wales, the government was urged by the Labour
Party in Wales to re-emphasize the fact that devolution was part of
Labour's socialist principle to extend both political and industrial
democracy.[258] Its views were further developed in a pamphlet entitled *Political and Industrial Democracy in Britain*, issued in May 1978.
In a summary, wide-ranging political reforms were listed, namely
the abolition of the House of Lords, reform of the House of
Commons and of local government, the creation of regional assemblies, and the abolition of undemocratic public offices and the
system of advisory committees for the appointment of magistrates.
On the industrial front, public ownership should be extended and
there should be an increase in industrial democracy. Moreover,

[256] Parl. Deb., vol. 949, cols 1007, 358, 364, 326.
[257] Ibid., vol. 954, cols 831, 815.
[258] Labour Party Wales, news release, 26 July 1977.

various ways were suggested in which ordinary people could participate in decision-making that affected their lives.[259] As J. Barry Jones
and Michael Keating explained, when *Political and Industrial
Democracy in Britain* was approved by the Labour Party in Wales it
'had come some considerable way to accommodating a policy of
decentralisation within the broader ideological and traditional
working class ethos of the party'.[260]

MPs opposed to devolution made a number of assertions, and
although the government tried hard to counter them it never really
succeeded in doing so. One of the arguments advanced was that,
with a reduction in the scope of the secretary of state's duties
following the transfer of functions to the assembly, his influence in
the Cabinet would be greatly reduced and, consequently, his office
might not survive.[261] John Morris had previously said, in the debate
on 4 February 1975, that there was no question of the office not
surviving, and he explained that the secretary of state would have
three important functions. He would watch over Welsh interests
when legislation was passing through the House, be an advocate for
Wales in the Cabinet when resources were allocated, and be a link
between the assembly and parliament.[262] It was well known that this
secretary of state was particularly anxious that functions should be
transferred to the assembly, and the views of those MPs opposed to
the proposal were summed up by Wyn Roberts, who claimed that
John Morris was prepared to hand over his powers to an 'untried
body'.[263] Perhaps MPs' fears and anxieties were justified to some
degree, because just before his appointment as secretary of state,
John Morris had said that the Welsh Office should not be regarded
as a 'sacred cow'.[264] Later, the secretary of state's comment that he
was the tier of government being transferred to the assembly
confirmed opponents' views that if an assembly were created, the
post would be more or less obsolete.[265] The continued existence of
the Welsh Office was important to Welsh MPs, partly because, with
three ministers, it offered opportunities for advancement, particularly
to those who were not likely to be offered posts in other ministries.

[259] Idem, *Political and Industrial Democracy in Britain* (Cardiff, May 1978).
[260] Jones and Keating, 'The British Labour Party as a centralising force', 27.
[261] Parl. Deb., vol. 903, cols 600, 300.
[262] Ibid., vol. 885, col. 1184.
[263] Ibid., vol. 949, col. 1115.
[264] *Western Mail*, 17 January 1974.
[265] Ibid., 1 December 1976.

Welsh MPs also feared for their positions as members of parliament. In the debates on the Scotland and Wales Bill they maintained that a reduction in their number would be inevitable following the establishment of an assembly; their workload would be reduced and by their votes they would be able to influence decisions that only affected England. Nigel Lawson (Conservative, Blaby) confirmed in January 1976 that English members would not tolerate such a situation.[266] John Morris had argued from the beginning in 1974 that there was no case for a reduction, because major decisions affecting the United Kingdom would still be taken at Westminster.[267] Many of the subjects in which Welsh MPs took a particular interest would become, under the government's proposals, the responsibility of the assembly, and they were simply not prepared to allow that to happen.[268] John P. Mackintosh's earlier observation, in 1968, that MPs from Scotland and Wales, more so than others, perhaps, were more interested in local affairs than in broader national issues is a pertinent one. If true, they might not want to see assembly members in Edinburgh and Cardiff having a greater role in such matters as housing, health and education than they themselves had at Westminster.[269] Labour MPs were also all too aware that a reduction in representation would damage Labour more than the Conservatives, and make Conservative governments more likely at Westminster, thus further jeopardizing their own career prospects.[270] After listening to MPs pleading their case during the committee stage of the Wales Bill in March 1978, Gerry Fowler invited Leo Abse to tell the House whether he thought that the Wales Bill was about the 'better government of Wales and the rights of the Welsh people or about the rights of the Welsh Members'.[271] The Welsh assembly's functions were to be executive only and a reduction in the number of MPs could not therefore be justified, but if in the future the assembly were to assume legislative functions, then obviously there would be a case for the number of MPs to be reduced.

---

[266] Parl. Deb., vol. 903, cols 683, 599, 706.
[267] Ibid., vol. 885, col. 1185.
[268] Ibid., vol. 903, cols 683–4.
[269] J. P. Mackintosh, *The Devolution of Power* (London, 1968), 165.
[270] Parl. Deb., vol. 924, cols 208, 108.
[271] Ibid., vol. 945, col. 504.

High costs are sure to deter people from supporting any scheme, and Welsh MPs opposed to the government's proposals never missed an opportunity to point out the financial implications. Neil Kinnock claimed in January 1976 that £12m would finance four hospitals, ten comprehensive schools, ten miles of motorway or two Welsh-language television channels; Leo Abse maintained later in the year that such spending set a bad example at a time when local authority spending was being cut and people were expected to accept a lower standard of living.[272] Emrys Jones was probably correct when he said in 1975 that the issue of the expense involved was being used by MPs who did not want to see any changes, 'by people who are too conservative to want to make a radical step forward'.[273] He was echoing Edgar L. Chappell's comment of 1943. Although John Morris conceded in December 1976 that democracy had to be paid for, he argued that in relation to the tasks allocated to the assembly, the additional number of civil servants would not be large.[274] Closely linked with the debate over costs was the question of whether or not extra resources would become available once the assembly was established. In January 1977 Neil Kinnock declared that unless the proposals meant extra resources, the suggestion that conditions in Wales would improve had to be rejected.[275] The secretary of state was unable to confirm that there would be additional resources, but he justified the additional costs on the ground that resources available for the devolved services would be better allocated.[276] The estimated annual running costs of the assembly were approximately £13.7m at November 1978 prices, and assembly elections would cost an estimated £0.7m.[277] Perhaps the expense was a small price to pay for democracy, but to people who had recently been required to pay higher rates and water charges the government's argument was not a convincing one. Cledwyn Hughes argued in the Welsh Grand Committee on 6 April 1976 that anti-devolutionists were able to exploit the issue of cost because the reorganization of local government undertaken by

[272] Ibid., vol. 903, col. 293; vol. 918, col. 1749.
[273] *Western Mail*, 6 November 1975.
[274] Parl. Deb., vol. 922, col. 1565.
[275] Ibid., vol. 924, cols 153–4.
[276] Ibid., vol. 949, col. 1002.
[277] Ibid., vol. 960, col. 81; vol. 953, col. 2.

the Tories had resulted in higher charges. He admitted that the argument was a damaging one in the economic climate, because the idea of additional costs naturally frightened people. Neil Kinnock and Leo Abse represented Gwent constituencies, and the new headquarters of the county council at Cwmbrân, opened in 1974, had cost £9 m.[278]

Leo Abse, in particular, voiced the fears of some English speakers that they would be at a disadvantage compared with the Welsh-speaking minority in Wales. He was well aware that in south-east Wales there had always been a good deal of opposition to use of the language, particularly among Labour representatives on local authorities who thought that support for the language was synonymous with support for Plaid Cymru. Their opposition intensified when Plaid Cymru began to win council seats at Labour's expense. Some Labour councillors in the region had objected to the huge expansion of Welsh-medium education, on the grounds that it was elitist, and certain Labour-controlled local authorities refused to make contributions to the National Eisteddfod because of its all-Welsh rule. Before the publication of *Our Changing Democracy: Devolution to Scotland and Wales*, Abse expressed fears in the Welsh affairs debate on 23 October that the assembly's civil service would consist only of Welsh speakers, so that the people of Gwent and similar areas would 'be regarded as second-class citizens in their own country'.[279] Later, in January 1976, he expressed the view that in effect Wales would be governed by 'a Welsh-speaking bureaucratic elite', and in the Welsh affairs debate in November 1976 he referred to 'a packed gravy train steaming out of the Cardiff City Exchange', with the 'first-class coaches marked "For Welsh speakers only"'.[280] On 22 February 1977, during the debate on the timetable motion, Michael Foot, an Englishman, took the opportunity to remind the House that there were no grounds for such fears.[281] In January, Neil Kinnock, though he was opposed to devolution, insisted that he would 'never use fear of the Welsh language', and in any case he could not see the English-speaking majority giving way

---

[278] Ibid., Welsh Grand Committee, 7 April 1976, col. 24; information from Treasurer Gwent County Council, 4 April 1985.

[279] Parl. Deb., vol. 898, col. 864.

[280] Ibid., vol. 903, col. 686; vol. 918, col. 1753.

[281] Ibid., vol. 926, col. 1324.

to the Welsh-speaking minority.[282] Kinnock's point was a valid one, but that majority were never to be convinced that Abse's claims were totally unfounded. Later, in November 1977, Kinnock was anxious to point out that he was not against the Welsh language as such. He said that he supported the expenditure earmarked by parliament for the promotion of the Welsh language, but he doubted whether an assembly would be as generous in its support, and that would be regrettable.[283]

Such arguments advanced by critics were damaging, and in order to rally support to its policy the government's spokesmen made repeated reference to the fact that devolution was a manifesto commitment which could not be discarded. Michael Foot emphasized that it had been a major proposal in the election manifesto and 'nothing could be more damaging to the Labour Party' than for the government to renege on the commitment given to the people of Wales.[284] In a speech in London on 6 March 1977, Ron Hayward declared:

> It is however a sorry practice if Members of Parliament are to be selective in their approach to Manifesto commitments . . . If we are now to face a situation where our Members of Parliament have second thoughts on items contained in the Manifesto then we stand to be indicted by the electors for not carrying out a promise, which was within our power to fulfil.[285]

In Wales, Emrys Jones had stressed in October 1975 that it was the duty of the party and of individual members to keep the promise that had been given. He also had said that it was his responsibility to ensure that MPs adhered to policies that had been democratically adopted after extensive consultations. Furthermore, some MPs had not even thought it necessary to attend the annual conferences where the decisions had been taken. He had been confident that MPs would loyally support the devolution proposals. If any MPs voted against them, they would be voting against their own party and government.[286] Constituency representatives, however, argued that when the decisions were taken not enough attention had been

---

[282]   Ibid., vol. 924, col. 155.
[283]   Ibid., vol. 939, col. 472.
[284]   Ibid., vol. 916, col. 1467; vol. 925, col. 502.
[285]   Labour Party Wales, news release, 6 March 1977; Labour Party Information Department, news release S46/77.
[286]   *Western Mail*, 30 October 1975.

paid to their views, and that the views of the Wales TUC had predominated, even though it did not necessarily reflect the views of rank and file trade union members.[287] That it was a commitment binding on all party members was again emphasized when the 1977 annual conference of the Labour Party in Wales carried a resolution that Labour Party members, from Cabinet ministers downwards, should canvass for the assembly, in line with decisions taken at Welsh and national conferences and the manifesto commitments.[288] Labour MPs claimed that many commitments over the years had been 'abrogated, pushed into pigeon-holes or conveniently forgotten'.[289] It was indeed a manifesto commitment, but few people in Wales who voted Labour did so because they supported devolution, and in England it had not been an issue at all. Harold Wilson later admitted that devolution was not seen as a core issue during the election campaign in February 1974. That campaign centred on issues that were in his view 'more immediate and contro-versial'.[290] Grant Jordan, commenting on the Committee Stage of the Scotland and Wales Bill, came to much the same conclusion, saying that 'there was a mood in the whole proceedings that the subject was seen as peripheral; marginal to the party programme. Rebellion wasn't "real" as devolution didn't really count.'[291]

In 1976 an attempt was made to bring the MPs into line. Then, when it seemed that no argument could deter the rebel MPs from opposing the devolution proposals, the executive of the Labour Party in Wales and the general council of the Wales TUC turned on them. The general council met the MPs in November 1976, when there was intense pressure for a referendum, and urged them to accept the decision of the Labour Party conference. Neil Kinnock, Leo Abse, Fred Evans and Donald Anderson were accused by the chairman, D. Ivor Davies, of 'attempting to black-mail the Government by threatening withdrawal of support for the Devolution Bill'. When the dissident Labour MPs were told by the Wales TUC 'to stop "sniping" at the Government', Abse retorted, 'I am not a sniper who lurks in the undergrowth: I have openly

---

[287] Interview, R. K. Blundell, 19 September 1983.
[288] *Report of the Annual Conference of the Labour Party Wales*, 27–8 May 1977, 20.
[289] Parl. Deb., vol. 922, col. 1625.
[290] Wilson, *Final Term*, 46.
[291] Grant Jordan, 'The committee stage of the Scotland and Wales Bill (1976–77)', *Waverley Papers*, 1 (1979), 31.

declared my opposition to this massive folly with the support of my constituents and I shall continue to do so as a full-frontal fighter.'[292] The Wales TUC had opposed a referendum, on the grounds that it would be both inconclusive and divisive; after it had been conceded, the MPs were subjected to further attacks. D. Ivor Davies accused them of acting in 'an irresponsible and maverick manner', and George Wright, the secretary, warned that 'It is not unfair to say to MPs of all parties that if they disregard the democratic decisions of their party that party will not forget it'.[293] A joint Labour and Wales TUC statement issued during the referendum campaign condemned the MPs' action. Attention was drawn to the fact that Fred Evans, Neil Kinnock, Donald Anderson and Ioan Evans supported the proposal in their election addresses, and that Leo Abse and Ifor Davies were members of the Welsh Parliamentary Labour Party which had unanimously supported an elected assembly in November 1973. George Wright added:

> By their behaviour they are not only reneging on their own commitments and that of their manifesto but they are dividing the Labour movement in Wales, indulging in personal attacks on fellow party members and acting in such a way that they could bring down the Labour Government.[294]

The MPs were not without support. In March 1976 the Welsh Parliamentary Labour Party decided to send a 'stern letter' to Emrys Jones objecting to the personal attacks on MPs and particularly to the 'obnoxious cartoons' that were being circulated.[295] And apparently George Thomas, a known opponent of devolution, gave them as much support as his position as Speaker permitted.[296] According to Tam Dalyell, writing in 1977, the criticisms that had been levelled at the rebel Labour backbenchers by their fellow members were 'gentle and civilised', which would not have been the case 'had a matter of fiercely held Socialist belief been involved'. Labour MPs had not been too worried that the devolution bill could be lost, but they feared that if it were lost the nationalists would vote against the government on other issues 'out of a sense of grievance',

[292] *Western Mail*, 1 December 1976.
[293] Ibid., 11 December 1976; 2 February 1977.
[294] Ibid., 21 February 1979.
[295] Ibid., 11 March 1976.
[296] Telephone interview, Donald Anderson, 24 July 1984.

thus putting the government's future in jeopardy.[297] Other Welsh Labour MPs who remained silent on the issue in public had also supported the rebels.[298]

The Wales Bill which was introduced in November 1977 eventually received the royal assent on 31 July 1978; Welsh Office minister Alec Jones admitted that devolution had 'been a very long haul'; in Harold Wilson's words it had also 'been a bore'. That was very true, because the debates had been both long drawn out and repetitious, and the rebuke of Myer Galpern (first deputy chairman of Ways and Means) to Tam Dalyell in April 1978 was indicative of the proceedings: 'It is unfortunate that the hon. Gentleman uses every amendment to ask questions which he himself knows are wholly irrelevant to the amendment under discussion.'[299] The period had been one of mixed fortunes for the Callaghan government. The value of the pound had risen against the dollar, and except for the first quarter in 1978 there had been a balance of payments surplus, but prices continued to rise and unemployment remained at a high level, and the number of working days lost in stoppages was much higher than in 1976. After losing the Ilford North by-election in March 1978, Labour succeeded in holding off the challenges of the nationalists in Garscadden in April and in Hamilton in May, and it seemed that the government's prospects were improving.[300]

THE REFERENDUM CAMPAIGN

In the referendum the Welsh people rejected the proposals by a majority of nearly four to one: only 243,048 supported an assembly while 956,330 voted against it. The Welsh, according to Kenneth O. Morgan, 'had been offered a real prospect of power being transferred from Whitehall to themselves' and 'when given the choice, they had thrown it out with contumely'.[301] Several factors contributed to this defeat of the Labour government's devolution proposals.

Timing is always of the utmost importance as far as referenda are concerned. In the first quarter of 1979, 5,442 working days were lost in stoppages, mainly as a result of the industrial action

---

[297] Tam Dalyell, *Devolution: The End of Britain?* (London, 1977), 141.
[298] Interview, R. K. Blundell, 19 September 1983.
[299] Parl. Deb., vol. 958, col. 1386; Wilson, *Final Term*, 212; Parl. Deb., vol. 947, col. 308.
[300] Butler and Kavanagh, *British General Election of 1979*, 20, 24–5.
[301] Morgan, *Rebirth of a Nation*, 405.

taken by the public sector employees. The number of days lost during that period was just over a thousand fewer than the 6,494 days lost in the first quarter of 1974, when there were a miners' strike and a three-day week in operation.[302] The referendum to decide the fate of the Wales Act 1978 was held in March 1979, when the widespread strikes were making the Callaghan government unpopular with the electorate. As Colin H. Williams explained, at such a time devolution seemed 'not the pivotal question of Welsh national development as some had claimed', and the argument advanced by the prime minister, speaking in Swansea on 21 February, and other Labour spokesmen that devolution meant better government seemed irrelevant to most people.[303] Furthermore, electors were not convinced that an assembly would result in more jobs, better housing and health services or greater influence on the United Kingdom government and on EEC institutions, as was claimed by the Wales for the Assembly campaign, which had Elystan Morgan as its chairman and Jack Brooks as its secretary.[304] The Labour Party in Wales's official 'Vote Yes' campaign, organized jointly with the Wales TUC, was allocated £35,000 from party funds, and local branches were instructed 'not to support the "vote no" campaign organised by others'.[305] Three groups were established to oppose the proposals. They were the Labour No Assembly campaign, the Vote No campaign based in the Caerphilly constituency, with R. K. Blundell as its secretary, and the mainly Conservative No Assembly campaign, with David Gibson Watt as its chairman. These groups emphasized that the proposals would lead to a divided kingdom and more bureaucracy, and that they were costly and a threat to local government. In his Swansea speech, the prime minister tried to allay a major fear by asserting that:

> Wales has a strong sense of being a Nation. And pride in being Welsh, pride in Welsh achievements, goes hand in hand with pride in being part of the United Kingdom. I respect the sincerity of my friends who fear a Welsh assembly would be a wedge dividing Wales from Britain. But they are mistaken. They underestimate our people.[306]

---

[302] Butler and Kavanagh, *British General Election of 1979*, 24.
[303] Colin H. Williams, 'Separatism and the mobilization of Welsh national identity', in Williams (ed.), *National Separatism*, 184; Labour Party, news release, 21 February 1979, 5.
[304] Wales for the Assembly Campaign, *The Wales Bill* (4 June 1978).
[305] Labour Party document, 'Devolution to Wales', 8–9.
[306] Labour Party, news release, 21 February 1979.

Rather surprisingly, he did not condemn the actions of the Labour rebels. An opinion poll conducted by Research and Marketing Wales and the West a week before polling day revealed that their message was getting through. When 'No' voters were asked why they had decided to reject the proposals, 61 per cent said that they were too costly, 43 per cent thought that they would create another level of bureaucracy, and 40 per cent considered that they would lead to the break-up of the United Kingdom.[307] Opponents also claimed that north Wales would be dominated by industrial south Wales, and that Welsh speakers would suffer at the hands of non-Welsh speakers.[308] In south Wales, the fear among the non-Welsh-speaking majority was that there would be discrimination in favour of the Welsh-speaking minority.[309]

As John Osmond demonstrated later, the 'No' campaigners also had the popular press on their side. In Wales the most popular daily newspapers, namely, the *Sun*, *Daily Mirror*, *Daily Express* and *Daily Mail*, had a combined circulation of 634,000 in 1979. It might be thought that as these newspapers paid scant attention to Welsh issues, their readers had little or no opportunity to acquaint themselves with the arguments for and against devolution and so voted to retain the status quo. Six Welsh-based English-language newspapers had a combined circulation of 421,000, but the *Western Mail*, with a circulation of 94,000, was the only paper in favour of an assembly. Not one of the newspapers opposed to the Wales Act 'matched the *South Wales Echo* (circulation 120,000) in its sustained campaign of vindictive fury against the Assembly proposals'. Most of the newspapers did not give the campaign a coverage that could be termed adequate, and that was partly because so much space was allocated to the industrial action being taken by lorry drivers and public sector employees. On 10 February, however, they all gave prominent front-page space to the BBC Wales opinion poll predicting that 45.8 per cent intended voting against the assembly. As author and broadcaster Harri Pritchard Jones pointed out, the Welsh-language weekly *Y Cymro* did likewise. *Y Cymro*, like the other weekly, *Y Faner*, supported the assembly, but the combined circulation of both papers was less than 10,000. In addition to the press, television and radio were potentially powerful influences, but it appears that they

---

[307]   Research and Marketing (Wales and the West) Ltd., 19–20 February 1979.
[308]   Morgan, *Rebirth of a Nation*, 405.
[309]   Labour Party, news release, 21 February 1979, 6.

did not make 'a measurable and observable impact', in the words of Geraint Talfan Davies, an assistant controller at Harlech Television, Cardiff. Television made very little impact on the 35 per cent of the population who, because they received their programmes from transmitters outside Wales, had to rely on the few programmes about Welsh issues transmitted from London.[310]

Apart from the arguments advanced at the time, other factors played a part in determining the fate of the Wales Act. In general, support in Wales for devolution had been steadily declining over the years. When the Commission on the Constitution commissioned its poll in the summer of 1970, support for it had declined to 36 per cent of respondents. There was a resurgence in November 1975, when a Marplan poll recorded a figure of 49 per cent, but a year later, in October 1976, support had slipped to 39 per cent, according to another Marplan poll. Support for the proposals was lower, according to three polls conducted by Research and Marketing Wales and the West. These polls, conducted between December 1975 and March 1977, indicated that only around 30 to 27 per cent supported the proposals. Two polls conducted for BBC Wales in May and September 1978 indicated a higher level of support, namely 40.8 and 37.8 per cent respectively, but by 1 February 1979 it had fallen to 30 per cent. Two other polls, conducted by Research and Marketing Wales and the West and by Marplan between 19 and 22 February 1979, were much nearer the mark. Both polls indicated that only 22 per cent of the electorate supported the proposals. The referendum was held nearly thirteen years after the Carmarthen by-election, and much had happened in that time to cause people to take a different view. Moreover, the debates in parliament had extended over a four-year period and that had not helped the devolutionists' case, as Ferdinand Mount, writing in the *Spectator* immediately after the referendum, explained:

> It was the very length of the debate that defeated the Yes campaigners. For the longer the argument went on, the more tirelessly and insistently Mr. Tam Dalyell, Mr. Cunningham, Mr. Leo Abse and Mr. Neil Kinnock exposed the weaknesses and illogicalities of the proposals . . . But now all the conviction and determination and passion seemed to be on their side.[311]

[310] John Osmond, 'The referendum and the English-language press', 154–62; Harri Pritchard Jones, 'The referendum and the Welsh-language press', 169, 171, 177; Geraint Talfan Davies, 'The role of broadcasting in the referendum', 192, all in Foulkes, Jones and Wilford (eds), *Welsh Veto*.
[311] Ferdinand Mount, 'The psychotics' revolt', *Spectator*, 10 March 1979, 4.

The fact that the proposals were unacceptable to large numbers of
Labour Party members and to a hard core of MPs was another
crucial factor. The way in which such proposals had come about
was partly responsible for that. Nationalist successes in 1974
enabled ardent devolutionists in the Labour Party in Wales to press
for the highest option, short of a legislative assembly, which Edward
Short, the minister in charge, would have supported.[312] As it was,
the proposals that emerged went far beyond an elected council to
control nominated bodies, which Welsh Labour MPs generally were
prepared to support. Consequently, the party in Wales was divided
on the policy with several constituency parties opposed to it. Just
before the Labour Party in Wales's annual conference in May 1976,
a survey carried out by the *Western Mail* revealed that twenty-one
constituency parties supported the policy, six were against it, and
nine were undecided; in March 1978 the *South Wales Echo* reported
that only fourteen constituency parties supported the policy, twelve
were opposed to it and ten were undecided.[313] Therefore, the
Labour Party in Wales did not reflect the views of its members, and
during the referendum campaign there was a dearth of canvassers.
Indeed, in some constituencies only a handful of Labour activists
campaigned for the proposals and Plaid Cymru supporters did
much of the work.[314] Labour Party activists were doing so little on
the ground that even in Michael Foot's constituency of Ebbw Vale it
was felt that only a greater effort by the prime minister could save
the day.[315] That the policy had been endorsed at successive Labour
Party conferences in Wales was due in no small measure to the
support given to it by the Wales TUC, though not all individual
unions supported the policy. The AUEW and the GMWU were
hostile, and within the NUM in Gwent there was lukewarm
support. Although the trade union movement was officially
committed to the policy, rank and file members were clearly not,
and that was evident during the referendum campaign.[316] Trade
unionists, though pledged to support the measure, said in private

[312] Interview, Edward Short, 19 December 1984.

[313] *Western Mail*, 13 May 1976; *South Wales Echo*, 1 March 1978.

[314] Interviews: Keith Jones, 18 March 1985; Ron Evans, 11 December 1984; private
information.

[315] Private information.

[316] Interviews: Michael Foot, 18 July 1984; Glyn Williams, 19 December 1983; Gwilym
Prys Davies, 4 July 1983.

conversation with Neil Kinnock that they agreed with him.[317] The executive of the Labour Party in Wales, led by Emrys Jones, and Welsh Office ministers had relied too heavily on the support of the Wales TUC and failed to take sufficient cognizance of the views of activists in the constituency parties and of those of Labour MPs. The more modest proposal for an elected council to control the nominated bodies could have been accepted without a referendum, and a basis for further development would thereby have been established. The executive of the Labour Party in Wales, while clearly disappointed with the referendum result, reiterated its policy. It emphasized that the 'problems which the Assembly was designed to deal with, will still remain' and that the policy, as set out in 1978 in *Political and Industrial Democracy in Britain*, was 'central to the whole purpose and existence of the Labour Party and to the well being of people in Britain'.[318] The general council of the Wales TUC in its statement said that it recognized that its own members had rejected its policy; while that and the referendum result should not in themselves lead to the policy being changed or abandoned, the general council tactfully admitted that a reappraisal was necessary.[319]

In Scotland the 'Yes' vote fell short of 40 per cent of the eligible electorate, but 33 per cent did vote for the proposals. While the government was deliberating on the next move, the Scottish National Party tabled a motion of no confidence and the Conservatives followed with their own no confidence motion. In the division at the end of the debate on 28 March, the government secured the support of the three Plaid Cymru MPs, but the motion was passed, and a general election followed in May.[320] A bill to give compensation to quarrymen suffering from respiratory diseases had been rushed through the House of Commons in order to secure the votes of the Plaid Cymru members.[321] Apparently, the government's defeat was viewed 'as a blessed relief' by many ministers, and, perhaps surprisingly, by the prime minister. He was sure that the election could be won.[322] It was ironic that the man who in 1968

[317] Telephone interview, Donald Anderson, 24 July 1984.
[318] Labour Party Wales, *Report of the EC to the Annual Conference*, 1979, 11.
[319] Wales TUC, *General Council Statement on Wales TUC Policy with Regard to Devolution (Post Referendum)*, 3.
[320] Butler and Kavanagh, *British General Election of 1979*, 125–6.
[321] Callaghan, *Time and Chance*, 562.
[322] Joel Barnett, *Inside the Treasury* (London, 1982), 187.

had proposed a Royal Commission to examine the devolution of government in order to ease the pressure on the Wilson government was forced out of office a decade or so later by that very issue. In its election manifesto, Labour offered no alternative proposals in place of a Welsh assembly. The manifesto merely stated that the party accepted the decision of the people of Wales.[323] The Conservative Party, however, still stood by the commitment that it had made in June 1974 that a parliamentary select committee should be appointed.[324] After the election, won by Margaret Thatcher and the Conservatives, the draft Wales Act 1978 (Repeal) Order 1979 was approved by the House of Commons on 26 June 1979; the House also approved a motion that a Select Committee on Welsh Affairs should be appointed 'to examine the expenditure, administration and policy of the Welsh Office and associated public bodies'.[325] As Harold Wilson later remarked, what decided the date of the general election was not 'industrial disputes, pay policy, or the piling up of garbage in the streets during the strikes of public service unions – it was the impasse caused by the response of Scots and Welsh in the devolution vote'.[326] The referendum campaign provided a platform from which the Conservatives could attack the Labour government, and effectively was the first offensive in the election campaign that followed immediately afterwards. Michael Foot saw the danger of a Conservative government being elected back in 1976, when he told delegates to the Labour Party conference, 'If we were responsible for that, that would be the worst possible betrayal, and I am sure that it is not one that any member of this Party wishes to commit'.[327] The sustained opposition of the so-called Labour 'rebels' to the devolution proposals led to a referendum, whose result brought down the Callaghan government. In the general election the Conservatives gained two seats in Wales, Brecon and Radnor and Montgomeryshire, where the sitting members had been active supporters of devolution, and a third, Anglesey, where the Labour candidate had been chairman of the Wales for the Assembly campaign.

[323] 'Labour Party Manifesto', *Keesing's Contemporary Archives*, 1 June 1979, 29631.
[324] Conservative Party, *Putting Britain First: A National Policy from the Conservatives* (London, October 1974), 27; *idem, Conservative Manifesto for Wales*, 1979.
[325] Parl. Deb., vol. 969, cols 359–61.
[326] Wilson, *Final Term*, 213.
[327] *Labour Party Annual Report*, 1976, 203–4.

At the end of the decade Labour's devolution policy was in ruins. The policy had been conceived in great haste in order to counter the menace of nationalism in Scotland and Wales, and it was not given widespread support at ward and union branch level. While some MPs supported it, others representing the south Wales valleys were openly hostile, and even some ministers expressed reservations. The policy aroused intense opposition in England, and the Labour Party had not taken that sufficiently into account when it reacted to what seemed a threat to its ascendancy in the Celtic countries. Although Labour was deeply divided on the issue, the government retained the support of many of its own MPs by conceding a referendum. It had also concluded a pact with the Liberals, and since the nationalists continued to lend their support it managed to survive until after the referendum. By then the government had virtually completed a full term in office, and, as it had been without an overall majority for most of the time, this was no mean achievement.

In 1896 the adherents of Cymru Fydd failed in their attempt to win over Welsh Liberalism; in the 1970s the devolutionists within the Labour Party, because of particular circumstances, succeeded in committing the party and the government to a Welsh assembly to give Wales a distinctive political identity. However, they failed to convince the electorate which, when it was given the opportunity to make a judgement on devolution, showed that it was overwhelmingly hostile. At the time it seemed that devolution had been removed from the political agenda.

CONCLUSION

When discussing the devolution of government, it is necessary to examine the political context in which the debates took place. After the formation of National and Coalition governments in 1935 and 1940 respectively, the United Kingdom from 1945 to 1979 was governed by either Labour or Conservative governments, each party holding power for a total of seventeen years or so. In Wales the situation was very different. Labour held the overwhelming majority of the Welsh parliamentary seats throughout the period. In the 1950s, when there were Conservative governments at Westminster, Labour held twenty-seven seats in Wales and in 1966 it reached a new peak by winning thirty-two seats, but by October 1974 its representation had fallen to twenty-three seats.[1] The Labour Party, then, was the dominant party in Welsh politics, and this inevitably meant that it was a major player in any devolution debate. Its response to demands for greater devolution was clearly governed by its nature and outlook and by the background of its leaders, both inside and outside parliament. The party was strictly centralist and its leaders, like those before them, 'were positively suspicious of the regions and disliked attempts to make use of the "nationalist" aspirations of the Scots and the Welsh', but it did, nevertheless, reluctantly yield to the demands of devolutionists when particular circumstances prevailed.[2] Wales's Labour MPs were clearly divided over the question of devolution. Some MPs were openly hostile towards it and, true to the party's centralist tradition, were adamant that any attempt to recognize Wales's identity as a nation should be resisted. At the same time, others believed that Wales's identity as a nation should be given constitutional status and therefore were keen advocates of devolution. The need to recognize Wales as a nation was one of the arguments advanced by devolutionists for a secretary of state and for a Welsh assembly. They were fully aware, however, that there was little enthusiasm

[1] Jones, *Etholiadau'r Ganrif,* 95, 99, 103, 111, 123.
[2] Ross McKibbin, *The Evolution of the Labour Party, 1910–1924* (Oxford, 1974), 241.

within the party for changes in the machinery of government, but they never gave up and, indeed, secured significant concessions.

In Wales interested parties have held conflicting views on the devolution issue, but in the 1930s and 1940s, when the demand was for a secretary of state, there was, rather surprisingly, a consensus in favour of such an appointment. It was supported by individual MPs of all parties, by the Welsh Parliamentary Party, by the local authorities and by the South Wales Regional Council of Labour. Later, it was the inability to achieve a consensus that slowed down and thwarted moves to secure changes in the machinery of government. The Conservatives opposed the appointment of a secretary of state and rejected a Welsh assembly, and although Labour eventually supported both there were divisions within the party's own ranks, particularly among MPs. Local authorities, too, opposed the creation of an assembly, because they feared a loss of their responsibilities. From the outset, devolutionists argued that Wales should be given parity with Scotland. The post of Scottish secretary was created in 1885; in 1926 it was raised to that of secretary of state and it was thought that the country had benefited as a result. Opponents, on the other hand, pointed out that the situations in Wales and Scotland were not parallel because Scotland had its own legal system whereas Wales did not. After a secretary of state had been conceded, the aim again was parity with Scotland and the Scottish Office was the model for the emerging Welsh Office. By the early 1970s, however, the thinking within the Labour Party in Wales on devolution of government was ahead of that in Scotland but, surprisingly perhaps, the party opted for an executive assembly, when a legislative assembly was being granted to Scotland. That decision went very much against the wishes of the Wales TUC leaders, who supported a legislative assembly. In the early post-war debates, devolutionists also claimed that a secretary of state should be appointed because Wales had special needs, but government ministers argued that Wales's economic and social problems were no different from those in the regions of England and that having a secretary of state would not resolve them. The English regions did have similar problems, and this was highlighted thirty years later when some of their MPs voted against the Labour government's devolution proposals because they feared that resources would be diverted to Scotland and Wales and that their areas would be disadvantaged. When the case for a secretary of state was being made in the 1940s, one of the arguments put forward was that there had been a substantial increase in bureaucracy and the power of the civil service at the expense of the elected representatives of the people. This was not an issue that was peculiar to Wales; as opponents pointed out, it applied to the whole of the United Kingdom. Opponents advanced the same argument during the devolution debate of the 1970s, when the power of civil servants and unelected members on public bodies was a major issue. At that time, to win support for the government's policy, the Labour Party in Wales argued that the proposals for Wales were part of a radical transformation of the machinery of government throughout the United Kingdom. The aim was greater democratization and accountability and that applied not only to Wales but to the English regions also. Aneurin Bevan, when opposing the appointment of a secretary of state in the 1940s, feared that whoever was appointed would have to be Welsh speaking and that, consequently, people in Anglicized south Wales would be disadvantaged. The Welsh language was not a major issue at the time, but it had become one in the 1970s, when MPs from south-east Wales again raised fears that if a Welsh assembly were established the country would be governed by a Welsh-speaking bureaucracy. This was a dangerous ploy and risked causing tensions between Welsh speakers and non-Welsh speakers where none had previously existed. In Wales the devolution debate was clouded by a language issue, but this was not the case in Scotland and, as a result, the debate there was less complicated.

After Labour grudgingly conceded an advisory council in place of a secretary of state, the Conservatives proposed a minister for Welsh Affairs, linked to a Cabinet post. The Conservatives had always been resolutely unionist, but by making this proposal they showed that they were prepared to give Wales the recognition at Westminster that the Labour government had refused. The reasons for this move on the part of the Conservative Party are not wholly clear; perhaps it hoped to stem the Labour tide in rural Welsh-speaking Wales. If that was the case, it failed, because Labour won Merioneth, Anglesey and other rural seats in 1951 when the Conservatives were returned to power. The appointment of a minister for Welsh Affairs was a significant move on the Conservatives' part, because for the first time a government had conceded that a territorial minister should be appointed. Now there was to be no turning back. Of the ministers appointed minister for

Welsh Affairs, only one, Gwilym Lloyd George, was a Welshman. This was so because the post was attached to either the Home Office or the Ministry of Housing and Local Government, and the minister who happened to be in charge of either department was given responsibility for Welsh affairs.

The Conservatives' innovation and the pressure of the Parliament for Wales Campaign forced a response from the Labour Party. It could have taken the initiative and suggested a bold, radical measure, such as the appointment of a secretary of state. Instead, it committed itself to the appointment of a minister for Welsh Affairs with a seat in the Cabinet but without a department, which was no real advance on the position prevailing at the time and was no different from the proposal by Ness Edwards that Attlee's government had turned down. The thinking of the Labour Party in Wales was strictly centralist, and even when the decision was eventually taken by the party centrally to appoint a secretary of state, the Welsh Regional Council of Labour still thought that the policy to appoint a minister for Welsh Affairs should stand. Prior to the election in 1955, S. O. Davies's bill to set up a Welsh parliament revealed divisions within the Labour Party in Wales. During the debate on S. O. Davies's bill, devolutionists were given a clear indication of the opposition that they faced from the Labour and Conservative parties. Opponents made several claims that were repeated in the 1970s, when Labour MPs joined forces with the Conservatives in opposing the creation of a Welsh assembly. It was maintained that a measure of self-government would lead to the break-up of the economic unity of the United Kingdom, that rural Welsh-speaking Wales would be dominated by Anglicized industrial south Wales and that, inevitably, there would be a reduction in the number of Welsh MPs at Westminster. If ever there were such a reduction, the chances of the Conservatives forming a United Kingdom government would, of course, be improved.

Throughout the period under review there were divergent views on devolution within the Labour Party, but, surprisingly, MPs who opposed the party line were tolerated and not disciplined. The Welsh Regional Council of Labour was anxious that MPs supporting a parliament for Wales be disciplined, but the party centrally thought differently and no action was taken against them. Four of the MPs represented rural areas, and in the 1951 election they had either retained their seats in a straight fight with the

Conservatives or had won them for the first time. In the 1955 election they kept their seats.[3] They were therefore in a strong position to oppose the party line on this issue. The other MP, S. O. Davies, had substantial support in Merthyr Tydfil, as was proved in 1970 when, standing as an Independent Socialist candidate, he defeated the official Labour candidate. Again, in the 1970s dissident MPs were not disciplined. Then, the Labour government was a minority government, and that made it vulnerable to defeat and strengthened the position of MPs opposed to a Welsh assembly. Some would say that they would not have been disciplined in any case, because devolution was not a major plank in the government's programme.

Devolutionists in the Labour Party gained a notable victory when the party, after James Griffiths had exerted considerable influence, compromised its centralist stance and agreed to create both a secretary of state and a Welsh Office. For Labour this was a major policy shift, one that was to have far-reaching repercussions. Griffiths argued that there was a demand for the appointment, and devolutionists in later debates also advanced the same argument in support of their claims. This argument was a difficult one to substantiate. The Labour government fulfilled the promise and appointed a secretary of state in 1964, but not all the functions listed in the manifesto were transferred. Subsequently, the Welsh Office was given extended powers by both Labour and Conservative governments, and by 1979 was a sizeable department of state. Its development, though, was rather chequered and unplanned. The real impact of the presence of a secretary of state in the Cabinet on the quality of life of the Welsh people is difficult to assess because some improvements were the result of United Kingdom policies, pursued by successive governments and which their ministers in Wales merely administered. There was obviously room for some initiative on the part of the Welsh Office, but whether or not this resulted in marked differences between Wales and England in the administration of policies is an open question. It seems, too, that although the Welsh Office had powers of oversight, it was not always consulted when decisions that affected Wales were taken by other government departments.

---

[3] Jones, *Etholiadau'r Ganrif*, 96–7, 100–1.

Plaid Cymru has always claimed that London governments acted merely because of the threat from the nationalist parties in Wales and Scotland. There was no such threat in Wales until the 1960s, when in successive by-elections Labour lost one seat to Plaid Cymru and came close to losing another two. Nationalist successes in Wales and Scotland prompted the Labour government to establish a Royal Commission on the Constitution, and when it produced its report, devolution was firmly back on the political agenda. Further nationalist successes in Wales, and particularly in Scotland, helped those within the Labour Party in Wales who wanted an executive assembly to press their claims when the devolution policy was being framed; their man, John Morris, was appointed secretary of state. However, following the success of the nationalists, the anti-devolutionists in the Labour Party became more resolute in their opposition, claiming that devolution was an attempt to appease nationalists and that the eventual result would be independence. In the elections of 1974 several Welsh Labour MPs who supported devolution lost their seats, and this weakened the devolutionists' position within the Welsh Parliamentary Labour Party and in parliament. Consequently, among Labour backbenchers the case against a Welsh assembly was put more forcefully than was the case in support of it.

In the 1970s, for the first time, government proposals for changes in the machinery of government were debated in the House of Commons. Previous measures, for example the appointment of a secretary of state with a Welsh Office, had been implemented without such a debate, although some Welsh Labour MPs had reservations at the time. MPs were able to debate the devolution proposals, and this gave Welsh Labour MPs and their English counterparts an opportunity to voice their objections and to withdraw support. This 'is a prime example of Parliament asserting itself and its opinions against those of the Executive'.[4] Consequently, for only the second time in the United Kingdom's history a referendum was deployed as an instrument of government. It was introduced to resolve difficulties within the Labour Party. Tam Dalyell put it thus: 'It is not being proposed as a constitutional check whereby the people, in their ultimate wisdom, may instruct the Government, but to bind together a political party that is deeply divided on an

[4] Mari James and Peter D. Lindley, 'The parliamentary passage of the Wales Act 1978', in Foulkes, Jones and Wilford (eds), *Welsh Veto*, 35.

awkward issue.'[5] The referendum is a 'powerful force for conservatism and stability' and the result of the referendum in Wales confirmed the status quo.[6] Now that a precedent had been set, it seemed that significant changes in the machinery of government would in future have to be approved in a referendum – as happened in 1997. The 1970s witnessed a strange situation in which Labour MPs, some of them on the left of the party, were campaigning, with the support of activists in the constituencies and in trade union branches, for a referendum and retention of the status quo. These opponents of devolution succeeded because they managed to persuade the overwhelming majority that, despite the high costs, they might not be better off; indeed, they could be worse off. When the electors were given the choice, they opted to retain the existing system. Welsh people, in the circumstances prevailing in 1979, were not prepared to embark on a venture whose material benefits were uncertain.

In the election that followed, the Conservatives were returned to power; the preceding devolution debate certainly contributed to their electoral success in Wales, where they gained three seats and increased their parliamentary representation to eleven members. The Conservatives' success meant that devolution was no longer a priority; however, subsequent events resulted in a Labour government making it a priority once again within twenty years. The creation of a Welsh assembly in 1999 does not mark the end of the devolution debate in Wales. It is a continuing debate; already there are demands that the assembly be granted more extensive powers (some have already been conceded), and the argument that there should be parity with Scotland, where there is a legislative assembly, is being advanced once again. This is an issue that is likely to confront United Kingdom governments in the twenty-first century.

[5]   Dalyell, *Devolution*, 146.
[6]   Bogdanor, 'Defeat of devolution', 13.

BIBLIOGRAPHY

1. Manuscript collections
2. Interviews
3. Newspapers and periodicals
4. Official publications (in order of publication)
5. Reports and works of reference
6. Published works
7. Unpublished works

1. MANUSCRIPT COLLECTIONS

Coleg Harlech
James Griffiths Papers.

Council minutes
Taff-Ely Borough Council, 29 December 1975.
Mid Glamorgan County Council, 6 January 1976.
Torfaen Borough Council, 27 January 1976.
Association of County Councils Policy Committee, 1976–9.
West Midlands County Council Policy Committee, 17 January 1977.

Glamorgan Record Office
S. O. Davies Papers.

Labour Party Archives (LPA)
Morgan Phillips Papers, 1945–57.
Home Policy Subcommittee Minutes and Documents, 1954, November 1966–
    December 1975.
Home Policy Subcommittee Minutes and Documents, 1959.
Tripartite Committee on Welsh Policy Statement, April–July 1959.
National Executive Committee Minutes, 22 April 1959–6 January 1960, 24 July–
    18 December 1974.
Commission on the Constitution, November 1969.
Devolution Working Group, May–August 1974, and Devolution Material, 1969.

Labour Party, Welsh Office
Correspondence, memoranda, news releases, policy statements, 1974–9.

National Archives (formerly Public Record Office) (TNA)
CAB. 65, CAB. 128 and 129, Minutes and Memoranda of the War Cabinet and
post-war Cabinets.
PREM. 4/36/9, Confidential Papers, and PREM. 8/1569, Correspondence and
Papers, 1945–51, in the files of the prime minister's office.

National Library of Wales (NLW)
Huw T. Edwards Papers.
James Griffiths Papers.
Plaid Cymru Papers.

Press Notices issued by Economic Planning Councils
South-East, 13 August 1974.
North-West, 29 January 1976.
West Midlands, 8 March 1976.
Yorkshire and Humberside, 20 March 1978.

Privately owned
R. K. Blundell Papers (courtesy of R. K. Blundell).

Reports
Joint Report of the Chief Executive and County Secretary to the West Midlands
County Council Policy Committee, 15 March 1976.
Background information for members of the Merseyside County Council
attending a seminar, *Devolution: The Prospects*, 4 March 1977.
Report on seminar, *Devolution: The Prospects*, organized by the Merseyside County
Council, 4 March 1977.
Devolution CSS/128/77, Report of the County Solicitor and Secretary to the
Merseyside County Council Policy, Planning and Resources Committee,
9 December 1977.

University of Wales Swansea Archives, South Wales Coalfield Collection (UWS)
S. O. Davies Papers.
Fred Evans Papers.
D. J. Williams Papers.

Views on Our Changing Democracy: Devolution to Scotland and Wales, 1975
(Cmnd. 6348).
North-West Economic Planning Council, 28 January 1976.
Northern Economic Planning Council, 28 January 1976.
Welsh Counties Committee, 16 February 1976.
Views on *Devolution: The English Dimension*, 1976.
Yorkshire and Humberside Economic Planning Council.
North-West Economic Planning Council, 4 April 1977.

2. Interviews

Donald Anderson, 24 July 1984 (tel.)
R. K. Blundell, 19 September 1983
Jack Brooks, 21 December 1984
Goronwy Daniel, 28 April 1983
Gwilym Prys Davies, 4 July 1983
Ron Evans, 11 December 1984
Michael Foot, 31 March 1984, 18 July 1984
Raymond Gower, 12 April 1985
Ian Grist, 31 July 1984
K. S. Hopkins, 13 April 1983
Cledwyn Hughes, 29 March 1983
Roy Hughes, 26 May 1984
Emrys Jones, 7 March 1983 (tel.), 29 March 1983
J. Vaughan Jones, 3 August 1982, 13 July 1983
Keith Jones, 18 March 1985
John Morris, 16 November 1999
Cliff Prothero, 19 December 1983
Wyn Roberts, 31 July 1984
Edward Short, 19 December 1984
Dafydd Elis Thomas, 24 January 1985
Trevor Vaughan, 2 October 1984 (tel.), 8 October 1984
Tudor Watkins, 5 March 1983
Eirene White, 26 November 1982
Glyn Williams, 19 December 1983

3. Newspapers and periodicals

Newspapers

Daily Express
Daily Telegraph
Guardian
Liverpool Daily Post
Scotsman
South Wales Argus

South Wales Echo
Sunday Times
The Times
Western Mail
Y Cymro

Periodicals

Barn
County Councils Gazette
The Economist
Labour Weekly
The Listener

Local Government Chronicle
New Statesman
Spectator
Tribune
Wales: Cymru Radical

4. OFFICIAL PUBLICATIONS (IN ORDER OF PUBLICATION)

Secretary of State for Wales and Monmouthshire Bill (29 October 1937).

Parliamentary Debates, Fifth Series, 1943–79 (Parl. Deb.).

Scottish Home Department, *Scottish Affairs,* 1948 (Cmd. 7308).

Secretary of State for Wales and Monmouthshire Bill (28 January 1949).

The Council for Wales and Monmouthshire, A Memorandum by the Council on its Activities, October 1950 (Cmd. 8060).

The Council for Wales and Monmouthshire, Second Memorandum by the Council on its Activities, July 1953 (Cmd. 8844).

Government of Wales Bill (15 December 1954).

The Council for Wales and Monmouthshire, Third Memorandum by the Council on its Activities, January 1957 (Cmnd. 53).

Government Administration in Wales. Text of a letter addressed by the Prime Minister to the Chairman of the Council for Wales and Monmouthshire, 11 December 1957 (Cmnd. 334).

Select Committee on Procedure, 1958–1959, Report, vol. I.

The Council for Wales and Monmouthshire, Fourth Memorandum (Government Administration in Wales) and the Reply of the Prime Minister, January 1959 (Cmnd. 631).

The Council for Wales and Monmouthshire, Report on the Rural Transport Problem in Wales, September 1962 (Cmnd. 1821).

The Council for Wales and Monmouthshire, Report on the Welsh Holiday Industry, March 1963 (Cmnd. 1950).

The Council for Wales and Monmouthshire, Report on the Welsh Language Today, November 1963 (Cmnd. 2198).

Parliamentary Debates, Welsh Grand Committee, Regional Development (11 December 1963).

Parliamentary Debates, House of Lords, Government Administration in Wales (8 December 1964).

Parliamentary Debates, Welsh Grand Committee, Functions of the Secretary of State for Wales and Constitutional Changes in Wales (16 December 1964).

The Council for Wales and Monmouthshire, Report on the Arts in Wales, May 1966 (Cmnd. 2983).

Local Government in Wales, July 1967 (Cmnd. 3340).

Commission on the Constitution, Written Evidence 1: The Welsh Office (1969).

Commission on the Constitution, Minutes of Evidence 1: Wales (1970).

Welsh Council, A Strategy for Rural Wales (1971).

Welsh Office, Welsh Council, 1968–1971, (1971).

Parliamentary Debates, Welsh Grand Committee, The Reform of Local Government in Wales (13 July 1971).

Commission on the Constitution, Minutes of Evidence 5: Wales (1972).

Commission on the Constitution, Written Evidence 7: Wales (1972).

Commission on the Constitution, Written Evidence 8: England (1972).

Commission on the Constitution, Written Evidence 9: United Kingdom (1972).

Parliamentary Debates, House of Commons Standing Committee D, Local Government Bill (16 March 1972).

Commission on the Constitution, Research Papers 5: Aspects of Parliamentary Reform (1973).

Commission on the Constitution, Research Papers 6: Aspects of Constitutional Reform (1973).

Royal Commission on the Constitution, 1969–1973, Report, vol. I, October 1973 (Cmnd. 5460).

Royal Commission on the Constitution, 1969–1973, Memorandum of Dissent, vol. II, October 1973 (Cmnd. 5460–1).

Welsh Office, Welsh Council, 1971–1974 (1974).

Office of the Lord President of the Council, *Devolution within the United Kingdom: Some Alternatives for Discussion* (1974).

Democracy and Devolution: Proposals for Scotland and Wales, 1974 (Cmnd. 5732).

Referendum on United Kingdom Membership of the European Community, February 1975 (Cmnd. 5925).

Our Changing Democracy: Devolution to Scotland and Wales, 1975 (Cmnd. 6348).

Devolution: The New Assemblies for Wales and Scotland (1976).

Parliamentary Debates, Welsh Grand Committee, Devolution (7 April 1976).

Devolution to Scotland and Wales: Supplementary Statement, August 1976 (Cmnd. 6585).

House of Commons Library Research Division, 'Devolution proposals, 1973–1976', Background Paper 54 (24 November 1976).

Devolution: The English Dimension (1976).

House of Commons Library Research Division, 'Scotland and Wales Bill', Ref. Sheet 76/20 (6 December 1976).

House of Commons Library Research Division, 'The devolution debate: regional statistics', Background Paper 57 (11 February 1977).

House of Commons Library Research Division, 'Scotland Bill, Wales Bill', Ref. Sheet 77/16 (9 November 1977).

Central Office of Information, *Devolution in the United Kingdom* (December 1977).

House of Commons Library Research Division, 'The Devolution Question: Regional Statistics', Background Paper 67 (22 February 1979).

House of Commons, First Report from the Committee on Welsh Affairs, Session 1979–80, *The Role of the Welsh Office and Associated Bodies in Developing Employment Opportunities in Wales, Report*, vol. I (30 July 1980).

5. REPORTS AND WORKS OF REFERENCE

Reports
Conservative Party
Annual Conference Reports: 1947, 1948

Labour Party
  Annual Reports: 1957, 1968, 1975, 1976
  Annual Conference Reports: 1943, 1948, 1954, 1969, 1974
  Scottish Regional Council
  Annual Report, 1957
  South Wales Regional Council and its successors
  Annual Reports: 1938–80
  South Wales Regional Council and its successors
  Annual Conference Reports: 1938–80

Works of reference
Butler, David, and Pinto-Duschinsky, Michael, *The British General Election of 1970* (London and Basingstoke, 1971).
——, and Kavanagh, Dennis, *The British General Election of February 1974* (London and Basingstoke, 1974).
——, *The British General Election of October 1974* (London and Basingstoke, 1975).
——, *The British General Election of 1979* (London and Basingstoke, 1980).
——, and Sloman, Anne, *British Political Facts, 1900–1975* (London and Basingstoke, 4th edn., 1975).
Jones, Beti, *Parliamentary Elections in Wales, 1900–1975* (Talybont, 1977).
——, *Etholiadau'r Ganrif: Welsh Elections, 1885–1997* (Talybont, 1999).
Keesing's Contemporary Archives, 1964–1979.
The Times Guide to the House of Commons, 1970 (London, 1970).
The Times Guide to the House of Commons, October 1974 (London, 1974).
Who's Who, 2006 (London, 2006).
Who Was Who, vol. III (1929–40) (London, 1941) – vol. VII (1971–80) (London, 1981).

6. PUBLISHED WORKS

Abse, Leo, 'Exploiting the natives', *Spectator*, 24 January 1979.
Andrews, J. A. (ed.), *Welsh Studies in Public Law* (Cardiff, 1970).
Balsom, Denis, and McAllister, Ian, 'The Scottish and Welsh devolution referenda of 1979: constitutional change and popular choice', *Parliamentary Affairs*, 32, 4 (Autumn 1979).
Barnett, Joel, *Inside the Treasury* (London, 1982).
Beckett, Francis, *Clem Attlee* (London, 1997).
Bevan, Aneurin, 'The claim of Wales: a statement', *Wales*, 7 (Spring 1947).
——, *In Place of Fear* (London, 1952).
Birch, Anthony H., *Political Integration and Disintegration in the British Isles* (London, 1977).
Bogdanor, Vernon, *Devolution* (Oxford, 1979).
——, 'The defeat of devolution', *Spectator*, 10 March 1979.
Borthwick, R. L., 'The Welsh Grand Committee', *Parliamentary Affairs*, 21 (Summer 1968).

Butt Philip, Alan, *The Welsh Question: Nationalism in Welsh Politics, 1945–1970* (Cardiff, 1975).

Callaghan, James, *Time and Chance* (London, 1987).

Calvert, Harry (ed.), *Devolution* (London, 1975).

Castle, Barbara, *The Castle Diaries, 1974–1976* (London, 1980).

Chappell, Edgar L., *Wake Up, Wales!* (London, 1943).

——, *The Government of Wales* (London, 1943).

Clarke, Sir Richard, 'The number and size of government departments', *Political Quarterly*, 43, 2 (1972).

Cledwyn, Lord, *The Referendum: The End of an Era* (Cardiff, 1981).

——, 'Trafod Materion Cymraeg yn y Senedd', *Y Traethodydd*, 138, 586 (Ionawr 1983).

——, *Wales Yesterday and Tomorrow* (Bro Colwyn, 1995).

Conservative Party, *The Conservative Policy for Wales and Monmouthshire* (London, 1949).

——, *This is the road* (London, 1950).

——, *The Manifesto of the Conservative and Unionist Party* (London, 1951).

——, *Some Questions and Answers on a Parliament for Wales* (Cardiff, 1954).

——, *United for Peace and Progress* (London, 1955).

——, *Wales with the Conservatives* (Cardiff, 1964).

——, *Action not Words: The New Conservative Programme* (London, 1966).

——, *Action not words for Wales* (Cardiff, 1966).

——, *A Better Tomorrow for Wales* (Cardiff, 1970).

——, *Wales into the 70s* (Cardiff, 1970).

——, *Manifesto for Wales* (Cardiff, February 1974).

——, *Putting Britain First: A National Policy from the Conservatives* (London, October 1974).

——, *A Conservative Manifesto – For Wales and Her People* (Cardiff, October 1974).

——, *The Right Approach: A Statement of Conservative Aims* (London, 1976).

——, Campaign Guides, 1950, 1951, 1955, 1959, 1970, 1974, 1977, 1978.

——, *Conservative Manifesto for Wales* (1979).

Cook, Chris, and Ramsden, John (eds), *By-Elections in British Politics* (London, 1973).

Craik, W. W., *The Central Labour College, 1909–29* (London, 1964).

Cross, J. A., 'The regional decentralisation of British Government departments', *Public Administration*, 48 (1970).

Crossman, Richard, *The Diaries of a Cabinet Minister*, vol. I (London, 1975).

——, *The Diaries of a Cabinet Minister*, vol. II (London, 1976).

——, *The Diaries of a Cabinet Minister*, vol. III (London, 1977).

Crowther-Hunt, Lord, 'Will England come off third best on devolution day?', *The Times*, 21 December 1976.

——, 'Whitehall: the balance of power', *The Listener*, 6 January 1977.

Dalyell, Tam, *Devolution: The End of Britain?* (London, 1977).

Daniel, Sir Goronwy, 'The government in Wales', *Transactions of the Honourable Society of Cymmrodorion*, part 1 (1969).

David, Rhys, 'Future of the Welsh Office', *Planet*, 1 (August–September 1970).

Davies, E. Hudson, 'Welsh Nationalism', *Political Quarterly*, 39, 3 (July–September 1968).

Davies, Gwilym Prys, *A Central Welsh Council* (Aberystwyth, 1963).

Davies, Gwilym Prys, *Llafur y Blynyddoedd* (Dinbych, 1991).

Davies, John, *A History of Wales* (London, 1993).

Drucker, H. M., and Brown, Gordon, *The Politics of Nationalism and Devolution* (London and New York, 1980).

Edwards, Huw T., 'What I want for Wales', *Wales*, January 1944.

——, *They went to Llandrindod* (Wrexham, Cardiff and Oswestry, n.d.).

——, 'Why I resigned', *Wales*, November 1958.

——, *Troi'r Drol* (Dinbych, 1963).

Edwards, Ness, *Is This the Road?* (Cardiff and Wrexham, n.d.).

Evans, David Myfyr, and Reynolds, John, 'A new constitutional structure for Wales', *Political Quarterly*, 42, 2 (April–June 1971).

Evans, Gwynfor, *The Fight for Welsh Freedom* (Talybont, 2000).

Foulkes, David, Jones, J. Barry, and Wilford, R. A. (eds), *The Welsh Veto: The Wales Act 1978 and the Referendum* (Cardiff, 1983).

Gowan, Ivor, *Government in Wales* (Cardiff, 1966).

——, 'The government of Wales', *Transactions of the Honourable Society of Cymmrodorion*, part 1 (1967).

——, 'Local government in Wales', *Local Government Chronicle*, 22 July 1967.

——, 'Nationalism: a great Welsh myth?', *Daily Telegraph*, 5 September 1974.

Grant, W. P., and Preece, R. J. C., 'Welsh and Scottish nationalism', *Parliamentary Affairs*, 21, 3 (1968).

Griffiths, James, *Pages from Memory* (London, 1969).

Griffiths, Jim, 'Wales, after the war', *Wales*, July 1943.

Gunn, Lewis, 'Devolution: a Scottish view', *Political Quarterly*, 48, 2 (April–June 1977).

Guthrie, Roger, and McLean, Iain, 'Another part of the periphery: reactions to devolution in an English development area', *Parliamentary Affairs*, 31, 2 (Spring 1978).

Hechter, Michael, *Internal Colonialism: The Celtic Fringe in British National Development, 1536–1966* (Berkeley and Los Angeles, 1975).

Heffer, Eric, 'Devolution and the Labour Party', *New Statesman*, 19 December 1975.

Henderson, Arthur, 'Home rule all round', *Welsh Outlook*, 5 (1918).

Hobsbawm, Eric, 'Some reflections on *The Break-Up of Britain*', *New Left Review*, 105 (September–October 1977).

James Griffiths and His Times (Cardiff, n.d.).

Jenkins, Geraint H. (ed.) *Cof Cenedl 10: Ysgrifau ar Hanes Cymru* (Llandysul, 1995).

Jones, J. Barry, 'The Welsh Office: a political expedient or an administrative inno-vation?', *Transactions of the Honourable Society of Cymmrodorion*, 1990.

Jones, J. Barry, and Keating, Michael, 'The British Labour Party as a centralising force', *Studies in Public Policy*, 32 (1979).

——, 'The resolution of internal conflicts and external pressures: the Labour Party's devolution policy', *Government and Opposition*, 17 (Summer 1982).

Jones, R. Brinley (ed.), *Anatomy of Wales* (Peterston-super-Ely, 1972).

Jordan, Grant, 'The committee stage of the Scotland and Wales Bill, 1976–77', *Waverley Papers*, 1 (1979).

Kerr, J., 'The failure of the Scotland and Wales Bill: no will, no way', *Scottish Government Yearbook*, 1978.

Kilmuir, Earl of, *Political Adventure* (London, 1964).

Kinnock, Neil, 'Bread of Heaven', *Guardian*, 8 August 1977.

Labour Party, *Labour is Building a New Wales* (Cardiff, 1950).

——, *Labour's Policy for Wales* (Cardiff, 1954).

——, *Forward with Labour (Labour's Plan for Wales)* (Cardiff, 1959).

——, *Signposts to the New Wales* (Cardiff, 1963).

——, *Let's Go with Labour for the New Britain* (London, 1964).

——, *Evidence of the Labour Party in Wales to the Commission on the Constitution*, 7 January 1970 (Cardiff, 1970).

——, *Now Britain's strong let's make it great to live in* (London, 1970).

——, *Let us work together. Labour's way out of the crisis* (London, February 1974).

——, *Labour's Policies for a Brighter Future for Wales* (Cardiff, February 1974).

——, *Bringing Power Back to the People* (London, September 1974).

——, *Labour Party Manifesto* (London, October 1974).

——, *Wales will win with Labour* (Cardiff, October 1974).

——, *Why Devolution: Some Questions Answered* (Cardiff, 1976).

——, *A is for Achievement* (London, 1977).

——, *Campaign Handbook: Wales* (London, 1978).

Labour Party, Welsh Office, *Speakers' Notes on Devolution* (Cardiff, January 1976).

Labour Party in Wales, *Devolution and Democracy* (Cardiff, June 1974).

Labour Party Wales, *Political and Industrial Democracy in Britain* (Cardiff, May 1978).

Lewis, Roy, 'Wales joins the world', *Contemporary Review*, 214 (1969).

Lewis, Vivian, and Walters, Donald, *Wales – A Blueprint* (London, 1974).

Lloyd, D. Tecwyn, 'Cyfraniad y brifysgol i wleidyddiaeth', *Efrydiau Athronyddol*, 1974.

Luke, Paul, and Johnson, David, 'Devolution by referendum? A look at the Welsh situation', *Parliamentary Affairs*, 29, 3 (Summer 1976).

McKibbin, Ross, *The Evolution of the Labour Party, 1910–1924* (Oxford, 1974).

Mackintosh, J. P., *The Devolution of Power* (London, 1968).

Mackintosh, John P., 'The Report of the Royal Commission on the Constitution, 1969–1973', *Political Quarterly*, 45, 1 (January–March 1974).

——, *The Government and Politics of Britain* (London, 4th edn., 1977).

——, 'The Killing of the Scotland Bill', *Political Quarterly*, 49, 2 (April–June 1978).

Madgwick, P. J., and James, Mari, 'Government by consultation: the case for Wales', *Studies in Public Policy*, 47 (1979).

Madgwick, Peter, and Rose, Richard (eds), *The Territorial Dimension in United Kingdom Politics* (London and Basingstoke, 1982).

Morgan, K. O., 'Welsh nationalism: the historical background', *Journal of Contemporary History*, 6 (1971).

Morgan, Kenneth, 'Inaction for Wales', *Socialist Commentary* (June 1967).

Morgan Kenneth O., *Wales in British Politics, 1868–1922* (Cardiff, rev. edn., 1970).

——, *Rebirth of a Nation: Wales, 1880–1980* (Oxford and Cardiff, 1981).

——, *Labour in Power, 1945–1951* (Oxford, 1984).

——, *Politics, Places and People* (Cardiff, 1995).

——, *Callaghan, A Life* (Oxford, 1997).

Morgan, W. J. (ed.), *The Welsh Dilemma* (Llandybïe, 1973).

Morris, John, review of Foulkes, David, Jones, J. Barry and Wilford, R. A. (eds), *The Welsh Veto: The Wales Act 1978 and the Referendum* (Cardiff, 1983), in *Barn*, 242 (1983).

Mount, Ferdinand, 'The psychotics' revolt', *Spectator*, 10 March 1979.

Nairn, Tom, *The Break-Up of Britain: Crisis and Neo-Nationalism* (London, 1977).

Newsam, Sir Frank, *The Home Office* (London, 1954).

No Assembly Campaign, *Keep Wales united with Britain: Vote No to the Welsh Assembly: A guide for the 1979 Referendum campaign.*

Osmond, John, *The Centralist Enemy* (Llandybïe, 1974).

—— (ed.), *The National Question Again: Welsh Political Identity in the 1980s* (Llandysul, 1985).

Parliament for Wales Campaign, *Parliament for Wales* (Aberystwyth, 1953).

Powell, D. Watkin, 'Carmarthen: before and after', *Contemporary Review*, 209 (October 1966).

Price, Emyr, *Yr Arglwydd Cledwyn* (Caernarfon, 1990).

Prothero, Cliff, *Recount* (Ormskirk and Northridge, 1982).

Prys-Davies, Gwilym, Lord, *Turning a Dream into a Reality* (Aberystwyth, 2000).

Purnell, Gerard, 'Nationalist or Labour for Welsh Radicals?', *Socialist Commentary*, May 1970.

Raison, Timothy, 'Devolution – the great divider', *Daily Telegraph*, 27 October 1977.

Randall, P. J., 'Wales in the structure of central government', *Public Administration*, 50 (1972).

Rees, J. F., *The Problem of Wales and Other Essays* (Cardiff, 1963).

Roberts, Alwyn, and Jones, Alun, 'Devolution and local government', supplement to the *County Councils Gazette*, July 1976.

Roberts, Michael, ' Devolution, Welsh connection', *Spectator*, 27 December 1975.

Rowlands, E., 'The politics of regional administration: the establishment of the Welsh Office', *Public Administration*, 50 (1972).

Smith, Brian C., *Advising Ministers (A Case Study of the South West Economic Planning Council)* (London, 1969).

Stacey, Frank, *British Government, 1966 to 1975: Years of Reform* (Oxford, 1978).

Steed, Michael, 'Don't leave the English regions high and dry', *Western Mail*, 20 May 1974.

Tanner, Duncan, Williams, Chris, and Hopkin, Deian (eds), *The Labour Party in Wales, 1900–2000* (Cardiff, 2000).

Thomas, Ian C., 'The creation of the Welsh Office: conflicting purposes in institutional change', *Studies in Public Policy*, 91 (1981).

Tonypandy, Viscount, *George Thomas, Mr. Speaker* (London, 1985).

Trades Union Congress, *TUC Policy on Devolution* (1976).

Trice, J. E., 'Welsh local government reform: an assessment of *ad hoc* administrative reform', *Public Law*, Autumn 1970.

Tyne and Wear County Council, *Devolution: The Case Against. Is This a United Kingdom?* (1977).

Wales for the Assembly Campaign, *Speakers' Notes* (3 June 1978).

——, *The Wales Bill* (4 June 1978).

Wales Trade Union Council, *Recommendations on Devolution* (Cardiff, n.d.).

Wales TUC, *General Council Statement on Wales TUC Policy with Regard to Devolution (Post Referendum)*.

Watkins, Percy E., *A Welshman Remembers* (Cardiff, 1944).

Welsh Nationalist Party, *TVA for Wales* (Caernarvon, n.d.).

Western Mail, Devolution: The Great Debate, 1964–74. As seen through the columns of the *Western Mail* (Cardiff, n.d.).

White, Baroness, 'The Report of the Kilbrandon Commission on the Constitution', *Transactions of the Honourable Society of Cymmrodorion*, Sessions 1972 and 1973.

'Wilkes, Jack', 'Lords and Commons', *Tribune*, 20 October 1944.

Williams, Colin H. (ed.), *National Separatism* (Cardiff, 1982).

Williams, David, *A History of Modern Wales* (London, 1950).

Williams, Glanmor, 'The idea of nationality in Wales', *Cambridge Journal*, December 1953.

Williams, Gwyn A., *When was Wales?* (London, 1985).

Williams, Philip M., *Hugh Gaitskell* (London, 1979).

Wilson, Harold, *The Labour Government, 1964–70* (London, 1971).

——, 'Democracy in local affairs', *Edinburgh Series of Policy Speeches*, 2 (1973).

——, *Final Term: The Labour Government, 1974–1976* (London, 1979).

Wise, Michael, 'The devolution debate', *Geographical Magazine*, L, 9 (June 1978).

Y Blaid Lafur, *Polisïau Llafur ar gyfer dyfodol gwell i Gymru* (Caerdydd, Chwefror 1974).

7. UNPUBLISHED WORKS

Byrne, P., McCarthy, J., Tudor, M., and Jones, J. W., 'The Welsh Office', UWIST, 1970.

Evans, J. G., 'British governments and devolution in Wales: attitudes and policies, 1944–1979', MA thesis, University of Wales, 1987.

Gibson, E. L., 'A study of the Council for Wales and Monmouthshire', MA thesis, University of Wales, 1968.

Randall, P. J., 'The development of administrative decentralisation in Wales, from the establishment of the Welsh Department of Education in 1907 to the creation of the post of Secretary of State for Wales in October 1964', M.Sc. (Econ.) thesis, University of Wales, 1969.

INDEX